The Day Trader's Guide to Technical Analysis

**How to Use Chart Patterns, Level II
and Time of Sales to Profit
in Electronic Markets**

Chris Lewis

McGraw-Hill, Inc.

New York San Francisco Washington, D.C. Auckland Bogotá
Caracas Lisbon London Madrid Mexico City Milan
Montreal New Delhi San Juan Singapore

Library of Congress Cataloging-in-Publication Data

Lewis, Chris (Christopher S.)
    The day trader's guide to technical analysis : how to use chart patterns, Level II and time of sales to profit in electronic markets / by Chris Lewis.
    p.   cm.
    ISBN 0-07-135979-6
    1. Day trading (Securities)—Handbooks, manuals, etc. 2. NASDAQ (Computer network)—Handbooks, manuals, etc. I. Title.

HG4515.95 .L49   2000
332.63'2—dc21   00-029202

McGraw-Hill
A Division of The McGraw·Hill Companies

Copyright © 2001 by The McGraw-Hill Companies, Inc. All rights reserved. Printed in the United States of America. Except as permitted under the United States Copyright Act of 1976, no part of this publication may be reproduced or distributed in any form or by any means, or stored in a database or retrieval system, without the prior written permission of the publisher.

2 3 4 5 6 7 8 9 0 FGR/FGR 0 9 8 7 6 5 4 3 2 1 0

ISBN 0-07-135979-6

The sponsoring editor for this book was Stephen Isaacs, the editing supervisor was Maureen B. Walker, and the production supervisor was Charles Annis. It was set in Palatino by Inkwell Publishing Services.

Printed and bound by Quebecor/Fairfield.

McGraw-Hill books are available at special quantity discounts to use as premiums and sales promotions, or for use in corporate training programs. For more information, please write to the Director of Special Sales, McGraw-Hill, Two Penn Plaza, New York, NY 10121-2298. Or contact your local bookstore.

 This book is printed on recycled, acid-free paper containing a minimum of 50 percent recycled de-inked fiber.

Real Tick™ is a trademark of Townsend Analytics, Ltd., copyright 1986–1999 Townsend Analytics LLC. Used with permission. Any unauthorized reproduction, alteration, or use of Real Tick™ is strictly prohibited. Authorized use of Real Tick™ by the author and publisher does not constitute an endorsement by Townsend Analytics of *The Day Trader's Guide to Technical Analysis*. Townsend Analytics does not guarantee the accuracy of or warrant any representations made in *The Day Trader's Guide to Technical Analysis*.

Disclaimer

This book is designed for educational purposes only. It is not designed to provide all the information required to be successful in day trading. Day trading may involve a significantly higher level of risk in comparison to other common forms of capital management such as long-term investments in stocks, bonds, or mutual funds. Proficiency at day trading may take a very long period of time to develop, depending on an individual's capacity to understand the high degree of risk involved, the aptitude to manage these high risks in order to preserve capital, and the potential to develop any and all necessary skills to create profitable results. Day trading may result in the loss of all of a trader's capital and, in cases that involve the use of extended buying power or margin, you may lose all your capital and assume liability for owing additional funds that are substantially more than your capital invested.

The authors and publisher will not assume any responsibility due, but not limited to, losses incurred as a result of applying what is discussed in this book. The authors and publisher do not claim or guarantee your success at day trading or suggest that any past performance mentioned in this publication indicates the same results will occur in the future.

Contents

Acknowledgments vii
Preface viii
Introduction x

Part I: Preparing the Plan

1. Why Day Trade NASDAQ Securities? 3
A Manifesto of Independence 4
Day Trading—What It Is and What It's Not 5
The Three Phases of the Trading Day 9
The Discipline of Day Trading 15
NASDAQ vs. Listed Exchanges for Day Trading 25
Who Wins and Who Loses in Day Trading? 31
What Is Technical Analysis? 33
The Basic Tools of TA 36
Answering the Criticism and Misperception 41

2. Trading Concepts That Have Stood the Test of Time 46
Dow Theory 46
The Basics of Trend 52
Essential Concepts of Trend in Security Prices 55
How to Identify Support and Resistance Price Levels 61
Common Reversal Patterns 64
Common Continuation Patterns 77

Contents   v

    Breakouts   88

3. Activities to Avoid   91

    Derivatives   92
    Overreliance on Complex Chart Analysis   96
    Overtrading   121
    Trying to Assimilate Too Many Variables   123
    Using the Wrong Tool at the Wrong Time   131
    A Potpourri of Helpful Hints   133

4. The NASDAQ Level II Screen   135

    The Components of the Level II Screen   135
    Level II Participants, Market Makers and the ECNs   137
    Look at the Flow Rather Than the Snapshot   140
    The Level II Screen at the Break of an Upward Trend   147
    The Level II Screen at the Break of a Downward Trend   152

Part II: Putting the Plan into Action

5. Executions   161

    Using the SOES Execution Route   162
    Why Island (Not Datek) Is the Preferred Route   168
    The Little Helper ARCA and the Other ECNs   174
    SelectNet Can Be a Good Friend   176
    Getting Shorts in the Market   178

6. A Trading Week   184

    Assessing the Market Direction: Charting Methods   185
    Assessing the Market Direction: Noncharting Methods   194
    Daily Premarket Preparation   199
    Market Open Patterns to Look For   205
    Trading the Post-Open Periods   212
    A Sample Trading Week   214
    Evaluation of the Week's Trading   237

7. Trading Psychology   239

    Learning to Love Stops   240
    Focus on the Process   241
    Obstacles to Trading Success   244
    Forming Your Own Set of Rules   247
    When Things Go Wrong   255

8. Keeping Track   257

Premarket Task Sheets   257
Screen Layouts   261
What to Keep Track of on a Daily Basis   263
What to Keep Track of on a Weekly Basis   263
Conclusions   265

Afterword   267
Index   270

Acknowledgments

I want first to acknowledge that, as always, without the loving support of my wife Claudia, I would never be able to complete a task of this nature. In addition to Claudia, my other inspiration is my son Ben, who at the tender age of one is able to give me all the fun I can handle. I want to thank Thomas Astuto for his fine work in taking my random scribblings and turning them into clear illustrations. I also wish to thank Stephen Isaacs for giving me this opportunity and Steven Elliot for making the introductions.

Janice Kaylor of Townsend Analytics was instrumental in securing the permission required to use the Real Tick™ displays used in this book. My thanks to her. To the folks at MB Trading I also wish to extend thanks for providing such high levels of service. Their efforts are essential in providing me with profitable opportunities every day.

Preface

Many texts on day trading mention the different styles of day trading that are most common, and students are urged to find which style of trading is most compatible with their abilities. As far as it goes, this is good advice, but it is incomplete. The choices offered tend to focus on scalpers, who go for lots of small gains and hold positions for only a few minutes at a time, on through to swing traders, who hold positions for more than one day. The reason I find the classification of scalper to swing trader to be incomplete is that it misses a vital element of how the exchanges operate in the U.S., and that is the change that trading on these exchanges goes through during each day. Trading at the market open is different from trading at the middle of the day, which is different from trading at market close. My advice is that you discover which period of the day you are most comfortable trading in and stick to that. In this text I refer to Phases 1, 2, and 3 as shorthand for market open, mid-market, and market close. Each has its own character, risks, rewards, and required disciplines.

Phase 1 trading can be classified as *momentum* trading, identifying and going with the flow of supply and demand. Phase 2 trading is better suited for those who are willing to constantly scalp small profits and those willing to hold positions for longer when a trend is in effect. Phase 3 trading requires much patience to wait for a breakout from a price level of support or resistance to occur.

For many reasons, my preference has been to focus on Phase 1 trading, primarily because I am more successful at it. With Phase 1 trading, I only have to hold positions for a short period of time, typically less than five minutes, because the biggest price swings of the day usually occur at that time and it leaves me with the rest of the day to pursue other things.

Preface

Personally, I find it difficult to maintain the level of concentration needed to trade profitably during the entire day, and I suspect lots of others do too. By restricting my trading mostly to Phase 1, I maximize my profits and virtually eliminate losses, which brings me to my next point.

Although it is possible to be profitable with only half of your trades making money, I do not like to trade that way. I trade once, sometimes twice a day, but only when all my indicators agree. By doing this, I miss out on a lot of opportunities for profit, but I also eliminate a lot of losses. By seeing small and regular profits, I reduce my stress level and keep trading fun. If my trade success rate drops below 80 percent, I consider something to be wrong and stop trading while I evaluate my actions.

The techniques I follow are intended to generate income, as opposed to a percentage return on a given level of capital. With more capital, there are more stocks available of which you can buy up to 1000 shares of (the safe limit for day-trading securities), so from that standpoint, more capital can give you better returns, but not much. For this book, I have traded an account with $20,000 in it for illustrative purposes. The returns can increase significantly with $50,000 available, but the increase in returns drops off dramatically after that. The reasons for this become clear as you progress through the book, but they are based on the safe trade size limit, defined by the safety net SOES system and the number of opportunities you can execute on at any one time.

The use I make of technical analysis in this book falls into two categories. First, there is technical analysis of daily charts that cover up to a year's worth of information. These charts tell you what the current market sentiment is and set your preference for long or short positions when trading. Within this type of analysis, we also assess trend and areas of support and resistance for individual securities. The specific securities for which we consider these levels are identified when certain premarket conditions occur, causing the security to become of interest. The trades that are occurring that day drive the second type of technical analysis. For this type of analysis we refer to the NASDAQ Level II screen, the time-of-sales screen, and realtime one-minute tick charts.

Using these inputs, the form of trading explained here draws upon the principles that Charles Dow laid down a hundred years ago. The nature of markets has remained constant, whereas the speed at which the markets change and the speed of making a trade have changed.

The techniques illustrated here do not require the market to go up, go down, or be in love with the Internet or IPOs. The one thing that is required is volatility, which is probably the only thing we are guaranteed for the foreseeable future.

Introduction

I have spent the last 12 years designing, implementing, and operating market data and trading systems for both data vendors and large financial institutions. During this time, it has been my privilege to meet both highly successful and notoriously unsuccessful traders, and to form my own opinions as to why they perform the way they do.

It does not seem to matter what trading method they used. There are successful traders using what appear to be the same methods the unsuccessful traders use. It seems also to be true that traders with superior academic skills are not necessarily more successful than those with none. What seems to separate the successful from the unsuccessful is that the successful trader uses a method of trading that fits with his or her personality. By that, I mean that a successful trader will analyze the market and make trading decisions using a method that naturally makes sense to that trader and complements his or her risk profile and innate capabilities.

To be successful at trading, you do not have to be Ph.D. material, and being Ph.D. material does not guarantee your success. The most important determinants of success in trading are that you (1) trade in a way that complements your nature, (2) have no problem admitting when you are wrong and taking the loss for that, and (3) are able to keep your emotions in check and maintain discipline at all times. Each of those points will mean different things to different people. The secret to any person's trading success lies within that person, and books like this one can only contribute one piece of the puzzle in each trader's path to self-knowledge.

For those of you who choose technical analysis as the path for daytrading activities, this book provides a framework for your trading deci-

Introduction

sions. I do not contend that technically driven day trading is the only or always the best way to make money in the market. It is right for some traders and wrong for others.

In conjunction with my work on systems, I have traded my own account during this 12-year period and learned by the only means possible how to trade profitably—experience. I have been and continue to be fascinated by the financial markets and their ability to distribute wealth to those able to take advantage of them. In this book I present methods that work for me and, in fact, have worked for many successful traders for a century or more.

Whatever method you study and choose to use for your trading decisions, the emotions brought into play by having your own money on the line dramatically change the way you behave in a trade. I steadfastly believe that unless you have traded a method with your own money, you don't know how well it performs for you.

Trading is a continual learning process, and during my own learning, I have read every book I could lay hands on, studied the principles presented, and tried most methods with my own cash. Like most small traders, I made some money, lost some money, and always wondered why, looking for a new method that would make me better.

Most of the books that got me fired up and convinced me that I had finally found the way to trade were written either by brokers who live by motivating people to trade and thereby generate commissions, or those offering expensive seminars or subscriber-only chat rooms. Broker commissions, seminar fees, and chat room fees are the only sure methods when it comes to getting profit out of the financial markets. I believe that although some of these people can probably help you, at the end of the day, a trading decision must be yours and yours alone. To trade and survive long term, you must make your own trading decisions and understand why you fail or succeed. If you enter a trade on someone else's recommendation, you can only exit it on their recommendation, which completely takes away your control.

What I have finally come to realize is that there is nothing new in market behavior. There may be new systems and mechanisms that speed up what happens in the marketplace, but the underlying dynamics remain, and it is these that must be studied and understood in order to trade profitably. I now rely on principles of Dow Theory that have been known for over a hundred years, and can successfully apply those principles to day trading on the NASDAQ market. The emphasis of this book is to look at how technical analysis can be used to determine the psychology of the market, and to that end, displays of NASDAQ Level II screens, tick charts, and time-of-sales displays are given where appropriate.

To show that I use my principles on a daily basis, I have provided details on numerous trades that I have executed with my own money. You will see trades that were losers as well as some that were winners. In fact, I think reviewing losing trades is one of the most productive activities a day trader can undertake. At the minimum, you should keep a daily log of why you made each trading decision and a printout of the daily chart to see where you made your entry and exit points.

The key to the approach I now use is simplicity. I do not rely on any sophisticated computer-generated models, but I do need to understand the psychology of the market and see where there are imbalances in supply and demand. This approach does not rely on forecasting what will happen. Instead, it is based upon putting yourself in a position to react quickly to events if they prove to be following one of the commonly repeated patterns presented in this book.

In day trading, the old argument of whether fundamental or technical analysis is most likely to produce the best results is moot. If you are only holding positions intraday, the only thing you are interested in is the market sentiment toward a given stock, which is almost always an overreaction to any change in the fundamentals of a company. Seeing regular daily swings of 5 percent to 100 percent or more in a company's share price cannot be explained by the fundamentals. Technical analysis is the analysis of price and volume, which represents the actions of the masses and is therefore really an exercise in crowd psychology. With an understanding of the motivations of the NASDAQ market participants and the tools to view their actions, it is possible to make sound trading decisions based on the reality of price movement, not the hope for a price movement. This is worth breaking out as a point of emphasis. It's

Hope
Versus
Reality

The methods of technical analysis in this book focus you on the reality of what is happening to the price of assets rather than the hope the price will move in your favor. Hope is one of the cruelest killers of capital in a novice day-trader's account. For technical analysis to work for you, you must be totally disciplined: As soon as the reason that you entered a trade is no longer there, you must exit as quickly as possible.

In this book we'll cover the following points in detail:

- Why the NASDAQ market is better suited to day trading and why listed securities are better for swing trades (the practice of holding stocks overnight).

- Trading concepts, such as Dow Theory, that have stood the test of time and how they can be applied to day trading.

Introduction

- Activities that get in the way of making profits.
- Understanding the NASDAQ Level II screen and time of sales, with special attention to why they may legitimately provide conflicting information.
- Getting the best price for your trade by critically appraising all the execution mechanisms open to you, like ECNs, SOES (which in many cases is no longer the fastest route), and SelectNet.
- Detailed tracking of real trading activity using these principles, including premarket preparation/stock selection: the analysis that is best applied to the open, middle, and closing periods of the trading day; and illustration of execution routes.
- Trading psychology and generating your own list of rules that will help maintain your discipline.

These points cover the essentials of day-trading success, which are identifying opportunities, executing effectively, and maintaining discipline.

Once you have read this book, I urge you to take from it what works for you and discard the rest. It is not possible to provide information that will make every trader successful, because we are all different. Your goal should be to develop your own style within the timeless principles presented here. If I can give you just one idea that improves your trading performance and that becomes part of the way you automatically think and react, then this book will have been worth the effort that went into it, from each of our perspectives.

Although this book may be used by those new to trading, it is likely to provide the most benefit to those with some trading experience. The trades illustrated here assume an account size of $20,000, which, with margin, provides $40,000 of purchasing power. This is the minimum I would consider for day trading. My goal is not to convince someone that they can start with a few thousand dollars and become rich. There are plenty of people out there making those claims. I also do not claim that this is easy, or that market makers are stupid people waiting to hand money over to anyone who opens a brokerage account. If this was easy, the economy of the U.S. would be in danger of not producing anything, because everyone would start trading and stop producing.

Realistically, with $20,000 you can generate a regular and reliable income—in excess of $50,000 per year. Once you get to a stake of $100,000, it gets increasingly more difficult to get these types of returns using the methods presented in this book. I can only hope that this is a problem you will eventually face. If you do get to that stage, you need to read *Reminiscences of a Stock Operator* and see how the hero of that book, Larry Livingstone, moved on to the next level in terms of market trading.

PART I
Preparing the Plan

1
Why Day Trade NASDAQ Securities?

This first chapter sets the scene for the information in the rest of the book. It is really an extended introduction to the topics that will be discussed in greater detail in subsequent chapters. To experienced day traders, most of the information in this chapter will already be familiar. I do not recommend that any reader skip this chapter, however, because here is where I lay the groundwork for the methods that will be used to make trading decisions and the thinking behind those methods. In fact, among the key differentiators of this book are that I prove my methods by showing you how market data screens provide trading signals, and that I give you access to my trading account over a given period so that you can see that these methods make money. There are several examples of trades I have made throughout the text, but you will find the most detail in Chapter 6.

In addition, you get access to the premarket analysis I used to determine trading candidates, copies of trade reports to show you how I was able to execute the trades, and margin reports over a period to show you that an account with $20,000 can grow quite rapidly.

A Manifesto of Independence

Please don't be tempted to skip ahead to Chapter 6. You should not read that material until you have read and understood the first five chapters. It is important that you understand the drivers behind my trading decisions before you can judge them in action. I know of no other books that offer such a demonstration of the trading techniques they present. Certainly none of the currently available books provide the premarket analysis, trade reports, and tick charts that give trading signals in real time. In reviewing the available material, I was struck by the same observation that most readers make when reading these texts: How do I know that a person can make money doing this? The closest I saw was one Level II handbook that showed a day's worth of trades that yielded a total of nearly $2000 in profit. There was no independent verification that those trades were executed, that they were the only ones executed that day, or, just as important, that they were executable at the price shown. In fact, as we progress through our analysis of these trading techniques and you learn to apply them to your own trading decisions, you will see that getting the execution you want is in many ways more difficult than identifying a low-risk opportunity. Without the knowledge and ability to execute the opportunities that technical analysis provides you, that analysis is of no value.

I was truly suspicious of that text. Anyone can record a day's activity, then look back on it and determine at what point to trade in order to make a given profit. The author claimed to use an oscillator chart as an indicator for the first trade of the day at 9:33 a.m. However, the settings used on the oscillator would not have allowed it to give a signal at the time claimed by the author. Moreover, as we shall see in later chapters, relying on any form of chart during the first 10 minutes of market open when trading an active NASDAQ security is very dangerous (meaning high risk). Market makers are allowed to report trades up to 90 seconds late during that period, which makes oscillator signals or any chart very unreliable until that time has passed. With an appropriate market data system that provides smoothed multiday displays for one-minute charts, oscillators can be used as a confirmation tool, as will be seen later, but certainly never as the primary indicator. Incidentally, a one-minute chart means that price points are recorded each minute. Later, you will learn about daily charts, so called because each point (or bar, if it is a bar chart) covers one day's worth of data.

The author of that Level II handbook just referred to makes money by getting people to pay subscription fees for an Internet chat room. I suspect that the majority of money made by that particular chat room comes from short-term subscribers who either lose money or learn from their own mistakes and go on to day trade by themselves. The vast majority of chat rooms of this sort are run by a guru who gives market commentary throughout the day that is intended to guide subscribers through their trading decisions. Typically, prior to market open, the guru will introduce a list of securities for the day and comment on the movement of these securities. My experience with these types of chat rooms is that the summary at the end of the day covering the winning recommendations made in the room does not match well enough with the actual commentary during the time the trades should have been made. In addition, when I have seen specific recommendations from one of these gurus, it has often been too late for anyone to make an execution at a favorable price.

The key point here is that if you are going to day trade for yourself, it is you who must do the research and make the trading decisions. Relying on someone else to provide you with a list of securities to watch and looking for recommendations as to when and where to take positions does not make you self-sufficient. It does not provide a path to independence.

Day Trading—
What It Is and
What It's Not

Let's get started and review what day trading is and how it differs from other forms of trading activity. Day traders by definition do not hold positions in securities overnight. Typically, the day trader makes and holds trades for only minutes at a time, most commonly for less than an hour. Operating in this fashion requires a very disciplined approach that includes accepting loss as part of the cost of doing business. It is not possible to make every trade a winner. In fact, I know of people who make lots of money being right only half the time in the trades they make. The key to making money while day trading is limiting your losses and taking profits when you can. Not only does this take a methodical approach, but the approach must be based on the reality of what is happening to the asset you hold, not the hope of what may happen to it in the future.

For those who have held investment accounts, concepts such as doubling down, which may work well for longer-term trades, are potentially disastrous in day trading. Doubling down is the practice of buying a security, and if its price falls, you buy more in order to lower your average cost. That way, you can make money even if the security does not get back to your original purchase price. When day trading, these types of tactics fall more into the hope than the reality column, and they definitely do not contribute to a disciplined approach. As I will say again and again, discipline is the key to survival and profitability in the day-trading game.

Making an investment decision to trade in securities that are then held for years at a time generally comes as the result of fundamental analysis of a company's business. You then apply some sort of valuation model to the share price and become convinced that the share price should be higher. The day trader cares nothing for this sort of analysis. Day traders only care about finding imbalances between supply and demand, and taking positions in securities that take advantage of those temporary imbalances.

Day trading is inherently different from swing trading too (swing traders hold a security over the course of one or two days). The day trader must keep tighter stop losses and have the discipline needed to keep them. In addition, swing traders rely heavily on several types of technical analysis, often far more sophisticated forms than a day trader will use. Day traders need to react quickly to take advantage of the low-risk, short-term moves that result from supply-and-demand imbalances. Using complex analytical methods will never be useful to pure day traders. To properly absorb the information delivered by that type of analysis will take so long that the best entry point will be long gone. Taking inappropriate trading methods that may work well in other circumstances and applying them to day trading is a sure path to high risk and, ultimately, losses.

Here is a useful analogy for describing how day trading differs in concept and execution from longer-term forms of trading. Think about someone taking a dog for a walk through some wooded land using an elastic leash. The paths that the person and the dog might take are illustrated in Figure 1-1.

Think of the path the dog takes as representing the intraday movements of a security and the path the owner takes as representing the closing prices of a security on a daily chart. We know that the elastic leash will tend to bring the dog back toward the owner, and that the things that make the dog dart from one side of the owner to the other are more predictable than the course the owner will take. The dog is a simple, predictable creature who will chase a rabbit or head off to sniff a tree. It is more difficult to predict the owner's path, because it depends on his or her skill at map reading and knowledge of the terrain. This analogy captures the basics of my day-trading approach. The technical indicators presented are quite good at predicting short-term intraday movements. They are less good, however, at telling you where the security is going to close for that day, or any other day.

However, back to a fuller description of this analogy. The dog owner wants to get from point A to point B. Due to the difficult terrain, she cannot go in a straight line. By plotting the paths that the dog owner and the dog take, we generate the graph shown in Figure 1-1 and can illustrate the differences between the three approaches to buying and selling securities (long-term, swing trading, and day trading).

The long-term investor looks for a return from an investment greater than what would be gained by placing the funds in an

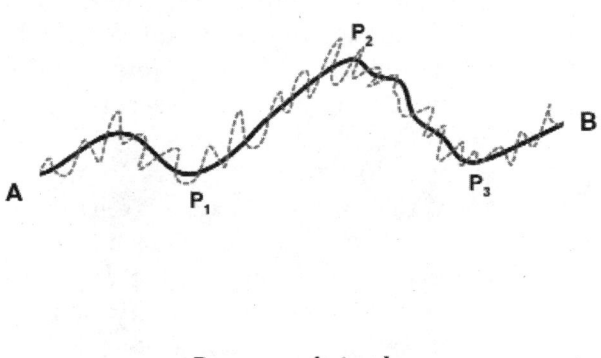

———— **Dog owner's tracks**

- - - - - - **Dog's tracks**

Figure 1-1. The difference between day trading and longer-term forms of trading.

interest-bearing account. The investor will pick a company with a management team in which he or she has faith to navigate the business landscape and return a profit at some point in the future. The company the investor picks may be viewed either favorably or unfavorably by the market at different points during the lifetime of the investment, but that is of little concern. As long as the fundamentals and management team remain intact, the investment is held in the belief that profit will come. This is the Warren Buffett type of trading decision. To make an analogy for this type of trading, we would pick a dog owner we believed would be able to navigate from point A to point B and not worry that detours are necessary to get there. In other words, the path the dog owner takes does not concern us. We firmly believe that the owner will get there in the end. The fact that the dog is pulling the owner off course occasionally only registers as insignificant noise in the overall scheme of things.

A swing trader pays more attention to patterns in the path of a security and seeks to capitalize on moves that occur over several days. For example, if we think of Figure 1-1 as a chart showing daily stock price movements, a swing trader might enter a position at point P1, believing the security has pulled back to levels of support, and exit at point P2, believing a topping formation is in effect. P3 might be viewed as another potential entry point. This form of trading focuses on the path the dog owner is taking. We're less concerned about whether the owner gets from point A to point B. Any effect the dog has of temporarily pulling the owner away from his chosen path is, again, seen as temporary, and not something that will take the owner off course. Here, the dog owner's path is analogous to the closing price of the security, and the dog's tracks are analogous to the intraday swings.

To apply the dog and dog owner analogy to day trading, we focus almost entirely on the tracks the dog takes. The idea that a stock price might behave like a dog, which, as a result of seeing a rabbit or some such event, might bolt in the opposite direction from its owner is key to day-trading activity. If the dog does indeed bolt in the opposite direction from its owner, the elastic leash will ultimately pull the dog back on track, and it will have to forget the rabbit or whatever it went in search of. We don't know when the dog will reach the limit of the elastic, or of his desire to chase the rabbit, and head back to the owner, but we do know that eventually he will. This concept is most easily applied when trading the market open, when we look for large premarket moves in a security that we expect to correct at least partly once the initial run has been made. We will see later that when trading at the market open, a security that makes a big move in the premarket (almost always due to a news story of some kind) is even more attractive when that move is in the opposite direction to the overall trend for that security. In this scenario, it is even more likely that the short-term move will expire and the price will come back closer to the premove price. In this little parallel world, news items are like rabbits, frequently enticing the dog offtrack with great strength, countered, of course, by such external factors as the leash and the owner's desire not to be diverted.

We can also use our analogy for trading stocks after the market-open period. During this time, we seek to identify a trend and trade in the direction of that trend on a very short-term pullback. That is analogous to seeing the dog go off to sniff a tree, first on one side of the owner's tracks, then on the other. We know the dog will lose interest in the tree fairly quickly and will then head off in another direction, most commonly on the opposite side of the owner. Applying that thinking to day trading, we seek to identify what the current trend of the security is, i.e., the direction the dog owner is headed, then trade at a point where we think the security has traded against that trend and reached support. Again, this is analogous to the dog straying away from its owner until it reaches the limit of its elastic leash and getting pulled back toward the owner.

As a day trader, you don't care where the security's price ends up. You are just interested in riding parts of the short-term intraday swings.

The Three Phases of the Trading Day

The approach to day trading presented in this book views the trading day in three phases, which vary in length depending on the trading day. The typical duration of each phase, however, is as follows:

10 Chapter 1

Phase 1: The search for overreaction, followed by reversal (first 10 to 40 minutes of the market).

Phase 2: The search for trends (about four hours after Phase 1 is finished).

Phase 3: The search for breakouts (the last two hours of the market).

A graph of a fictitious security that exhibits these three phases can be seen in Figure 1-2.

It would be meaningless, of course, to say that securities will conform to that pattern of trading throughout a day. Figure 1-2 is only intended to illustrate the types of movement one can expect to see in a typical trading day (if there is such a thing). Not all securities will conform to this mode of trading, but that doesn't matter. My job is to seek out those that show signs of an early reversal in the first phase, show a trend during the second phase, or are experiencing a breakout in the third phase. While it is extremely unlike-

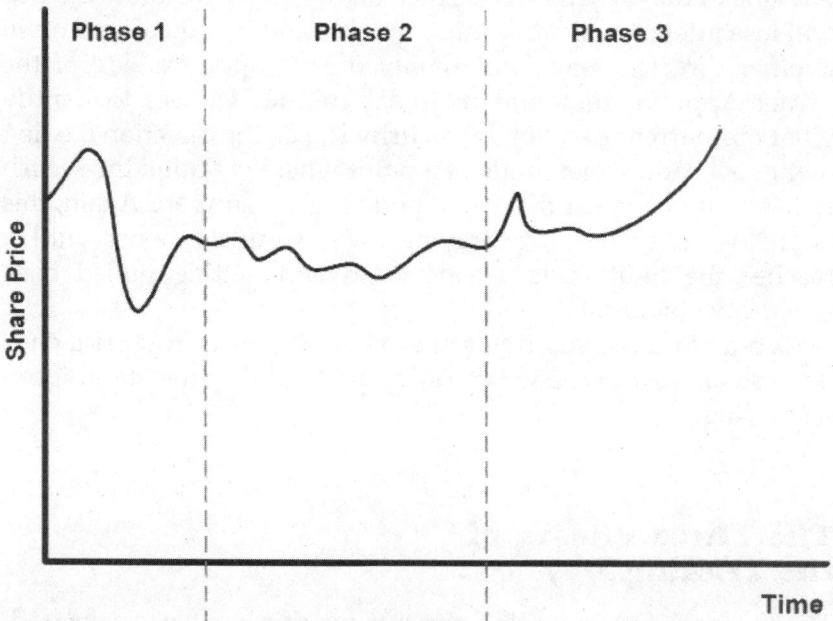

Figure 1-2. Illustration of expected market behavior in the three phases of market operation.

ly that any one security will do all three in one trading day, it is not unheard of. The focus here, though, is to seek out securities that fit a certain mold and trade these securities in a fashion that stacks the odds in our favor.

In Figure 1-2, the Phase 1 portion of the graph shows the typical market action of a stock that has been bid up strongly in premarket action, probably due to some good news. Most commonly, the stock will continue up for a short while after the open and then reverse quite strongly. The opposite tends to be true for stocks whose ask prices have moved down significantly in premarket action. The odds that any given security will follow these patterns increase if the premarket action is in the opposite direction to the prevailing market and security trend. For example, if the market and sector the security is in are in a confirmed downtrend and some news comes out that makes the premarket action very positive, the odds that the security will quickly reverse down early in the day are greater than if the market and sector are in an uptrend. For Phase 2, we are looking for trends (defined as higher highs and higher lows for an uptrend and lower lows and lower highs for a downtrend) that are in line with the overall market and sector trends for that day. The majority of the risk in any given security derives from what is happening in the overall market and what is happening to the sector the security is in. For Phase 2 trading, we have to lower our risk by going with the prevailing market trends at that time. Figure 1-3 shows a classic uptrend, and Figure 1-4 shows a classic downtrend.

Phase 3 trading should be a fairly rare occurrence. It is not where the majority of lower risk trades appear. It is often said that the public controls the open, but the professionals control the close. I am not sure how true this is, but there is enough of a pattern to the trading around the close to make it worthwhile studying. The majority of the time, I do not trade around the close. More often than not, there will be no breakout activity. When it does occur, however, it can be very rewarding. The way to operate in this phase is to identify a security that seems to be trading within a band during the day, set alerts if either the upper or lower limit of the band is breached, and then trade in the direction of the breakout. The entry point during Phase 3 is completely different from that used in Phases 1 and 2. In Phase 1, we are looking for an early

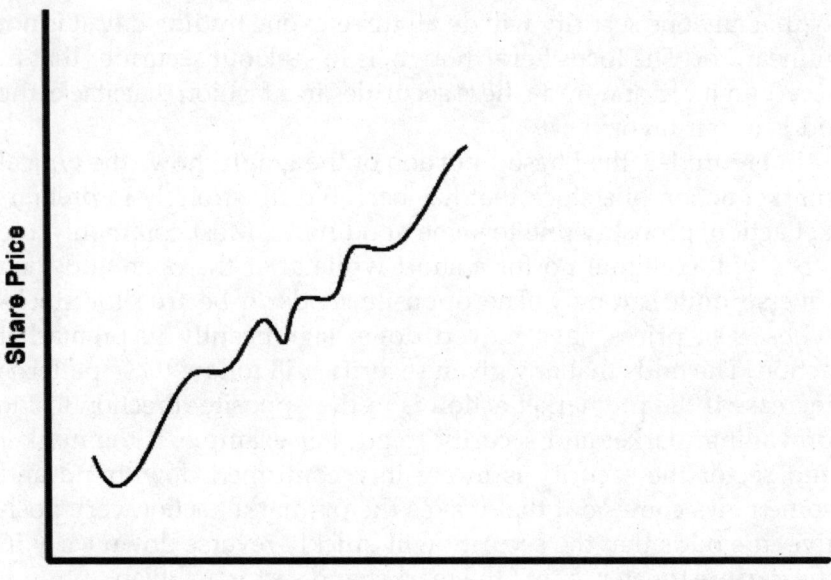

Figure 1-3. A classic uptrend.

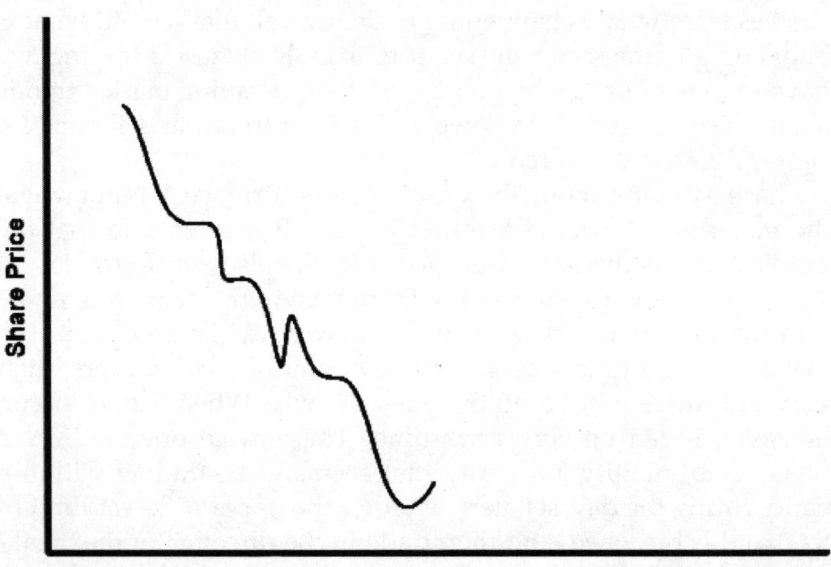

Figure 1-4. A classic downtrend.

top or bottom. In Phase 2, we look to enter either an uptrend on a dip or a downtrend on a small rally. With Phase 3, we don't know where the breakout will run out of steam, so we look to get in and ride the movement as far as it goes.

These ideas on timing entry for the three phases may be somewhat foreign to those who have used technical analysis for investment accounts. One of the key things to know about timing entries when you are holding a security longer-term (several days, weeks, or years) is that it is very difficult to pick tops and bottoms. Looking for continuation patterns within an established trend yields the lower-risk trades. Picking the early reversal in Phase 1 may seem like trying to pick a top, but it differs from picking a top on a daily chart of a security's price movement. The early reversal is due not to identifying a reversal pattern in a daily chart but to the unique operation of the NASDAQ market-maker system, and it is based on the psychology of market participants. You will see that these reversals are generally of the type that I call *point reversals,* as illustrated in Figure 1-5. When taking a position for several days or more, a swing trader will never trade a point reversal on a daily chart, since a point reversal does not announce

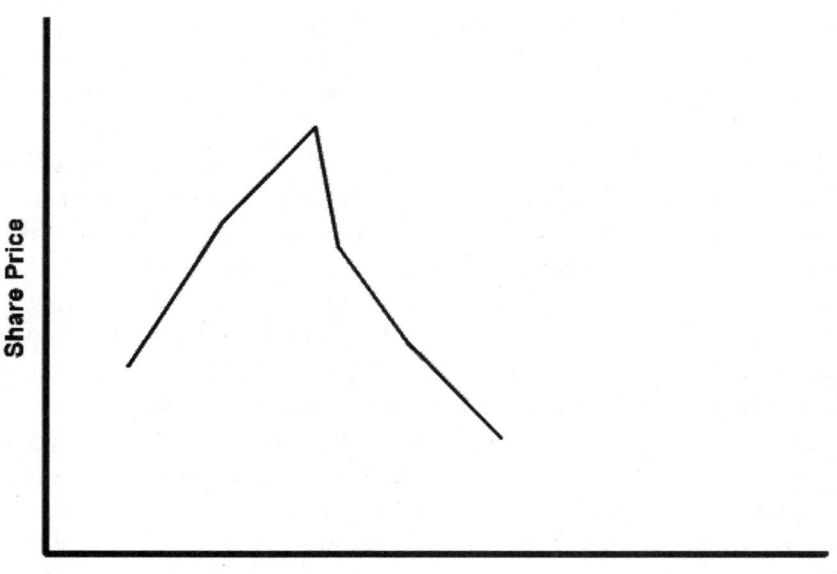

Figure 1-5. Typical point reversal as seen during Phase 1 trading.

itself, it just happens. Swing traders look more for multiple bottoms, head-and-shoulder patterns, or other, more predictable reversal patterns that we will discuss later, as they have relevance to Phase 2 and Phase 3 trading.

This point reversal phenomenon is more simply explained if we take a specific example. Suppose ABC Inc. has just had some positive news come out that it has obtained a major new distribution channel through a dominant supplier in its industry. The premarket price will start to be bid up by the market makers. It may seem on the face of it that the good news alone is increasing the value of the security and that that is being reflected by the market makers. This is not the case. What is happening is that the market makers know that the public, seeing this positive news, will want to buy the security, so they bid upward the price in the premarket. No market maker wants to be the one offering the lowest price, so bids are raised in the knowledge that there will be lots of buying by the public. When the market opens and the public starts buying, the price will generally tend to continue upward for a while until the demand from the public has been met. Once that buying pressure subsides, the price will fall, which is typically accompanied by members of the public realizing they have made a mistake and selling at lower prices to market makers who may well have sold short at earlier higher prices. This drying up of demand is seen as a slowing of price appreciation, accompanied by a decrease in the pace of transactions, and is finally characterized as a reversal in the direction of price movement. The goal in these circumstances is clearly to short the security as it reaches its peak. To get an execution in a case like this requires that you act quickly once you determine that a reversal is happening. Essentially, there is a balance to be struck. The earlier you enter a position, the more likely you are to get your order executed, but the more risk you take that you have not identified the reversal. However, the later you enter the position, the less likely you are to get your order filled at the price you want. My personal preference is to err on the side of entering later rather than sooner. There will always be another opportunity to trade. But once you lose capital, it is gone for good. I may miss the chance to get an execution for some good trades, but I decrease the number of losing trades I have.

The Discipline of Day Trading

When the time comes to review the trades I execute, I find the majority take place in Phase 1. This is because the majority of lower-risk trades occur at this time. Certainly, trends and breakouts do occur after the opening period, but trading them profitably is more difficult. Phase 1 is usually when the heaviest trading of the day occurs, and because of that, it is more difficult for any one group of market participants to affect the short-term movement of a security. I am not suggesting that price manipulation is what drives the price of a security over the course of a day, but I do believe that the purchasing power of some of the larger market participants and the interpretation of their actions by individual traders can temporarily distort a trend or suggest a false breakout that can catch you unaware. We'll cover this in more detail later when we discuss getting shaken out of positions and the proper time to enter a position in a trend.

Trading this way will lead to small, but regular profits and typically amounts to no more than three trades per day. The goals are to gradually increase your capital, avoiding the greed that will make you aim for big gains, and to trade less rather than more in order to limit your spending on commissions. If you have $20,000 and expect to regularly get more than $1000 per day when you win and never to have a losing day, you are in serious need of a reality check. In Chapter 6, I illustrate an average *week* of trading that yielded $3400 on a $20,000 account.

Books that suggest that day trading is an effective means for those in dead-end careers to elevate themselves to the status of financial independence are dangerous. Many people that consider themselves in dead-end careers will find raising $20,000 to start trading to be a significant challenge. From there, the amount of time before that person is making rather than losing money at day trading varies. If, in addition, that person relies solely on the income from trading to meet regular living expenses, the pressure to succeed will be so great that trading discipline is likely to be compromised, and ill-advised trades will result. I never recommend that anyone give up their primary income to take on day trading as an occupation until they have been consistently able to trade profitably while keeping another means of income. Even taking on afternoon or evening shift work can free up time to start trading, and it is much less risky than quitting a job completely. As we'll discuss in the chapter on psychology, you must focus on identifying and executing lower-risk, higher-percentage trades and keeping discipline with stops, while seeking to grow your capital slowly. If there are no opportunities that you feel good about, do not trade. For most individuals, it is only possible to approach the market in this disciplined fashion if they are not dependent upon its returns for their living expenses.

There is an old story about how even experienced traders perform badly if they view the market capable of supplying profits when they want rather than when the profits are really available in the market. The story goes like this:

> *A tailor enters a café that is frequented by successful traders and offers for sale an exquisitely tailored coat that carries an exorbitant price tag due to the cost of the fur used in its trim. All of the traders agree that it is a fine coat, but no one is willing to pay the asking price. Eventually, one of the brasher traders says he will not pay the price, but will take the money from the market and let the market buy the coat for him. He takes the coat from the tailor and tells the tailor that he will pay him when the market has delivered the coat's asking price.*

Needless to say, this trader has moved from the mindset of seeing his job as searching for opportunity. The trader forces trades and in his haste to pay for the coat, seeks opportunity when it is not really there. The coat passes from trader to trader this way, each in turn making the same mistake, until the coat ends up back with the tailor. Each trader realizes that trading failure results from executing trading decisions based on a desire to make money, rather than a desire to trade well.

The point is that unless you can approach trading without the *need* to make a certain amount of money by a certain time, you should not be trading. If you do consider trading for a living, I urge you to have enough money to meet all your commitments for at least six months before you give up other forms of income. Naturally, this six months' worth of expenses has to be totally separate from your trading capital.

With the methods covered here, as with all trading methods, it is possible to produce examples of near-clairvoyant predictive capability. It is possible as well to pick examples of market action in which the method directed you to losses. The goal is not to present these methods as foolproof, because frankly, they are not. What I want to stress is that the patterns we will discuss repeat themselves often enough and for legitimate enough reasons to warrant searching for them. That is the key. We will search for stocks that behave the way we expect and trade them, discarding all others. We will also cut our losses quickly should something unexpected happen to a position we hold.

Positioning ourselves to react should a stock behave in accordance with our expectations enables trading to occur profitably no matter what the prevailing market conditions are. By making use of shorting techniques, it is as possible to make money when the market is falling as when it is rising. There are some challenges in getting a short when you want it, but you will learn how to improve your chances when we discuss executions in more detail.

There are several steps to learning these techniques. The first and simplest is identifying the patterns themselves. Next comes the ability to identify when those patterns are in effect. Third, and most important, comes the discipline to exit trades appropriately. This can mean cutting your losses if the security does not behave as expected, or it can mean taking profits by getting out when you can, not when you have to. Once you reach the point that you see a day of market activity where you decide that there are no opportunities worth risking your capital, you are well on the way to long-term success. I do not advocate inactivity, but I do believe there is a greater tendency to convince yourself that a pattern is forming and try to force trades than to be patient, maintain discipline, and only trade when the market presents real opportunity. I will repeat time and again that it is better to lose an opportunity than to lose capital, because more opportunities will always come along, whereas the same cannot be said of capital.

Of course, this does imply a certain degree of execution skill. With proper use of ECNs (electronic communication networks), SOES (small order execution system), and Selectnet, all of which will be illustrated later, you increase your chances of getting the fill you want. As we discuss the patterns and appropriate entry and exit points, however, remember that even with the mandatory SOES in place, if no one wants to buy a security that you want to sell, there is no way out for you until buyers come into the marketplace, which can be several dollars away from where you wanted to get out. I will speak more on this subject later.

To reach the stage of control in trading activity, in which you can actually decide not to trade in a day if nothing of value presents itself, requires weeks, months, possibly even longer. Reaching this stage of the day-trading experience will probably come at the expense of varying degrees of damage to a novice's opening balance. I was both lucky and unlucky during my initial application of these techniques. I hit a period in the market where the stocks I was trading were in a powerful bull run, and all the technical indicators for trend were pointing me toward quick and easy profits. The luck was that it allowed me to build my capital before the inevitable change in market conditions occurred. The bad luck was that it gave me, temporarily, the belief that I really did understand the market and was doing everything right. Starting with that mindset meant it took me longer to accept that my gains were due to fortunate timing rather than real knowledge. As will inevitably happen when you do not adapt in time to market changes, all the gains I had made disappeared, and I lost nearly 20 percent of my original capital before I was able to regain control, trade with discipline, and start to win again.

So how should one approach the markets to maximize the chances of success? Apart from using the technical analysis tools presented in this book and having the know-how to execute properly, the essential and most influential driver of your profitability as a trader comes from the mindset you use to approach trading. To get a winning mindset, you have to, as much as possible, view trading in a completely detached and unemotional way. You must concern yourself with discipline and the process of entering and exiting trades at the best points, as opposed to thinking about making big bucks and hoping that the market is going to run wildly in your favor. It usually does not. Your goal is to become a disciplined trader, not to make money. If you can trade with discipline, the money will come. If you sit there focusing on how much money you can make or what you will do with it, it is very unlikely that you will succeed as a trader.

In Chapter 7 we will look at the psychology of trading in more depth. It is at least equal to any other factor in determining trading success. I have kept a journal of every trade I have made, which now spans years of activity, and I still see myself repeating the same mistakes. The reasons for this vary, but common to all instances is some type of temporary weakness that leads to a lapse in discipline. Just knowing what to do does not guarantee that you will always do it. Fortunately, my lapses are getting fewer and fewer, along with my losses, and that is the trend to follow. Thinking that you will eliminate all mistakes is unrealistic. What you can hope for is to know that you have made a mistake, realize why it happened, and make future avoidance of that same mistake part of your trading discipline.

So what does keeping discipline mean? In the main, it means keeping to your own set of trading rules, both generic trading rules, such as exiting a trade immediately when a security stops behaving the way you expected it to, and the unique trading rules that identify your own trading style. Generating, maintaining, and reviewing these rules are the keys to long-term survival and trading profits. In Chapter 7, I share with you my set of rules, generated through analysis of my trading successes and failures. Not all of these rules will apply to all people. Everyone needs to create rules to help them avoid repeating mistakes that result from their unique, personal trading activities. Having said that, there is a core set of rules that everyone needs to follow.

Develop a Premarket Plan

Part of the discipline of day trading is that you must have a premarket plan. Going into a trading day with no idea of what you expect to happen, no plan of what you will do if the market either does or does not conform to your expectations, is a very risky proposition. The premarket plans we will look at include a plan of attack for the first two phases of the market. The plan for the third phase is developed as the trading day goes by.

In outline, the plan starts with forming a view of where the overall market is heading on a given day, which generally comes from looking at the premarket activity and a number of technical market indicators. This sets a bias for whether we will prefer to go long or short that day. We then search for securities that are either significantly up or significantly down in premarket activity. We watch these securities before the market opens and assess whether they are continuing or reversing the move they are in. Once the market opens, we will use the Level II screen exclusively to decide when to enter a position. Once entered, the job is to assess whether the reversal is continuing or is just a temporary breather. If we entered in a breather, and the security is poised or starting to continue in its original direction, the aim is to get out as quickly as possible. If, in fact, the security is reversing, we stay with that move for as long as it remains, typically aiming for somewhere between a $3/8$ and a one-point gain. If none of the securities that are up the most or down the most in premarket trading show a reversal, I rarely trade the open.

It is sometimes the case that a reversal occurs in premarket activity and the security continues in that direction after market open. This underlines the need for monitoring the market prior to the open and having the tools to do that. To perform this type of analysis puts stringent requirements on your market data system and requires an in-depth understanding of what that data is telling you. We will review in a little more depth what the market data system requirements are in Chapter 6. However, we will discuss here in overview what is necessary for proper premarket analysis.

The NASDAQ market is what is known as a quote-driven market, meaning the prices of securities are determined by the prices at which certain market participants (generally market makers) are willing to buy or sell the security. These prices can be seen as bid prices, indicating what the participant will pay for the security, and ask prices, which list the desired selling price of the security. For premarket activity, the prices advertised by market makers are not prices at which the market makers have to trade. These prices are more indicative of a market maker's interest in a security. In those cases in which a security is rising in price during premarket activity, the market makers will raise the bid price, but generally they will leave the ask price alone until close to market open. This leads to what is called *backwardation* in the quote price, where it appears that the market is willing to buy at a higher price than the one at which a security is selling. Of course, this backwardation does not lead to an arbitrage profit, because the market makers will not sell at the price that the security is advertised for during premarket activity.

Similarly, if a security is trading down in price prior to market open, the ask price is the one that the market makers alter in a downward direction.

So the first requirement of a market data system in helping us generate a premarket plan is to find NASDAQ securities that are significantly up or down. What does significant mean? For me, it means something that is moving 10 percent of its value or more. In addition to the price movement, we need premarket volume to indicate that the price movement is real, meaning that at least 50,000 shares traded prior to open. Of interest is how we calculate that a security has changed its value in premarket trading, which is related to how change on the day is calculated by your market data system. In general terms, change on the day is calculated as the difference between yesterday's closing price and the price of the most recent trade. Yesterday's closing price will not take into account postmarket trading, so it is the price when the official market ends, currently 4 p.m. EST. There is a convention, however, that change for NASDAQ securities (during normal market hours) is calculated from yesterday's closing bid to the current bid price. This provides a more consistent indication of change values and eliminates the effect that occasional wide spreads can have on change calculations. What this means here is that if a security has a spread of $1 or more between the bid and ask, the change value can alter by that $1 amount just through market participants buying at the bid or selling at the ask, without any real change in the market's view of that security. Calculating change off the bid eliminates this type of discrepancy.

So, for premarket activity, up securities are found by comparing the current bid price to yesterday's close, and for securities trading down, we look at the current ask price against yesterday's close. Once we find these securities, they must be tracked to see in which direction their price is moving, which requires that for the 15 minutes prior to market open, the market data system must show the current best bid and ask of the securities we want to track. Not all systems do this. Some will keep yesterday's information in the monitor (or market minder, whatever your system calls a Level I display) until five minutes before market open, which is too close for my comfort. However, systems that operate this way for the Level I information generally will still allow you to track your chosen securities properly in a Level II window.

This method of searching for what are termed *premarket gaps* does have some weaknesses, depending on how your search engine works. Typically, securities that undergo a split or stock consolidation will appear in the search because the current bid or ask will be well away from yesterday's close, but the large change is not due to a change in the market's view of the security and is therefore of little interest to a day trader. Also, this search will on occasion turn up test securities, like TESTA, the NASDAQ test symbol. Seeing that TESTA is up big in premarket with healthy volume does not mean that you should track it and try to trade it!

Some other day traders who also look for premarket movers as sources of securities to trade early in the day use news search engines to look for keywords like *upgrade, downgrade, merger,* and so forth, or to look at services like the Dow Jones "Hot Stocks to Watch" headline. It is true that you can generate a list of securities that will move nicely in early trading using this method, but it does take a lot more effort to get the same result. The downside to using news search engines is that you will get lots of securities touted as "hot" that do not move, or they have very little volume. I do not care so much what the news is on a security. I'm more interested in how the market reacts to that news; therefore I look for movement and volume directly. Also, when you think about it, to set up your screens to monitor between five and eight securities and get a feel for which ones are continuing to move in premarket, all within 15 minutes of market open, is quite a tall order. If you are trying to do that by searching and evaluating news, you are likely to have a problem.

Getting the Phase 2 Picture

For Phase 2, we look for securities that are showing consistent highs and lows on the intraday chart, which form a sustainable trend, that is also in line with their overall direction as seen on a daily chart, and we look to take positions on pullbacks.

This parallelism is important, since you will often see a stock on the daily chart that is trending strongly in one direction, but whose intraday indicators show moving the other way. I tend to give these securities a miss, because I have lost more than I have won by trading against the overall trend of the security. It is better to look for another stock that has intraday indicators in tune with its main trend. Owing to the nature of intraday reversal patterns, I have probably lost more than I have gained by taking intraday positions contrary to the overall trend of the security. When you look at intraday charts, one of the key differences you'll see between them and daily charts is that there are more point reversals in the intraday variety. These are more difficult to trade outside Phase 1.

The securities we trade in Phase 2 will not be the same ones traded in Phase 1. To trade trends in Phase 2, you need to know well the security you are trading. You need to know how it moves typically, so that you can spot anything out of the ordinary. You also need to know whether that security is in an uptrend, downtrend, or trading range, and how it is performing relative to its sector.

In addition, when we come to look at Level II screen data, we will see that each security has its own patterns in Level II screen motion. What that means to us as day traders is that the same Level II display can mean one thing for one security and something else for a different security. It is only your own knowledge of the way a particular security normally trades that lets you understand what the Level II screen is really telling you during this second phase. Perhaps an example would be beneficial here.

Securities like Microsoft, Dell, and Intel are very heavily traded every day. It is not uncommon to see Microsoft in a sustainable trend (for argument's sake, let's make it an uptrend), to see 30,000 shares offered for sale at the ask, and have the uptrend remain intact. A similar amount of shares being offered at the ask for a much smaller company would almost certainly indicate that further upward movement was unlikely.

Of course, plenty of instances could be pointed out when on a specific day, following this advice would make you miss an opportunity. However, keeping this discipline will save you from losing capital in the long run.

Some Tips for Phase 3

The plan for Phase 3 trades, as we have said, is generated as the trading day progresses. The securities we trade during Phase 3 are also from the pool of securities we monitor on a daily basis. As the day progresses, the one-minute tick chart will identify areas of support and resistance that can be drawn, and alerts can be set if a breach of support or resistance occurs. Other than close to the end of the trading day, there are typically many false breakouts during the Phase 2 period of trading, and it is for this reason that trends, rather than breakouts, are the mainstay of Phase 2 trading.

I have seen other methods for day trading that take the high and low values set within the first hour of trading and assume that those values will be the highs and lows for the day. With those highs and lows identified, the plan then becomes to trade in the opposite direction as the security reaches either its high or low value, i.e., short when the security reaches its high value and buy when it reaches the low. This technique will provide some winning and some losing trades, but it does not present a sufficiently high success rate. The only time I like to take a position on a point reversal that is happening is during the opening period. Past that time, they happen with far less predictability. The main problem with this method is that there is no guarantee that the high or low will be set during the first hour of trading.

In the next chapter, where we examine Dow theory, one of the key concepts introduced is that trends tend to persist for much longer than most people expect. During market open, no trends have established themselves and the reversals are due to overreactions. In Phase 2, trends have established themselves and you don't bet against them. The only time you determine that a trend is no longer worthy is when it has given a signal that it is no longer in effect. For an upward trend, this signal could be the failure to make a new high after a pullback, or making a low that is lower than the previous low. We'll look at this in more detail in Chapter 2, particularly with reference to what time frame should be used for real time charts. This is important because a one-minute tick chart can give you different information than a five-minute tick chart. Basically, the chart patterns will differ depending on the time frame over which you are looking at them, and it is important to use the right time frame for the right situation.

When trading a trend, you will be aware of such things as support or resistance, and your knowledge that the trend will expire at some point, often after an exhaustion run (also covered in Chapter 2). During Phase 2, however, it is important to not try to trade the reversal until a new trend has established itself. For now, let's just look in more detail at why the NASDAQ is a better exchange for day traders than listed exchanges.

NASDAQ vs. Listed Exchanges for Day Trading

First of all, let's just review how NASDAQ operates compared to the more traditional listed exchanges, such as the NYSE. On an exchange that deals listed securities, each security is assigned its own specialist, who is responsible for maintaining an orderly market in that security. To do this, the specialist is essentially responsible for providing liquidity to the market for that security. This means the specialist may have to sell from his own inventory when the stock is rising and there are more willing buyers than willing sellers. He may also have to buy in a falling market when there are more willing sellers than willing buyers. On the surface, this does not sound like a good deal. For providing liquidity, however, the specialist gets information in return. The specialist is the only person in the market who knows about *all* the orders, both buy and sell, for the security he or she is responsible for. This enables the specialist to set the buy and sell price that will most likely yield a profit via the spread he makes in the security.

One of the byproducts of the single-specialist system is that you will see far more halt conditions on NYSE securities than you will in the NASDAQ. A *halt condition* means that there is an imbalance between the amount of buy orders and sell orders seen by the specialist, and he temporarily halts trading in that security until he can work out what to do. Often, it means that limit orders put in near-market value prior to the halt will not be executed after the halt is lifted. Essentially, the specialist eliminates the imbalance by moving the price of the security to where there is balance. Halting securities on NASDAQ is far less common. There, each market maker is doing what the name suggests, making a market. No single entity knows all the orders that are out there; therefore, no single person can determine that there is an imbalance of orders. The way that order imbalances work themselves out on NASDAQ is that the price moves rapidly, but you still have the opportunity to trade while the move is taking place. Trading is not halted. That is not to say that there are no NASDAQ halts. They are just less frequent, so you have a better opportunity to trade these big, fast moves.

The specialist, at the heart of the NYSE operation, is there to hold auction in his security and match buyers with sellers. The way the specialist does this is to advertise the best bid and ask, as represented by brokers placing orders with the specialist, along with the size of the order available at that price. The best bid is the highest price someone is willing to pay for the security, and the best ask is the lowest price someone is willing to sell it for. The size (generally in hundreds of shares on most market data systems) lists the number of shares available at that price. If you want to buy more shares than are being offered at the best ask price, it is likely you will have to buy some at a higher price to get the amount you want. These are supplied either by other traders willing to sell only at that higher price, or from the specialist's inventory.

On listed exchanges, a broker's goal is to trade in between the best bid and ask, that is, not pay the full asking price and sell for more than the best bid price. This is usually done by advertising a bid or ask in between the current price and hoping that one of the existing buyers or sellers will move on the price at which he is willing to deal and take the price the broker is offering. This is, of course, a little riskier than executing on an existing order, since the market can move away from that newly advertised price and leave the broker without a fill. This is something you will become familiar with when day trading for yourself on ECNs like Island or Archipelago. Oftentimes, these in-between offers are executed immediately and do not result in a change to the bid and ask maintained by the specialist.

A common question asked by traders is whether the trade reported was a buy or a sell. The trader is trying to get a feel for whether or not there is demand for a security. In an order-driven market, such as the NYSE, where the bid and ask prices are reflections of orders placed with the specialist, this is a difficult question to answer. The reason is that in the majority of cases, there is both a buyer and seller; they just have to agree on the price of exchange. The trader asking this question is really trying to get a feel for where the action is in the marketplace. If a string of orders is executed at the asking price, the trader interprets this as buying pressure, whereas a string of orders at the bid will be seen as selling pressure.

This leads to the age-old question of what makes prices rise or fall, to which one of the standard answers is: Prices rise when there are more buyers than sellers and fall when there are more sellers than buyers. This is not strictly accurate. Every transaction requires two parties, buyer and seller. What we have to examine is how willingly the two participants enter into the transaction. This may at first seem a curious idea, that a market participant would make a trade unwillingly. That is, however, the case for both listed and over-the-counter (OTC) markets like NASDAQ. On the NYSE, the specialist is the one charged with keeping an orderly market and will buy or sell when no one else wants to. On NASDAQ, market makers have to offer a two-way price during market hours, so there is always a price to trade against there as well. It may not be the price you want to trade at, but there will be one.

As I will show throughout this book, identifying the nature of a single trade in the market or the value of a security or index at any one point in time does not help us in making our trading decisions. It is the flow, the direction or trend of a security's price at the time that is important. So trying to determine whether any given trade was a buy or a sell is meaningless on several levels. Our job is to assess demand and supply for a security and take a position in that security that takes advantage of any imbalance. It is demand and supply that cause price movement. Simply put, prices rise when there is capacity in the market to consume all stocks available at the best ask price, thus making the next highest ask the best available. When this happens and you see bids increasing, indicating that market makers are willing to pay a higher price for the security, then you know that you are, at least temporarily, in an uptrend. The number of stocks available at a given ask price will change based on two inputs, the number being offered and the number being bought. We will examine this idea more thoroughly when the NASDAQ Level II screen is discussed in detail in Chapter 5. For now, all we need to know is that the ask price can rise even without purchases of the stock, if those parties advertising stock for sale at the best ask remove their offers.

On the NYSE, the only information we get to see is the best bid and ask and the size at that price. We do not get to see the supporting offers or whether these bid and ask prices are changing due to orders being removed from the market or as a result of a transaction taking place. The specialist is the only one to see this information, which is one of the reasons day trading on NYSE is not recommended.

So how is this different from what happens on NASDAQ? The NASDAQ, or OTC market, as it is sometimes termed, is a quote-driven market. The bid and ask price are set by market makers (or unmatched orders on ECNs) indicating the price and size they are willing to deal at for a given security. In the case of market maker quotes, these are often not firm orders like they are on listed exchanges, but rather an indication of a willingness to trade should someone else wish to act upon the offer. In practice, the real difference is that on a listed exchange, the size represents a firm number of shares that someone is willing to transact, whereas in the OTC market, if a market maker lists a given size, she can transact several trades at that price before changing the quote. The exception to this is the best bid or ask from an ECN, which is in fact a firm customer order that will be immediately executed should you like the deal offered. As we shall see, however, in fast-moving markets, market makers have many ways of disappearing from the screens and avoiding transactions that they do not want to make. Also, we'll see that market maker prices can be posted in such a way that they hide their true intentions. It is not unusual for a market maker to look like a seller of a security when in fact, the ultimate goal is to acquire stock.

The NASDAQ market is best understood with reference to a Level II display, which is shown in Figure 1-6.

This shows the main market participants, along with the price and size they are prepared to trade at on the security in question, which in this case is Dell. Of all the texts I have seen on the sub-

Security	DELL						
tick dir ↑							
mm	Bid	Ask	Size	mm	Bid	Ask	Size
SHWD	49 3/8	49 5/8	10	SBSH	49 5/16	49 7/16	1
NITE	49 3/8	49 1/2	10	MADF	49	49 1/2	200
SBSH	49 5/16	49 7/16	1	DEAN	48 3/4	49 1/2	90

Figure 1-6. A typical NASDAQ Level II display.

ject of day trading, none provide a dynamic display of the Level II screen, which is the only real way to view and understand the information it is giving you. Chapter 5 provides successive screen snapshots that show how the Level II screen changes under different market conditions. The most common description of how the Level II screen operates is that when prices are moving from right to left, or counterclockwise, the price is moving up. Conversely, when the prices are moving from left to right, or clockwise, the price is falling. This is possibly the most useless information you'll come across regarding the Level II screen. If you only needed the Level II screen to see this movement in prices, it would be of no value. It would be far easier to watch the bid or ask prices on a Level I display or a real-time tick chart to see if prices were rising or falling. The real value of the Level II screen is in its ability to show potential areas of support or resistance before they can be seen on a tick chart, or to show you if a previous support level will hold. More on this later, but for now let's concern ourselves with a basic description of the Level II screen as presented.

In Figure 1-6, the left-hand column shows the market makers with the best bid in the market along with the supporting bids in descending order. In this case, both SHWD and NITE are offering the best bid of $49^{3}/_{8}$, with SBSH one-sixteenth (or a steenie) lower at $49^{5}/_{16}$. Like most Level II displays, this one shows the size that each market maker is willing to buy at that price, and it also lists that market maker's asking price. In this display SHWD is bidding on blocks of 1000 shares (as represented by the value 10 in the size column; size is normally quoted in hundreds). Similarly, on the right-hand side of the display are those market makers with the best asking prices. SBSH is on its own, offering stock at $49^{7}/_{16}$, with a size of 1, followed by DEAN and MADF at $49^{1}/_{2}$. This information is condensed down into a Level I quote of bid $49^{3}/_{8}$, ask $49^{7}/_{16}$, size 10×1.

This Level II display is showing you the essential elements of the NASDAQ market. The Level I quote is derived from the best bid to buy and the best offer to sell of all the market makers operating in that security. The prices change on NASDAQ depending on how all the different market makers perceive demand at the time, which is the key to the difference between trading on NYSE and NASDAQ. NASDAQ prices are set by group consensus, and none of the group members have access to complete information. On NYSE, by contrast, one person manages the prices, and that one person has access to all relevant information for that security. It is this essential difference that leads to the opportunities that exist for day traders on the NASDAQ market.

The Execution Imperative

As has already been stated, just identifying opportunities is not enough. You must be able to execute orders at favorable prices in order to turn opportunities into capital, and here again, NASDAQ scores over NYSE for day trading. For OTC securities, there are ECNs which provide a way for traders to match orders with other traders and bypass the market makers, or actually post a bid or offer on the Level II screen. The largest ECN is Instinet, represented by INCA on the Level II display. Instinet has traditionally been accessible only to institutions. However, it has recently signed a deal with E*Trade to give access to the public. Some other important ECNs that we will discuss in detail in Chapter 5 are Island and Archipelago. And there are still others, but they are of less significance.

With all the restrictions that are now in place with SOES, which protect the market maker from traders executing on the prices the market makers advertise, these ECNs have taken on even more significance than just allowing traders to offer stock for sale at the asking price or offer to buy at the bid price. Because fills on Island and other ECNs are virtually instantaneous, you can often get away with offering stock for sale at a price higher than the best ask and still have someone accept it. This is because the dreaded SOES queue will often make an ECN the only way to execute a trade at close to the current best price in a fast market. We shall cover this in more depth with some examples in Chapter 5. In fact, in that chapter you will learn how and why Island is currently the preferred route for order execution. Even though one can only enter limit orders on Island, the liquidity and speed of execution are so far unmatched by any other system. Of course, if no one enters a matching order to yours, you will not get your stock bought or sold on Island, but more on this topic later.

Who Wins and Who Loses in Day Trading?

So now another interesting question arises: If your buy only goes against someone else's sell, is the practice of day-trading stocks a zero sum game? I do not believe so. Anyone trading on an exchange adds liquidity, and liquidity is what makes a market successful. Securities do not have time values in them the way that derivatives do. In the equities market, real wealth is both created and destroyed on a daily basis. Consider this example: Microsoft is climbing on good news. A day trader buys 500 shares at 92, then sells them at $92^1/_2$, happy with a $250 gain for holding Microsoft over the course of 15 minutes. The trader sells those securities to a long-term investor who sees Microsoft appreciate to over $100 several months later. Both have won—which is not a zero sum game—because Microsoft is creating wealth by writing software that more and more people are using. If a security is falling in price, the reverse is true. In other words, those in the chain who buy the security and then sell it at a loss have lost money, essentially because the value of the falling security as a whole has decreased, not because one group of market participants has that money at the cost of another group. The equities market is not a fixed-size pie in terms of the amount of money to be distributed. The size of the pie is constantly changing, and typically it is increasing, if you look over the course of several years. What keeps the stock market from being a zero sum game is that there is no preset time constraint on when you decide to realize your gain or loss, also that buying a security is buying part of something real. This is not the case with derivatives, as you will see later. If day-trading securities were truly a zero sum game, it would not be possible for very many individuals at all to profit by it. The professional institutions would have all the money, as invariably ends up the case in options trading.

I was interested to read a recent *New York Times* story that quoted a government report investigating day-trading practices after a tragedy in which a disgruntled day trader shot brokers at the brokerage company he was using. Clearly, this particular trader was a lunatic, and no general conclusions can be drawn from his actions.

It is worth noting, however, that if you blame anyone other than yourself for trading losses, you are missing the point. One should always do one's own analysis and decide on appropriate entry and exit points for oneself. Relying on others is just not a viable option in day trading.

It is possible to make regular profits by day trading. If you do not, it is because of a fault in analysis, execution, or more commonly, in discipline.

The government report on the shooting incident only looked at 17 accounts and concluded that most people do not make money day trading. This, of course, was lambasted by the brokerage community as not being a representative sample. My main criticism of this government report is that it suggested that options trading offers greater leverage and is a better vehicle for those who want to profit from short-term movements in a security's price. The conclusion as to why traders do not use options trading was that this leads to a quicker loss of capital, whereas trading the securities themselves leads to a slower loss of capital. I totally agree that trading derivatives will, over time, lead to a loss of capital for the vast majority of people, and these reasons will be covered in Chapter 3. To suggest, however, that options trading and day trading NASDAQ securities are the same activity, only being executed using different financial tools, is a crass misrepresentation. The methods presented in this book will, when executed with total discipline, yield small (by the claims of many day-trading brokers and seminar providers) but regular profits that add up over time. Applying the same techniques to options trading would be disastrous.

It is still most likely that the majority of people currently day trading will not make money over the course of several months. This is not because it is impossible to make money day trading. I will be giving independently verifiable proof that I do make money day trading using the methods shown in this book. It is because the primary sources of information for the beginning day trader are supplied either by brokers or providers of expensive seminars, and not by those who spend every day in the market looking for low-risk, profitable trades.

What Is Technical Analysis?

There are no formal qualifications or standards applied to those offering advice on day trading. All you need is a convincing story to tell. I'm not writing this book as a taster to get you to sign up for an expensive course, or to motivate you to trade, just to generate commissions. In all honesty, much of the content here is well known. It's just not widely disseminated. What this book does do is remind readers about some trading methods that have stood the test of time and that are focused on more reliable means of capital appreciation rather than on get-rich-quick hype. These techniques are illustrated in the context of making day-trading decisions for OTC securities, so without further ado, I'll provide the overview necessary to get you started in technical analysis (TA) if you are new to it.

Essentially, TA is about observing a security's price movement rather than the reasons for it. Most technical analysts can get by without any type of fundamental research or news service at all. The pure TA view is that everything known about a security is already discounted into its price. The current price results from the summation of all the views of all the market participants that have an interest in the security. This view contends that all factors, from politics and interest rates to job figures and market psychology, are already reflected in the price, and anything new is quickly assimilated. TA does not believe that these factors have no impact on the price of a security; just the opposite. TA recognizes that fundamentals drive the market, but it sees analysis of price movement as a shortcut to understanding a security's likely future price movement.

I, personally, am purely interested in the likely price movement of a security as the basis for my investment, so the price movement is what I study. I have seen apparently good news result in a price decline too many times to rely on fundamental analysis alone. The content of news is not the important thing. It is how the market reacts to that news that is important. And only the price movement of the security tells you how the market is reacting.

The TA view also believes that history repeats itself. This view is grounded in the knowledge that the financial markets are driven by the psychology of the humans who participate in them, and as with history, the future largely repeats the past. Fear and greed are constant factors in the markets and generate predictable patterns in price movement. Those who do not learn from the past are going to repeat the mistakes of the past. Unfortunately, the majority of people seem to have difficulty learning from the mistakes of others, and they repeat these mistakes themselves. This prime tendency among humans results in price movements repeating themselves in the financial markets.

The key concept behind TA is the identification of trends. One tenet of TA is that once a security has started to move in one direction, either up or down, it will continue to move in that direction. Predicting the end of a trend is tricky business, and it requires a definite signal that the trend has expired. This is shown in Figure 1-7 for United Technologies. The security is in a strong trend from January 1999 until May. Once the trendline is broken, that trend is no longer in effect and the security has no overall direction. Although this is a daily chart, the same is true of intraday charts as well.

One of the main benefits of technical analysis is that it helps take the emotion out of trading decisions. There is enough emotion built into a trading decision just by having one's capital at risk. In addition, those who trade based on analysis of news and market forecasts invest something of themselves in the forecasts they make. It is their view of what should happen. If the market does not agree, the temptation is strong to believe that the market will come around to their point of view at some stage, at which point they can cash in. Technical analysts do not do this. Rather, they study the direction the market is taking a security and trade in harmony with the market, not attempting to predict when a change of heart will occur, merely taking action in response to the market doing whatever it decides.

There are, however, plenty of critics of TA. The main criticism is that TA is a self-fulfilling prophecy. Essentially, the argument goes that if there is a trend in existence, technical analysts will see that trend, buy into it, and in that very act of buying force the trend to continue. Baloney. No single group of market participants is big enough to control the market, certainly not the technicians, who represent only a minority among traders. Financial markets have a diversity of participants: long-term investors, swing traders, market makers taking the spread. To suggest that TA can dominate the

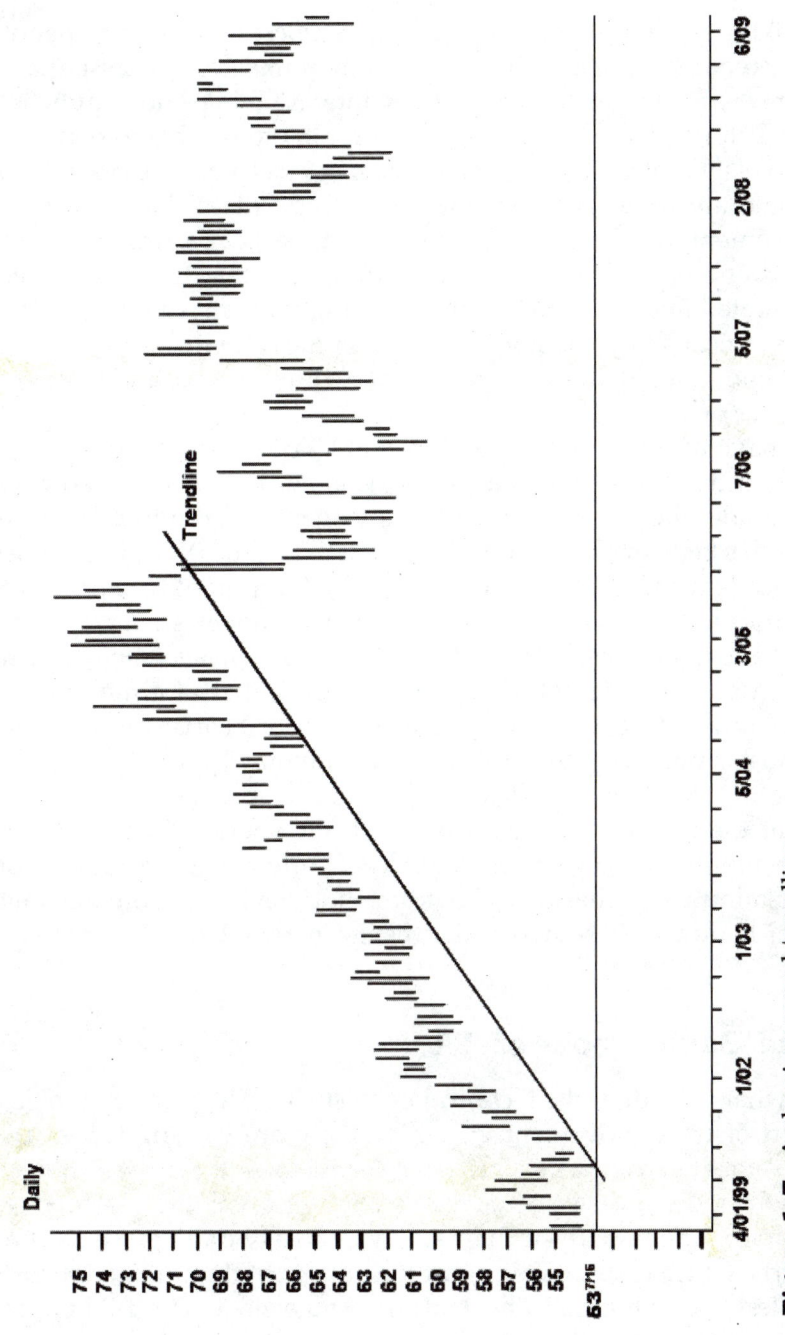

Figure 1-7. A classic upward trendline.

thinking of all of them is simply fantasy. Besides, very few people are prepared to apply the discipline required for TA. Essentially, there are too many people out there interested in rumors, hunches, gut feeling, or the latest news hype for TA to be able to drive the markets. What we tend to see in the markets is that the majority of people are more apt and willing to trade ideas than real price movement. It is because the majority of market participants trade ideas and become victims of fear and greed that the patterns get generated in the first place and get continually repeated after that. A technical analyst is not interested in the reason for the crowd's behavior, merely in the effect that their buying and selling has on market prices.

I have also heard the criticism that chart patterns only exist in the minds of technical analysts. This is not too far removed from the academics' view that market movements are random in nature and markets revolve around their *intrinsic* value. But just because an academic (few of whom have much, if any, trading experience) cannot see patterns, does not mean they do not exist.

I have a more valid criticism of technical analysis when applied to day trading. Many times, you can see a pattern forming but do not know which type of pattern (bullish or bearish) until it has almost completed itself. By this time, you may have difficulty getting an execution in order to take advantage of the price movement the pattern predicts. Moreover, the chart patterns seen on one-minute tick charts may look very different when viewed on five-minute tick charts, so what time horizon is the more informative? I address these two criticisms in Chapter 2.

The Basic Tools of TA

So what tools does the technical analyst use? The primary tool is a chart of price movement, of which there are varying types. The movement of a security's price is referred to as its *price action*. Price action is always the primary indicator, with volume a secondary indicator. In the analysis that is relevant to day trading, we use line charts, which display volume at the bottom of the chart. Bar charts are less useful for real-time analysis. And even less useful in intraday charts are candlesticks.

Bar Charting

When we look at assessing the overall market environment in Chapter 6, bar charts, point and figure, and candlesticks can all come in handy. Examples of line charts have already been provided in Figures 1-3, 1-4, and 1-5. Bar charts are somewhat different. Whereas a one-minute line chart (which I call a one-minute tick chart) will place a point on the chart at the price at which the security last traded within that minute, you will have no knowledge of how the security fluctuated in price during that one-minute period. The bar chart provides that information. The top of the bar represents the high price for that period, the bottom the low price, and the dash on the right-hand side of the bar represents the close. Some charts also show a dash on the left-hand side of the bar to indicate the opening price during that period. These features of the bar chart are shown in Figure 1-8.

When assessing general market conditions, I like to see two, and preferably three, different indicators all agree before I make my decision on where the market is heading.

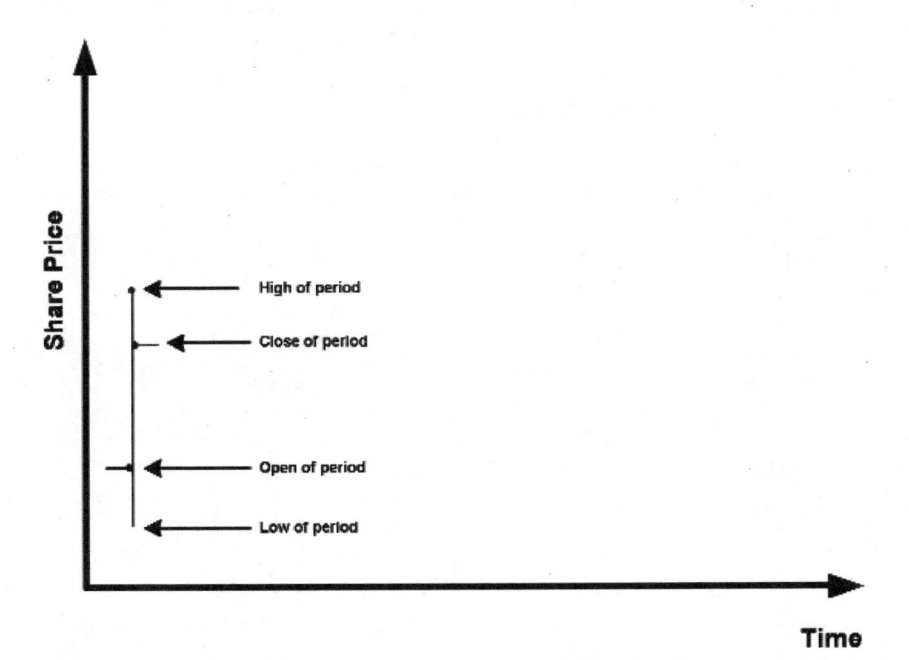

Figure 1-8. A typical bar chart.

We do not use indicators of overall market direction to control exactly how we behave. They merely provide a bias for our actions, pointing us toward looking for long opportunities in rising markets and shorting in falling markets. That is not to say that we will not sometimes trade against the prevailing market trend if there is an exceptionally strong movement happening in one security. It just means that we will be more careful about trading against the overall trend.

Candlesticks

In Chapter 6 we will discuss the basic (and most useful) candlestick patterns. Here, now, I will stick to main concepts.

Each candlestick is made up of a real body and two shadows, as shown in Figure 1-9.

The real difference between this and the regular bar on a bar chart is the information provided by the real body. In Figure 1-9, the upper end of the real body is marked with the letter A, and the bottom of the real body is marked with the letter B. These represent the open and closing prices for the period the candlestick

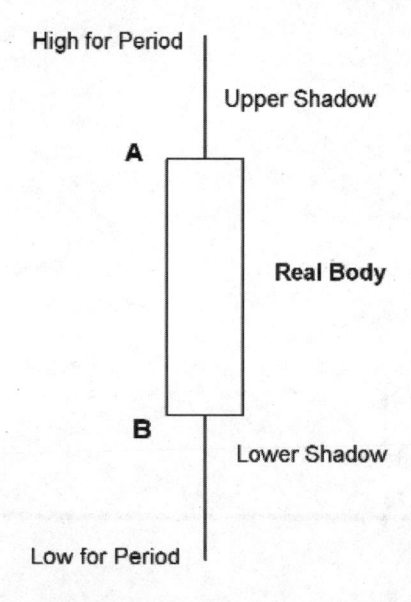

Figure 1-9. Elements of a candlestick.

spans. If the open is higher than the close for that period, the real body will be black, indicating that prices declined in the course of the day. If the open is lower than the close for that period, the real body will be white, indicating that prices closed higher than the level at which they opened. As we shall see later, it is the combinations of candlesticks that form the useful patterns, not analysis of any single candlestick.

Point-and-Figure Charting

The point-and-figure method is a little more difficult to understand, at least initially. Point and figure is a really good method when looking for stocks that may break out, either to the upside or the downside. I have heard of people using intraday point and figure, but I have not done so. Point-and-figure charts will be discussed when we are assessing overall market direction, to give us a bias for the direction in which we will look to trade securities. Again, just as with candlesticks, the point-and-figure information only gives us a bias. Should the price action for a given day contradict the point-and-figure information, we go with that instead. Day traders should always use the day's price action as the primary driver for trading decisions. Should the day's price action disagree with the point-and-figure indicator, the day's price action takes precedence. The basic point-and-figure chart is shown in Figure 1-10.

This is an odd display, no question. It represents price movement only, disregarding both the time element and volume. The vertical axis represents price, and the horizontal axis has no assignment. The concept behind the point-and-figure method is that a column of X's represents a rising trend, and a column of 0's a falling trend. As such, the point-and-figure chart highlights trend reversals and price breakouts very well, in fact, far better than a line or bar chart.

113	X					X
112	X	O	X			X
111	X	O	X	O		X
110	X	O	X	O		
109			O		O	

Figure 1-10. A basic point-and-figure chart.

In point-and-figure charting the box size is of paramount importance. In Figure 1-10, the box size is one dollar, and we can see the first column is one of X's, indicating that the price moved from 110 to 113 without any fallback. This could have happened over minutes, weeks, or months, because time does not matter in point-and-figure charting. The next feature to note is what degree of retrenchment will cause the chart to reverse into a column of 0's. That is selected, but for argument's sake, let us make it 3, which means a reversal of three box sizes is needed to shift the chart display to the next column on the right. To make this clearer, let's us look at some data that could be used to generate the display. These figures represent the closing price taken at regular intervals. They could be at the end of the day, a week, every hour, or even every 15 minutes. The rate at which data is collected is the only area where time has an effect on the point-and-figure chart. The first set of data is as follows:

110, 113, 109, 112, 109, 113

Here, a three-point reversal happens after each consecutive data point, which causes a new column to be created. The same display would be generated with the following data.

110, 111, 112, 113, 110, 109, 112, 112, 111, 109, 112, 113

This shows the runup from 110 to 113, which is immediately followed by a three-point reversal to 110, then a further decline to 109. The reversal happens again at 112 and holds there as the price falls to 111. The reversal does not happen until the fall to 109. The final reversal happens with the move to 112, followed by 113.

I have not come across a good source for intraday point and figure, although I would dearly like to, so I cannot use it for timing day trades. However, point-and-figure charting becomes important when it comes to assessing the overall market and sector health of securities.

Answering the Criticism and Misperception

To conclude this first chapter, I want to go over a few general points that come up when those who lack substantial day-trading experience criticize TA in day trading. First of all, the most common criticism is that it is riskier than buy-and-hold strategies. In my experience, this has not been the case. Inexperienced traders of all kinds are more likely to lose money, regardless of the method they choose to employ. Risk in the markets is determined by the length of time assets are held. The longer you hold a security, the more things can happen to its price, both good and bad. I share the view of day trading presented in *Reminiscences of a Stock Operator*, by Edwin Lefevre. That book's hero, Larry Livingstone, initially makes his money through bucket shops in late nineteenth-century New York. Bucket shops allowed clients to bet on the next movement of a security without buying the security. That was a perfect form of day trading: no execution delays, as there were no executions. Although Larry was able to generate a fair-sized trading stake through this day trading, he realized that to make real money, he had to be able to predict major market moves and take positions in securities or commodities to take advantage of those moves when they occurred. This reinforces the view of day trading as largely a reactive activity, whereas investing is a predictive activity. Taking a position in the market in anticipation of a move happening rather than getting in on an existing move has to be the higher-risk proposition.

This opinion has been confirmed by my own experience in trading. My biggest wins and biggest losses have come from buying and holding securities over a period of a few weeks or a few months. The balance in my day-trading account has changed far more slowly than the account that held securities over a longer term. Being able to time the purchase and sale of an individual security to take advantage of a significant move that it is about to make is a skill to which I still aspire, and it is possibly the most difficult one of all. Currently, I approach the markets from two angles, the first being to accrue small, consistent profits from day trading that add up over time. The second is the long-term holding of a diversified portfolio. The overwhelming probability is that a well-diversified portfolio will outperform interest-bearing accounts if it is held for several years, which makes this a boring, but fairly low-risk decision.

I agree with the lessons of Larry Livingstone's experience: that pursuing day trading is a good way to build capital while learning about market movements. Perhaps it is possible to learn enough that timing major market moves becomes feasible.

Another main misconception is confusing day trading with online trading, or perceiving services such as Datek or Ameritrade as suitable vehicles for executing day trades. These online brokers are certainly a step up in value from the average full-service broker, who makes a living through commissions. Full-service brokers can add value if they are managing your risk for you and work off some fee-based arrangement. This type of service is very different from the broker who receives your order and charges several hundred dollars for giving you a poor execution. I lived with that experience for many years in my early days. You can get the same executions at a fraction of the commissions by using the online brokerages, but don't be fooled into using them for day trading. These online brokerages are not giving you direct access to the execution systems themselves, like SOES, Selectnet, and the other ECNs. They have a trader in the middle making money out of executing your order at a price that is favorable to them rather than you. If you are buying securities to hold for many weeks or months, this is not likely to matter much, but in day trading, getting an extra $1/8$ or $1/4$ is essential to profitability. Many new traders ask me if executing on Datek is the same as executing on Island, and, of course, it is not. Datek is part owner of the Island ECN, and it is one of the paths of execution open to their traders. The easiest way to understand the difference is to know that Island only accepts limit orders, and only for NASDAQ securities, whereas Datek accepts orders for listed securities as well as market orders for NASDAQ securities.

So, besides pursuing the highly criticized activity of day trading, I choose to use the much criticized TA approach. To be fair, I can understand much of the criticism of these techniques, and I even side with some of them. In my early experiments with TA, I fell into the "vendor trap." Systems vendors have an incentive to sell more and more systems and come up with increasingly complex forms of analysis that require more and more sophisticated and powerful hardware and software to run. These complex systems are backed up with full marketing support, and it is easy to be sucked into believing that the holy grail of TA profits will be delivered by ever more complex analysis. This just has not proven to be the case. TA is a study of human psychology that is best manifested by simple chart analysis, which also happens to be simple enough to allow it to provide valuable input for the quick decisions required in day trading.

Yawning All the Way to the Bank

So if TA is such a good tool, why aren't there popular TV shows and high-circulation periodicals devoted to technical commentary? It probably is just not interesting enough to people for it to be covered in that fashion. TA is is more about trading with discipline and having a plan than anything else, and those things are just not sexy enough to hold the interest of the average trader. Trading plans require a lot of hard work to get in tune with the rhythm of the market being studied and to identify the significant trends in force at the same time. Even when novice technicians do write a plan, the most common approach is to search for reversal patterns, looking to identify when the market is going to turn, so they can feel they got it right when everyone else got it wrong. But as we shall see in Chapter 2, reversal patterns work better as warnings to exit existing positions rather than invitations to initiate new ones. The less glamorous, but more profitable, continuation patterns are often ignored.

   Also of great difficulty for novice technicians is to stick to a plan once it has been created. It is all too easy to listen to the opinions of others and be swayed from your original course. It is essential, though, to keep your convictions and let only the market movement change your mind, not someone else's opinion of what that movement will be. With a plan generated by TA, you won't need a news service, research reports, or even newspapers or financial reports on TV. All you need is your ability to read the state of the market from the charts. If you do actually watch reports, you will find that they really are reportive. They identify stocks that have moved, but they are not usually timely enough to catch part of that movement. Worse still, many of the reports are plain wrong. My favorite example (and the last time I listened to any financial report from the mass media) is when Dell missed expected earnings by a penny and dropped $10 after the close in early February 1999. The reason I heard this report was that my computer system was down, I had to call my direct access broker to place an order over the phone, and was put on hold to listen to a financial radio show. Now the commentary on Dell was that it was getting beat up badly in the market. The expert said there was little activity in the market other than Dell and that was all to the downside. Yes, Dell was significantly down, but no, it was not all negative. In fact, I made almost $3 per share by going long on Dell soon after market open. Here's my trade report from that day:

```
Terra Nova Trading, LLC DAILY TRADE LIST Page 1
STCS 4.4.51 (SWST) 2/17/99 15:13:02


Account: XXXXXXX-YYYY
                              Unit      Total                               Broker
Tick  #Typ Symbol B/S  Shares Price     Price     Comm   System Time       IP
5265  2    DELL   Buy  500    80 1/4    40,125.00 22.95  SOES   09:47:     DKNY
8970  2    DELL   Sell 200    83        16,600.00 22.95  ACTT   10:20:     TNTO
9087  2    DELL   Sell 300    82 15/16  24,881.2  0.00   ACTT   10:21:     TNTO


Trades 3
Total Gain 1,356.25
Commission 45.90
Total Net Gain 1,310.35
```

What had happened was that the out-of-hours trading had taken Dell down too far for the small shortfall in earnings. It was a typical market overreaction. Dell rose quite steadily in premarket trading. Then once the market opened, all stock offered at the bid was being purchased by the market. As soon as a new bid price came available, Knight Securities filled it to ensure it was the first at the best bid and took all the stock available in the market at that time. This trade was among the lowest-risk trades I have entered in my life. I bought at the ask to make sure I got a fill in this quickly rising market, then sold at the bid while the uptrend was still in effect.

The whole time I was seeing my position appreciate, I was hearing what a bad day it was for Dell. I guess it's a more compelling story to talk about Dell missing the numbers and how that is viewed by market analysts and so forth, rather than say that Dell fell to support levels and value buyers were pushing the price back up.

I suppose the human side of trading appeals to more people—the opinion, the rumor, the machismo of predicting. A technical analyst does not care for any of this. I often liken the job of a technical analyst to that of an airline pilot. The pilot must make and adhere to a flight plan and spends most of his or her time merely monitoring the situation, only taking the controls at takeoff and landing. The reason pilots are well paid is because high levels of concentration must be maintained while doing what is essentially boring, yet potentially dangerous work. A technical analyst must create a plan and stick to it. He must also spend a lot of time monitoring the market and his securities of interest, which is boring for most people when compared to the excitement of listening to rumors and predictions. Direct control of a trading system is only taken when it comes time to enter or exit a position. The ability to keep discipline and hold to a plan, combined with the ability to maintain concentration when monitoring a market through the trading day, are hallmarks of the successful technician. If you find yourself drawn to making a trade for no other reason than to relieve boredom or in reaction to some rumor or other, then technical analysis may not be for you. However, if what you want is to be able to make high-percentage trades that come out of your own research, without the need for any input from others, move on to Chapter 2.

2
Trading Concepts That Have Stood the Test of Time

It is not uncommon for a trader's first exposure to technical analysis (TA) to be some kind of complex, advanced technique like oscillators. Usually, the trader will see the oscillator produce some correct and some incorrect predictions and then, over time, drift away from TA altogether. Trying to go straight in and use an oscillator—or any such advanced technique—without first having a firm understanding of the principles of TA and knowledge of the market conditions that are appropriate for oscillator analysis (oscillators are not well suited to analyzing trending markets) is like building a house without a foundation. The basic principles of TA, which were laid down by Charles Dow in his *Wall Street Journal* editorials in the late nineteenth century, are as true today as they were then. Every technical analyst should know them.

Dow Theory

Dow never actually wrote his observations down in one manuscript, so the principles of Dow theory gathered together here have come from several different locations, not from one comprehensive source. You will find different interpretations of what Dow theory is. Here, though, are the six key principles in what I believe to be the most convenient grouping of Dow's thoughts.

1. The market indexes cover the whole market and discount all market information.
2. Markets have three time horizons for trends: primary, secondary, and tertiary.
3. Each trend goes through three phases.
4. For a trend to be in effect, it must be confirmed by volume.
5. For an overall market trend to be confirmed, the market indexes must agree with each other.
6. A trend is in effect until a clear signal is given that it has reversed.

The first point to note when looking at Dow's theory and applying it to today's markets is that he was working in a world where the industrial average (referred to as the Dow these days) and the transportation average covered all listed securities. There was no NASDAQ. The aspects of Dow theory that refer to market indexes are only relevant when assessing the overall direction of the market, which we do as day traders to give us a bias on the direction in which we prefer to trade. In other words, those aspects of Dow theory are presented mainly for the sake of thoroughness. Let's examine each principle in turn and see how it relates to trading today.

1. *The market indexes cover the whole market and discount all market information.* Dow's industrial and transportation indexes covered the whole market at the time, and he believed that their prices reflected the sum total of knowledge and opinion at any give time of how those indexes should be priced. All factors related to the supply and demand of securities are assumed to be represented by the movement of the indexes. Dow also asserted that any significant information gets quickly assimilated into the price, things like wars, unexpected interest rate changes, and the like. Dow was therefore able to reduce his market study to keeping up with the two averages and drawing his conclusions about market direction on the basis of their movement.

2. *Markets have three time horizons for trends: primary, secondary, and tertiary.* This is a general rule that can still be seen today. At the time of Dow's study, he determined that the primary trends that represented the overall direction of the market lasted between one and two years. A secondary trend occurred as a temporary interruption of the primary trend and acted as a temporary correction. (When we examine them later in this chapter, secondary trends will be seen as continuation patterns.) At that time, Dow considered that such corrections took between three weeks and three months to complete, and he viewed them as temporary as long as they corrected no more than 66 percent of the primary trend.

Tertiary trends were identified as fluctuations within secondary trends and could last for up to three weeks. They could be in the direction of either the primary or secondary trends.

These classifications are useful in terms of placing short-term movements within the context of an overall trend. This concept is essential to proper trading when the market is in the Phase 2 stage identified in Chapter 1. As a means of analyzing the overall market, however, the time scales for each trend are not applicable any more. It is much more useful simply to be aware of the fact that countertrends exist within the overall trend, often identifying themselves as pullbacks to areas of support in the main trend.

3. *Each trend goes through three phases.* His description of the three phases is probably the most important Dow rule for day trading. Dow's explanation of these phases almost exactly describes how trends exist in the intraday movements that day traders can profit from. This is not surprising. In Dow's day, the flow of information was remarkably slow compared to today's speed of information delivery. What we see, therefore, is a concatenation of time scales for what happened in the past. In other words, what Dow described as taking place over the course of days or weeks, we can see taking place in the markets within minutes or hours. Here, then, are three phases, first for an uptrend, or bull move, then for a downtrend, or bear move.

In a bull move, the first move up is caused by those with superior information or those with superior insight as to the market's appetite for the security. During this stage, the majority are selling the stock, believing worse is to come, which allows those better informed to purchase the security. Since as day traders we merely react to trends that exist, the first phase is of no interest in terms of attracting our capital. The second phase is where the day trader hopes to identify and take advantage of the trend. Price accelerates out of the initial trend and the trend becomes established for everyone to see. The final stage is characterized by rampant speculation following up the significant price rise that professional traders have enjoyed. This is when the professionals sell into what are referred to as "weak hands," those who do not follow the market as closely as the professionals and therefore only get in on the end of the trend. The price falls when there are no more weak hands left to buy the stock. The professionals have sold out and the weak hands are driving the price down in their urgency to get out and limit their losses.

This is what I mean when I advise getting out of a winning position when you can, rather than when you have to. If you have a positive position, sell when there are still plenty of buyers. You will miss out on catching the top and, therefore, the most gain, but over time you will do better by not having to execute a trade when there are next to no buyers.

Bear market moves are similar in concept, but, of course, in the opposite direction to bull runs. Bear declines start when the professionals sell, either as a result of taking profits, or, in anticipation of a decline, selling short. The second move is typified by investors selling out their positions as they realize they have made a mistake with that investment. The last gasp is when the overly optimistic or those who say they are in it for the long term finally lose faith and take big losses.

These observations by Dow are critical for the day trader to internalize, because they really nail the notion of when a trend should be entered and exited. By the last gasp run, whether in the upward or downward direction, the professional should already be out, or for sure making an immediate exit.

4. *For a trend to be in effect, it must be confirmed by volume.* This is best illustrated with reference to Figure 2-1.

Here we see an uptrend, always the easiest to trade, especially in this case, since it is clear that the volumes are confirming the direction of price movement. As price moves up, volume picks up, indicating that the market is in agreement with the price movement. When the price moves down, volume falls, indicating that the mar-

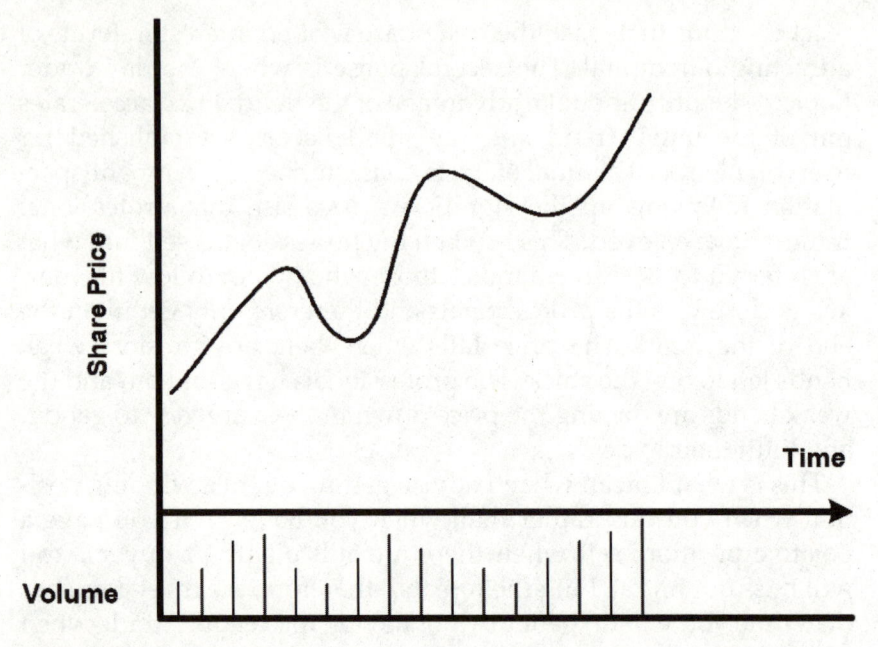

Figure 2-1. A chart with volume shown as confirming a trend.

ket as a whole does not agree with the downward direction in the price movement and that more people are waiting for the price to turn up again before buying in.

This point of Dow theory is less directly relevant to day trading than the last. It does, however, bear consideration as a secondary indicator. Most commonly, you will see this illustrated on intraday charts as a significant move in the security coinciding with heightened volume. It is not much of a predictor for the day trader because the price movement itself is telling you all you need to know. That volume is confirming it is nice, but not essential. Where a day trader can get value from this Dow point is that you tend to see an increase in trades, i.e., an increase in volume, when a security is starting to run up, which is better seen by judging the pace of trades through a time-of-sales screen than by looking at the volume bars on the chart.

5. *For an overall market trend to be confirmed, the market indexes must agree with each other.* This Dow point is really only of value to the day trader when assessing overall market health. It places a bias on the direction that day trades should be made in. In Charles Dow's day, the industrial average and the transportation average

covered all securities in the market, and Dow thought that both had to be trending in the same direction for it to be said that the market was in a confirmed trend. These days, those indexes clearly do not represent the market. They do not include any of the NASDAQ securities we will be trading, so as it stands, this Dow point is useless. We can, however, update it a bit by saying that perhaps the market is best represented by the S&P 500, which must be trending for the market to be considered in a trend. In my own experience, the S&P and the S&P futures have not provided much help in terms of deciding how to trade an individual security. There are some market gurus who will advise closely watching the S&P futures, the price of oil, and a whole bunch of other indicators in order to decide how to trade an individual security. I have not seen reliable enough signals from these indicators to make them part of my decision to put capital at risk, or more accurately, for the type of trading we will examine in Chapter 6.

6. *A trend is in effect until a clear signal is given that it has reversed.* This is a very important Dow point for the day trader to know and appreciate. During Phase 2 trading, when we are looking for trends, this point should be paramount in our minds. If you see a trend that has pulled back to support a couple of times, it is definitely worth entering that trend the next time support is reached. If, however, that turns out to be the point at which the trendline breaks, a swift exit should be made. Time and again, I have seen traders convince themselves that the market would turn in their favor and watch their losses mount as they wait for the bounce back. Occurrences like the break of a trendline should be seen as signals that the existing trend is no longer in effect. The astute day trader waits for the next trend to be established. This Dow point also helps to stop us from prematurely entering a short in the market just because we believe the market is too high. If, indeed, a strong bull run has pushed a security to all-time highs, it is probable that a pullback will happen, but we don't know when that pullback will occur until something definite signals it, like a reversal pattern. This Dow point should also stop people from buying a favorite security that is in a confirmed downtrend just because they believe it is too cheap.

This is not to say that as day traders we should wait for a signal that the trend has finished before exiting a winning position. It is always better to protect your profits and get out while you can, when there are plenty of buyers, even if it means missing out on some further appreciation. I myself prefer to wait for a sign of weakness, rather than a complete signal, before selling out. This thinking is covered in more detail in the next section, which discusses trend more fully.

The Basics of Trend

Dow did actually identify some trend reversal patterns in his work, which he referred to as *failure* and *nonfailure swings*. It seems appropriate to discuss these patterns now, before moving to a fuller discussion of trend, particularly since they introduce the concept of a sign of trend weakness, as opposed to a signal of the trend ending.

The first Dow pattern we will look at is the failure swing topping formation, illustrated in Figure 2-2.

The formation is given the name failure, because it comes about by the failure of the trend at point E to make a new high. Remember, an uptrend is defined as consistently higher highs and higher lows. At point E, the chart now shows weakness in the trend. It

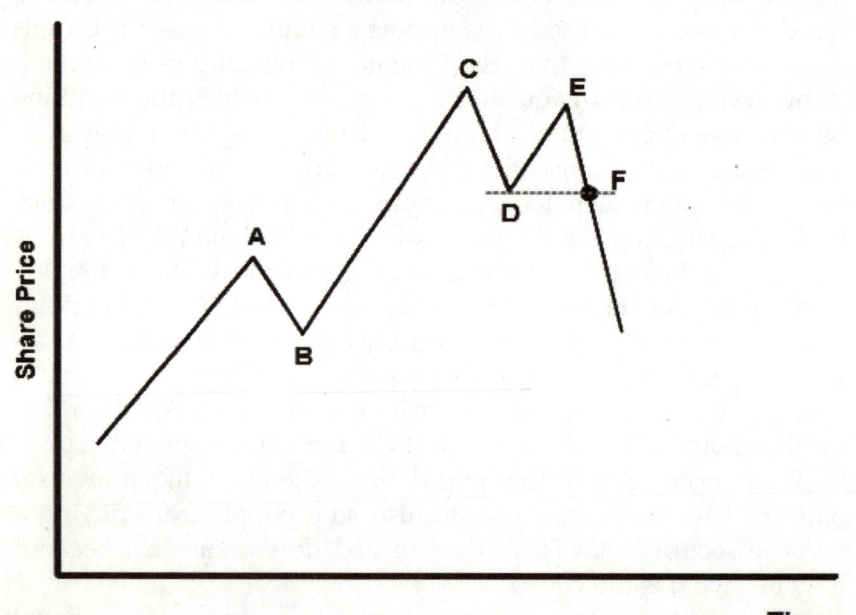

Figure 2-2. Dow's failure swing topping formation.

does not mean that the price cannot move higher on the next upturn. But it does mean that we are now cautious about the sustainability of the trend. In day-trading terms, if you saw this on a chart, you would not enter a long position on the next pullback to support levels. If you were already long, you would probably consider closing out to maintain profits. The next crucial point on this pattern is point F, which gives the signal that the uptrend is over: The price action has failed to make a new high and is about to make a lower low. Long positions should have been closed by now, and you might even consider examining the strength of the downtrend to see if it warrants a short position.

The cousin to the failure swing topping formation is the nonfailure swing topping formation. This is a very awkward name, and not very helpful in understanding the formation. In concept, however, this formation is quite simple. It is illustrated in Figure 2-3.

Here, the trend is progressing happily through points A to E, and then the weakness shows up by a new low being made. The confirming signal occurs when a lower high is made and a downtrend starts at point G.

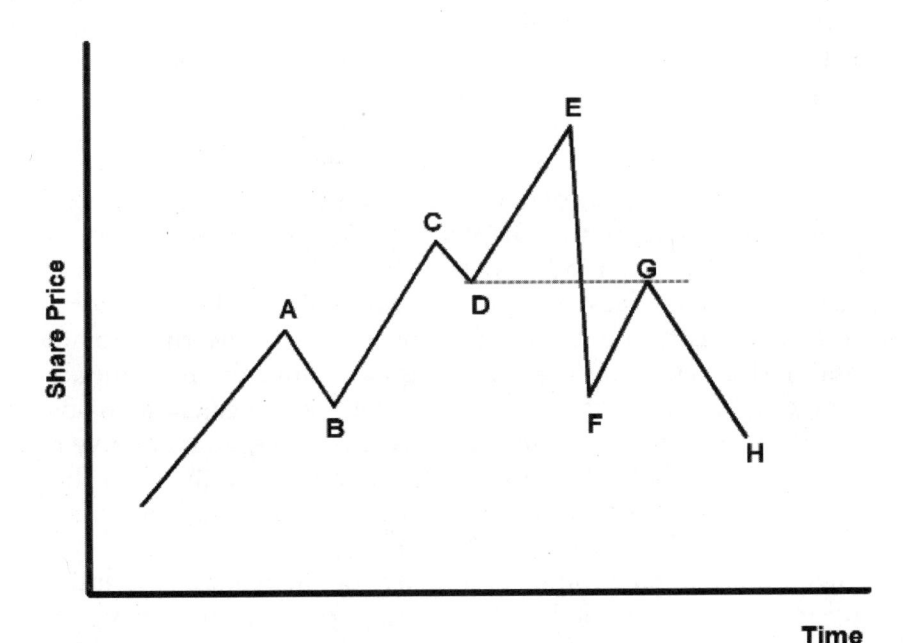

Figure 2-3. Dow's nonfailure swing topping formation.

Dow's bottoming formations are essentially the same as those in Figures 2-2 and 2-3, but upside down. Anyone who has real experience with trading patterns like these knows there are a number of uncertainties that surround their use. The first is that the failure swing pattern looks an awful lot like a double top or double bottom (covered later in this section), which are simpler to identify, so there seems little reason to bother. I tend to agree. What is most important for making decisions in a timely enough manner for day trading is being able to internalize the general principles behind these formations and act upon them quickly. Let us discuss these general principles when applied to an uptrend. The essential general principle is that if prices do not make consistently higher highs and higher lows, the trend has questionable strength. The goal is to enter a trend after a definite signal of the trend being in place has appeared, and to exit the trend on a sign of trend weakness. In a nutshell, enter on the signal, exit on a sign. This will certainly lead to smaller profits on many profitable trades, but over the long term, it will preserve your capital and allow it to grow steadily. In fact, during Phase 1 trading, I often exit winning positions even before a sign is given. The reason is that during this phase of market trading, reversals can come without warning and be so violent that winning positions can turn into losing positions before any order execution route will let you out.

Another concern with the use of these patterns is that until they have fully completed themselves, it is difficult to know whether they are really reversal patterns or are perhaps continuation patterns (covered later in this chapter). In some instances, analysis of the volume generated in the various up-and-down movements of the pattern can suggest which type of formation is being generated, but that is by no means guaranteed. This concern is totally valid and is why I do not enter positions until the formation is complete. This does, of course, mean that I do not catch the whole move of a new trend, and in some circumstances, I am not able to get in at a price that will allow me to catch enough of the move, but that is fine. Opportunities will continue to come along many times a day. Catching one or two of them in a safe fashion is enough to generate substantial profits. It is much better to maintain discipline and trade in a controlled way than to guess how an incomplete pattern will pan out.

Essential Concepts of Trend in Security Prices

When trading outside of Phase 1 market behavior, identifying trends and being able to trade within them is the most important determinant of day-trading success for the technical trader. The job is to identify whether the security is in an uptrend, downtrend, or is range bound, then to determine if the trend has shown any sign of trend weakness and see if an appropriate entry can be made to take a position in the security. I do not advocate trading a range-bound security when day trading. If you spot a range-bound security, it is better to monitor it, wait for a breakout from that range, and trade in the direction of the breakout.

We have already said that an uptrend consists of a series of higher highs and higher lows and a downtrend consists of a series of lower highs and lower lows. Let's look now at how to properly draw a trendline onto a chart. Initially, this should be done using a printed-out chart, with a transparent ruler for drawing the lines. As you become more proficient at drawing trendlines and deducing trading actions from them, you will be able to mentally draw trendlines on the real-time one-minute tick charts that are used for day-trading analysis. Printing out a one-minute tick chart and drawing a trendline on it when deciding to enter or exit a day-trading position is not realistic. Mentally picturing trendlines is just something you have to practice.

The key point about a trendline, whether for an uptrend or downtrend, is that all the price action exists on one side of the trendline. Let's examine this in Figure 2-4a.

Here we see part of an uptrend. The trendline is drawn from left to right underneath *all* the price action during which the trend is in effect. The angle of the trendline is determined by the last two lows on the chart (at A and B) prior to the current price of the security, point C. Of course, the second low must be higher than the first low for this to be an uptrend. The greater the number of times the price action has bounced off the trendline, the more significant that trendline becomes and the more significant any break of that trendline becomes.

A downtrend line is shown in Figure 2-4b.

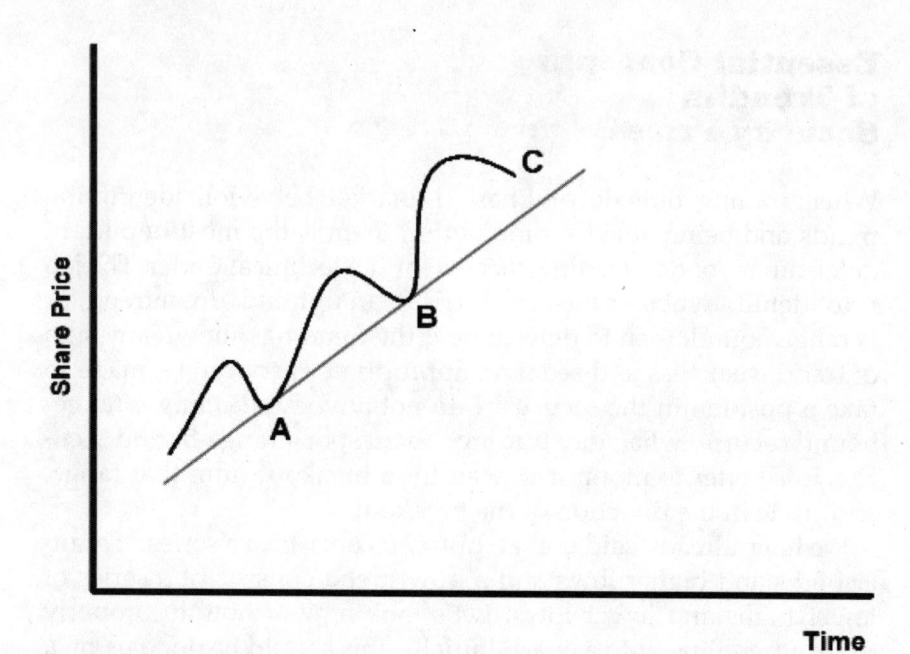

Figure 2-4a. Correct drawing of a trendline in an upward trend.

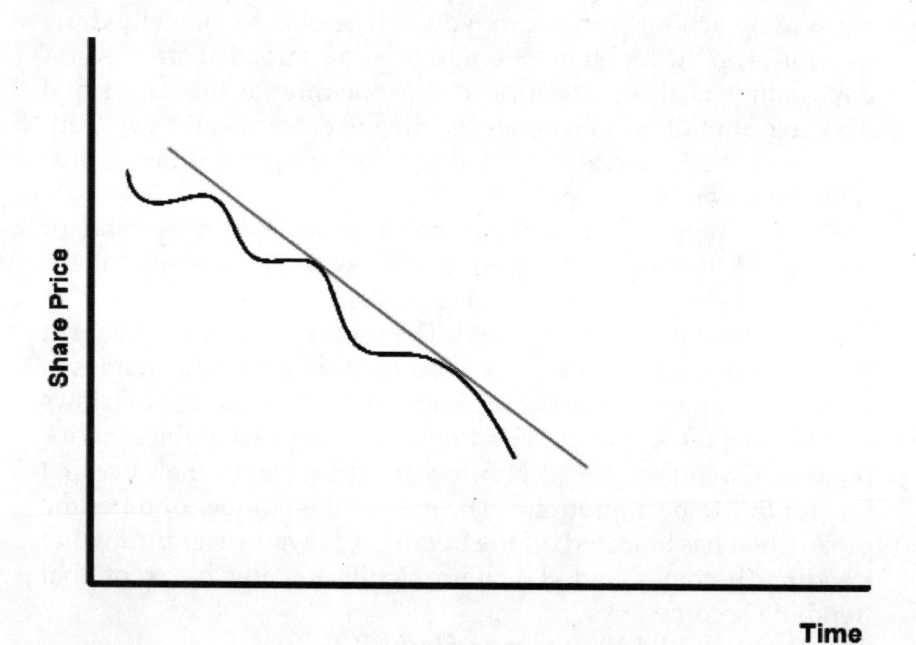

Figure 2-4b. Correct drawing of a downward trendline.

Again, a downtrend line is drawn from left to right, but in this case the line is drawn *above* all price action for the duration of the trend. The angle of the trendline is decided by the most recent highs prior to the current price of the security. The second high must be lower than the first high for a downtrend to be in effect.

These two charts are easily distinguishable from the range-bound security, as Figure 2-5 shows.

As I said before, it's advisable to stay away from range-bound securities (at least for day-trading purposes) that show this type of behavior. Seeing a pattern like this on a one-minute tick chart shows that there is a battle between equally matched bulls and bears in the security, and there is no real way of knowing who will win or even when that win will occur. Once either the bulls or the bears win and a breakout occurs, the security tends to move in the direction of that breakout with some velocity. During Phase 1 market operation, I will trade on breakouts. Typically during Phase 1, I will have identified a security that is either gapping up or gapping down, then wait for it to reverse part of that move before buying in. Often a security will spend the first few minutes within a range, then break out of the range in the reverse direction of the gap.

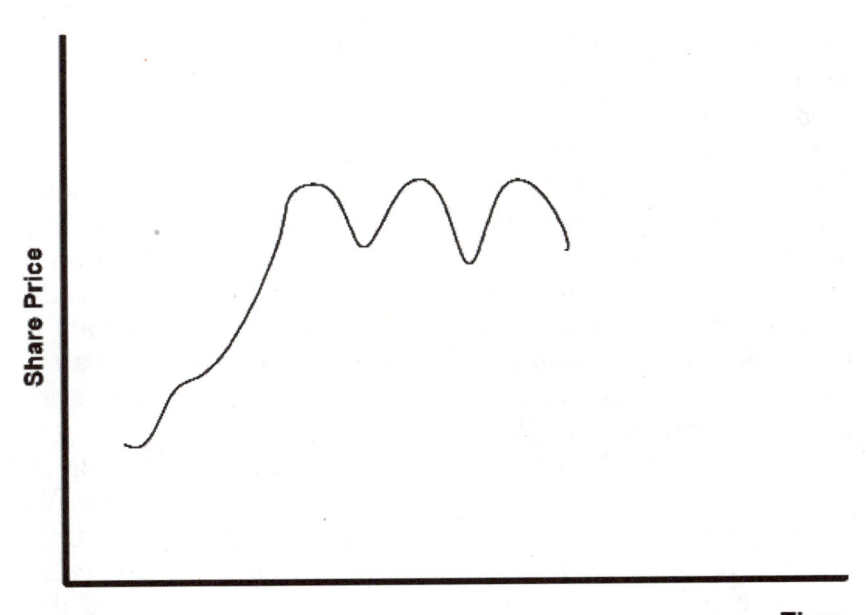

Figure 2-5. Depiction of a range-bound security.

For Phase 2 trading and beyond, I tend to treat a breakout as the beginning of a new trend and wait for that trend to be established before buying in. The reason for this is that during Phase 2 in particular I see a significant number of false breakouts. It can only be surmised that certain professionals know some traders will trade this pattern, push the security slightly out of a trading range, wait for the unwary to buy in, allow the price to retrench, and leave those unwary traders attempting to minimize their losses.

The essence of trading a trend is that prices will tend to move in the path of least resistance, which is in the direction of an established trend, when one exists. The correct way to enter a trend is when the price has pulled back to touch the trendline. When you have seen lots of trendlines and can recognize one when it is in effect, you will realize that entering a trend this way is a very low-risk proposition. Certainly there will be times when you enter the trend just as the price action enters a break of the trendline and you have to cover your losses. Later, when we examine the Level II screen in Chapter 4, we will see how it warns you of an imminent trendline break, allowing you to minimize the number of times you enter a position under those conditions.

This is part of doing business, and as long as you exit at the earliest stage (if you get in at all) and don't hang around hoping for the market to go your way, the losses should be minimal. The probability of consistently picking the point at which a trendline is broken is very small, though. Of course, any break of a trendline will be taken as a sign that the trend has weakened and may finish soon, so the risk-averse day trader would exit at any break of a trendline. Once you have a little experience spotting trendlines, you will realize they tend to be a bit elastic, which is to say that the price action may move through a trendline by a fraction only to move back over and maintain the existing trend. This is the art of TA. You have to get enough experience to be able to judge when the break of a trendline is likely to be temporary or hold on for real. There are no formulas for this. You just have to know the individual stocks well enough that you know when the pace of trades going off in one direction has the strength to break a trendline, or if the move shows signs of dying and succumbing to the strength of the trend. This is why for Phase 2 trading, I recommend that when you look for trends, you do so within a small, 15 to 20 stock universe that you can get to know intimately. With all TA, there are no absolutes, only probabilities. Anyone who tells you otherwise has not traded enough to know.

There's another thing when you are trading trends. There are two strongly opposed tenets of TA that require experience to judge appropriately. The first is that TA indicates that trends persist, in general, longer than anyone expects them to. The opposing point of view is that a trend will end, usually with an acceleration move, as the weak hands buy in at the end. So if you do spot a trend, what do you do to determine whether it has life left in it and is worth trading, or is nearing its end? Again, this is an art, not a science. In general, if the angle of the trendline connecting successive lows in an uptrend is accelerating much beyond 75 degrees on your one-minute tick chart, the probability is that there is some euphoria in the market action, which provides a hint that the trend may be about to expire. This is a sign and not a signal. Upon seeing this strong acceleration, the wise trader who is already long the security, will look to post an offer via an ECN and get out while the uptrend still exists. It is not a signal that the risk-averse trader would use to enter a short position, because confirmation of the trend ending and a new one beginning is necessary for that.

This effect is seen not only in one-minute tick charts, but also in time horizons greater than a day's worth of data. Most bull runs end with a steep rise. Just about everyone is bullish, pumped up by positive market comments from periodicals and newspapers. The reason for the precipitous falloff in price at this point in the trend is that everyone is fully invested and there are no more buyers. The market has grown unable to absorb any bad news. At this point, the same bad news that could easily have been absorbed earlier in the trend when there were plenty of buyers becomes disastrous. There are no willing buyers to take up the number of shares offered, which leads to a sharp and accelerating falloff.

The falloffs from bull runs tend to be more violent than the reversals in bear markets. This, again, is due to psychological factors. Now, I know that for every transaction there is a buyer and a seller, so by definition the number of buyers has to be the same as the number of sellers. However, the NASDAQ market can be viewed as divided into two halves: There are those making the markets by posting bids and offers, and there are those, generally the public, taking those bids or offers. When I say there are more buyers than sellers, I am referring to the fact that there are more members of the public with a buying or selling bias. When you see more purchases at the ask, it is an indication of more buyers in the public. More sellers in the public will be indicated by more sales taking place at the bid. It is generally accepted that it takes three times more buyers to establish an uptrend than it takes to establish a downtrend. If this is true, you can see that the effect of a given number of sellers will be far greater on the speed of downward movement than the same number of buyers in an uptrend. I have no statistical proof of this claim and have never needed it. Just comparing the velocity of downtrends to uptrends tells you all you need to know.

We have established that you need to pay close attention to the acceleration of trendlines, basically for two purposes. The first is to make sure that you don't get sucked into the crowd buying into the security at the end of the trend. The second is to know when to get out of a position safely before the correction occurs, even if this means missing out on substantial further appreciation. By getting out when there are still buyers, you are not trying to call the end of a trend. It is just good money management on your part. Calling the end of the trend is not feasible, and closing an existing position does not mean that you think you should be taking a position in the opposite direction. Always be aware of the two levels of indications from the market. A strong signal must be given in order to take a position, but you will close out positions on a sign that the existing trend is weak. Sometimes, however, the will to do this is weak. The reason for this is peer pressure, where your peers are other traders in the market who reveal their actions to you via market data screens. It is difficult to get out when you see your position continuing to appreciate.

Back in the 1960s, there was a seminal study done on the power of peer pressure. The study placed four stooges and the subject of the experiment in a panel. The panel was presented with a piece of paper that showed five black lines, and they had to decide which black line was the same length as the first one. All four stooges identified the same, incorrect, line. When it came time for the subject of the experiment to give his response, although there was some internal conflict evident on his face, he sided with the majority. The subject of the experiment was an intelligent college student, easily able to identify the correct line. He did not because of the power of his peers.

The same effect can be seen in the markets. If a stock is moving up rapidly, the urge to get on the bandwagon is almost overwhelming. The two times when this is almost always going to cost you at least some of your capital are at the end of trends at the close of Phase 1 trading, and during false breakouts in Phase 2 trading. Some may consider this as contrarian to the view that you can't fight the market. I'm not suggesting that you try to trade in the opposite direction of the overall market. I am only warning against entering positions when the weak hands enter the trend, that being when the trend is about to expire. When the market is in a trend, you have to trade in harmony with it. The advantage a technical analyst has is that he or she is studying crowd behavior (via chart patterns), will enter trends early in securities that have been studied prior to the market opening, and only trades securities that behave according to known patterns. The technical trader also has the opportunity to gracefully exit positions before overzealous traders exhausting the trend into a reversal, or at least a temporary pullback.

How to Identify Support and Resistance Price Levels

At this point we are reviewing chart patterns only, so the discussion of support and resistance that can be seen on a Level II screen will be left for Chapter 4. The concepts of support and resistance are essential when selecting entry and exit points for trading a trend. These are not esoteric theoretical concepts for notions based in voodoo or some other mystical realm. They are reflections of the repetitive nature of market participation. First of all, let us talk about a resistance level in an uptrend, as illustrated in Figure 2-6.

At point A, traders operating without knowledge of when best to enter a trend buy in. Instead of receiving a price appreciation, however, they see the price fall after their purchase. Feeling sore, they look for an exit that limits the damage to their capital. That point comes at B, when they can get out even, which most people will settle for when they have a negative perception of the position they hold. This then causes a wave of selling when those that pur-

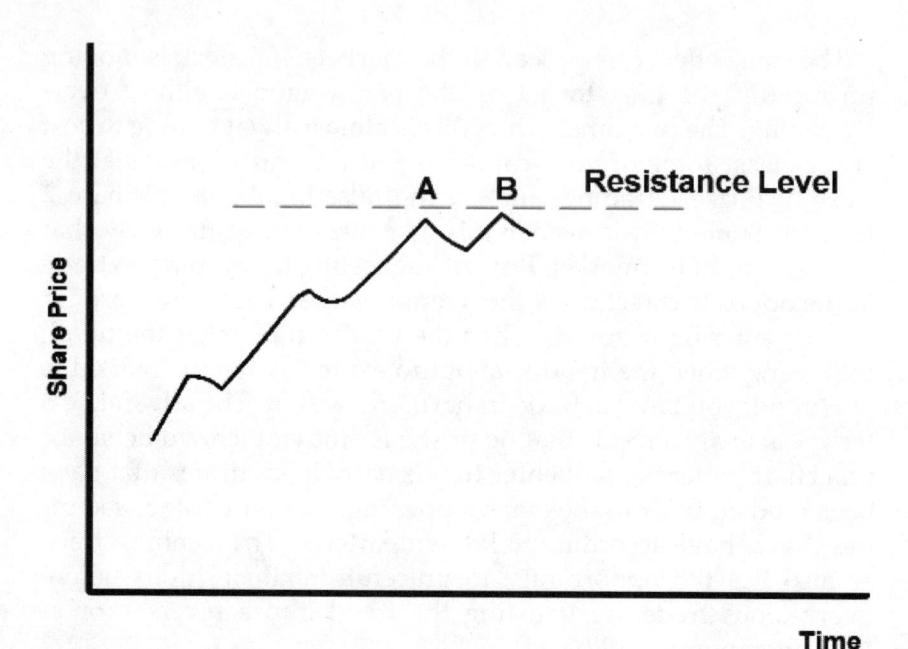

Figure 2-6. Resistance in an uptrend.

chased at point A decide to get out. This cycle can go on and on. If there are sellers at the resistance level, it probably means that there were members of the public buying at that level and the cycle can repeat. The obvious question is why the buyers at point A did not cause a further price appreciation? The reason is that trends always move in a zig-zag formation, and there were more eager sellers than willing buyers in the public at that time. As a technical analyst, you don't care why this happens, you merely note the effect and try to profit from it.

Support occurs when the price action takes a security down to a level where there are willing buyers in the public. This can happen for various reasons. Buyers may come in to cover short positions that did not work out as intended and seek to get out even, just as long holders did in the uptrend discussed previously. It can also be that for whatever reason, the stock is perceived as cheap once it has reached that level. Again, there can be many reasons, and we are only interested in trading the effect, as and when it happens.

Another important effect to be aware of is that support becomes resistance if that support level is broken. Consider Figure 2-7.

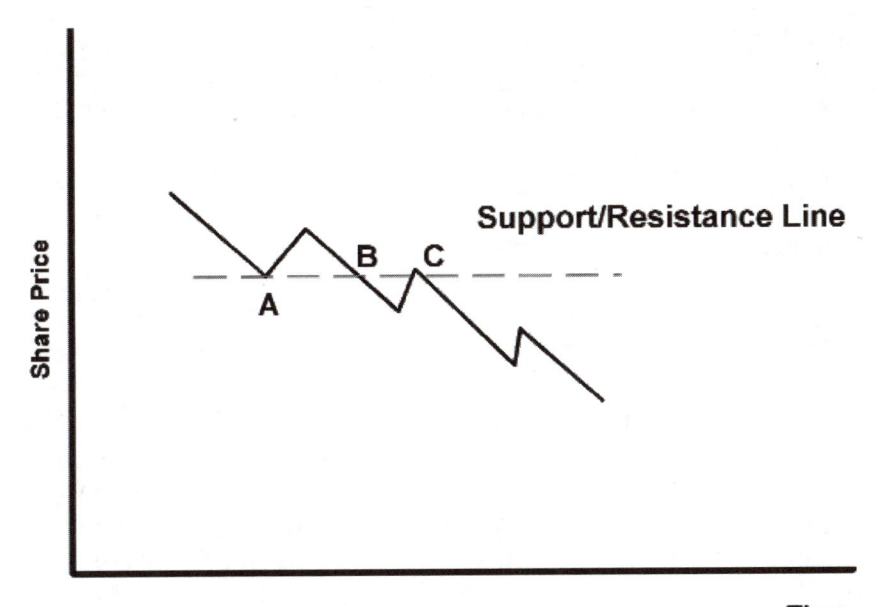

Figure 2-7. Support becoming resistance in a downtrend.

In this figure, we see the usual downward zig-zag formation of an established downtrend. At point A, we can imagine some traders thinking that the security has gone as low as it should and that the trend is reversing (these are clearly not disciplined technical analysts), and they buy the security. The security rallies briefly, but the strength of the trend carries it lower and these traders find themselves in a losing position. When the security rallies briefly, the traders look to get out even, so as soon as the price reaches their initial entry point, they exit in a wave of selling, pushing the security down further.

Support and resistance levels can arise from many other causes. The trendline itself is important as a support or resistance indicator. The greater the number of times the price action has bounced off a trendline, the more significant a break of that trendline becomes. What this means in terms of concrete action taken by day traders is that if you have a position in a security that has seen more than six bounces off a defined trendline, any break of that trendline should immediately trigger liquidation of that position. The breach of a long-established trendline tends to be followed by a rapid move in the opposite direction of the recent trend. In addition, round numbers can become significant levels in a stock's price action. Under certain market conditions, the fact that there are lots of bids at a certain level can create support; conversely, a lot of stock offered at a certain ask price can create resistance. This is by no means the whole story, as we will see in Chapter 4. Round numbers as support or resistance certainly ranks as a secondary effect. Day traders should be aware of it, but not driven to action by it.

These levels of support or resistance are used to time entry and exit points in trends. We have already discussed the correct place to enter a trend: on a pullback to resistance. Should the expected bounce in the price action not take place immediately, however, at what stage should traders close their losses? That question has no definitive answer; it depends on many factors at the time of the trade. The main concern is that we believe the trend to have been broken by the unexpected move. When we are convinced of the break, the time is right to cut our losses. When entering the trade, it is wise to have a level in mind that will trigger you to cut your losses. If that number is reached, you will invariably do best by exiting immediately. This is illustrated in Chapter 7 in the discussion of a typical trading week.

When we are in a trend and see it weakening, there is also a decision to make as to when to lock in profits. During Phase 1 trading, if I have a long position, I usually exit a position at the first sign of a slowdown in the buying of that security. During Phase 2 trading, however, if I have correctly bought into a trend and see immediate price appreciation, I allow the trend to mature and test the trendline on pullbacks in anticipation of further gains. In general, I do not let the price drop more than a 1/4 past where I perceive the trendline to be without closing my position in these circumstances.

Common Reversal Patterns

Reversal patterns seem to get all the attention from those new to TA. It seems that the urge to call the turning point in a market or security is almost irresistible. In fact, it is far more likely that you will be able to produce consistent profits by trading continuation patterns within a trend. Be that as it may, reversal patterns are important. They warn us that it is time to close a position and take profits. Now, the most important thing by far regarding reversal patterns is that for the pattern to mean anything, there must have been a distinct and sustained trend for the pattern to reverse. Time and again, I have seen traders detect what looks like a textbook head-and-shoulders or a double-top (which will be discussed shortly) and take a position based on that pattern signaling a move up or down. The problem is that there was no prior trend for the pattern to reverse, so the fact that a perfect head-and-shoulders pattern appeared really meant nothing. Although the head and shoulders is one of the most common reversal pattern in charts spanning several months, it is less common in intraday charting. The most common reversal patterns seen in intraday charting are multiple tops or bottoms (double, triple, quadruple), spike tops and bottoms (referred to as *point reversals*), and rounding formations. Less common in intraday charts are head and shoulders, or triangle formations as tops or bottoms. Let's deal with each in turn.

The multiple tops are generally of the double-top variety, and less commonly of the triple- or quadruple-top kind. The double top is shown in Figure 2-8.

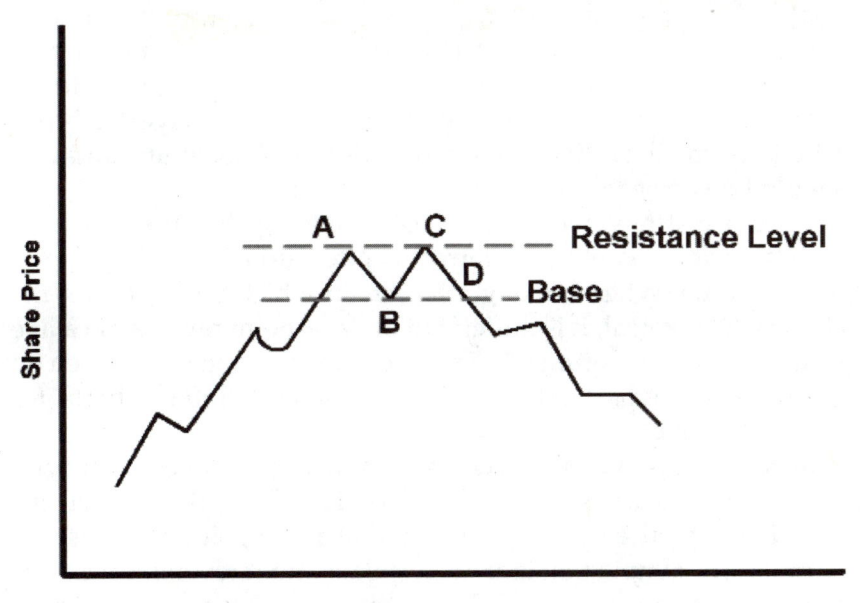

Figure 2-8. The double-top formation.

This is not dissimilar to Dow's failure swing formation. It is really a specific case of the trend not being able to make a new high on its current upswing. The concept and result are the same. If you were long on the security shown in Figure 2-8, you would look to exit your position as close to point C as you realized that a failure to make a new top had occurred. If you see this pattern in a security in which you have no holding, you would avoid entering a short until after the formation had completed beyond point D. Typically, this pattern has predictive value insofar as the move down after point D will be equal to the distance between the base of the formation and the line of resistance. Should the move continue down, it is due to a new trend being in force, not to the effects of the double-top itself. The same is true in reverse for a double-bottom.

Triple-tops or -bottoms are just extensions of the double-top/bottom concept. The existence of a triple or quadruple formation however raises the question of how that differs from a flag continuation pattern (to be discussed in the next section). As we shall see, the only difference between a typical continuation flag and a triple-top is the direction of the price action when it breaks out of the pattern. This should drive home the point that the disciplined trader only initiates positions after a pattern has been fully qualified; in other terms, the pattern has completed. It is acceptable to close positions when a pattern of this type is being formed, owing to the uncertainty of what that pattern will turn out to be. Protecting profits is always a good thing. You will never go broke by taking small profits when you have the opportunity, and that should be your goal in day trading.

Since it just has one point in its formation, the spike, or *point reversal*, as it is sometimes referred to, offers little in the way of predictive value. When looking at charts in which one point on the chart is the reversal, it is difficult to trade. A point reversal on a line chart is shown in Figure 2-9. This type of formation can be seen on many days, in particular when looking at intraday charts for Internet stocks.

In bar charts covering several weeks' worth of price action, with each bar representing a day's worth of data, the spike reversal can reveal its presence by a key reversal day at the point of reversal. If we take an example that looks at a spike bottom reversing a downtrend, the reversal day will be characterized by the price action moving sharply lower during the day, but the close will be near the

Figure 2-9. Typical point, or spike, reversal at the beginning of the trading day.

high for the day. In intraday charting, we do not have that type of information, so we have to rely on information that can be gleaned from the Level II display instead, as will be discussed in Chapter 4. The only time I advocate looking for and trading a spike reversal is during the Phase 1 part of the day. It is here (typically before 10:00 a.m. and most commonly at around 9:40 a.m. in the current market) that early reversals take place, and they tend to be of this type. During Phase 2 and Phase 3 market periods, you will not search for point reversals to initiate positions, but should they occur and cause a weakening of a trend, you may use them to initiate closing positions.

The spike reversal naturally occurs during the heaviest periods of the day's trading because a steep runaway move is required prior to the reversal for it to occur. These steep runaway moves typically occur when a security has made a significant (15 percent or more) move in premarket with plenty of premarket volume. This premarket move often carries over into the beginning of the trading day, and as was discussed above, when the initial drive is over, an immediate reversal occurs. Of course, the likelihood of premarket movers reversing after market open is impacted primarily by two factors: (1) the overall direction of the market, and (2) the direction of the premarket move relative to the prevailing trend of the security. For example, if the overall market is in a strong bull phase and a quality stock that is in an upward trend pulls back in value by 15 percent or more, an early reversal of part of this premarket move is likely. In the same market, however, a stock appreciating by 15 percent or more may go even higher through the day's trading. This is something that will receive more attention in Chapter 6.

Rounding formations are reversal patterns that commonly occur later in the day than point reversals and among the best patterns to trade for those with patience. The typical rounding formation can be seen in Figure 2-10.

The reason this formation usually occurs outside of the opening or closing periods is that it is a characteristic of quieter markets. It represents a slow drift in the balance of supply and demand. Generally speaking, the first clue that a bottom rounding formation is taking place is that the lows fail to make lower readings and eventually each successive low registers a higher

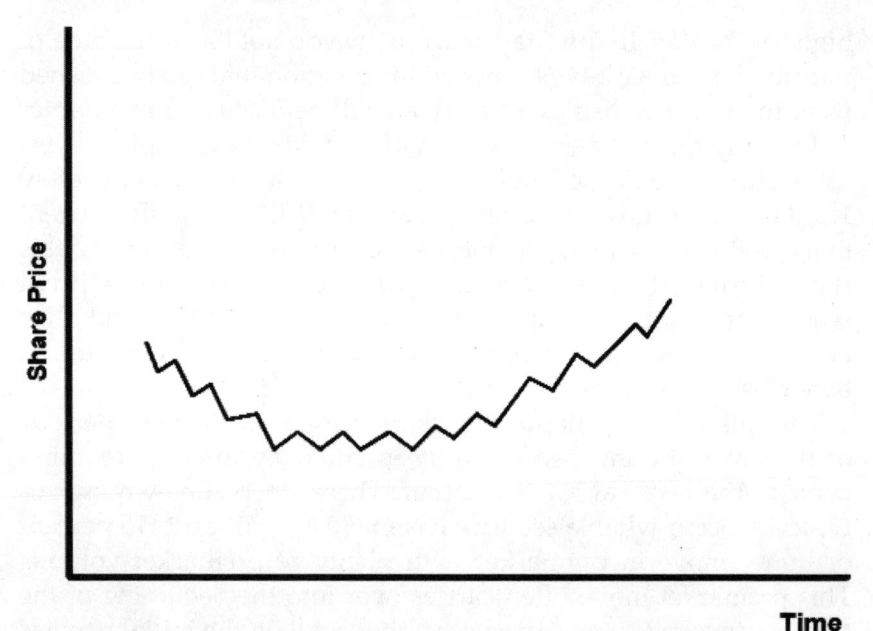

Figure 2-10. Typical rounding formation.

value, which indicates that the uptrend is now in effect. These patterns require a lot of discipline to trade profitably. It is essential to enter a position on a pullback within the new trend and exit before the pace of trading picks up and any new trends establish themselves. If you are going to trade it, the most important feature to note about the rounding pattern is that the zig-zag of the price action must be small and regular. In other words, there must be no sharp increases or decreases in the price action. If sharp movements do occur, that indicates high market activity and it is not a rounding pattern.

The next reversal pattern we will look at, the triangle pattern, is relatively rare, but it can be traded on intraday charts with a high degree of success. Triangles can be of various types and can as easily indicate the continuation of an existing trend as a reversal. Given this duality of triangles, it becomes even more important to let them complete before initiating any new positions as a result of seeing the pattern.

The most important thing to remember is that even though triangles are quite accurate, it is a 50/50 bet which way they will go until the triangle is complete and a break of one of the sides of the triangle occurs. We will, therefore, give a fuller treatment of the triangle pattern here.

There are four types of triangle patterns that are worth trading:

- The symmetrical
- The ascending
- The descending
- The broadening formation

The symmetrical triangle is illustrated in Figure 2-11. The essential concept with triangles is that they graphically depict a war of attrition between the bulls and the bears operating in a security. The bulls are represented in the upward trendline and the bears are represented by the downward trendline. These two opposing trendlines constrict the price action into an ever-narrower space, building up pressure as the price action is constricted. It appears that the two trendlines would eventually cross over, but of course this never happens. So when one of the trendlines is broken, the pressure built up within the triangle is released and a move in the

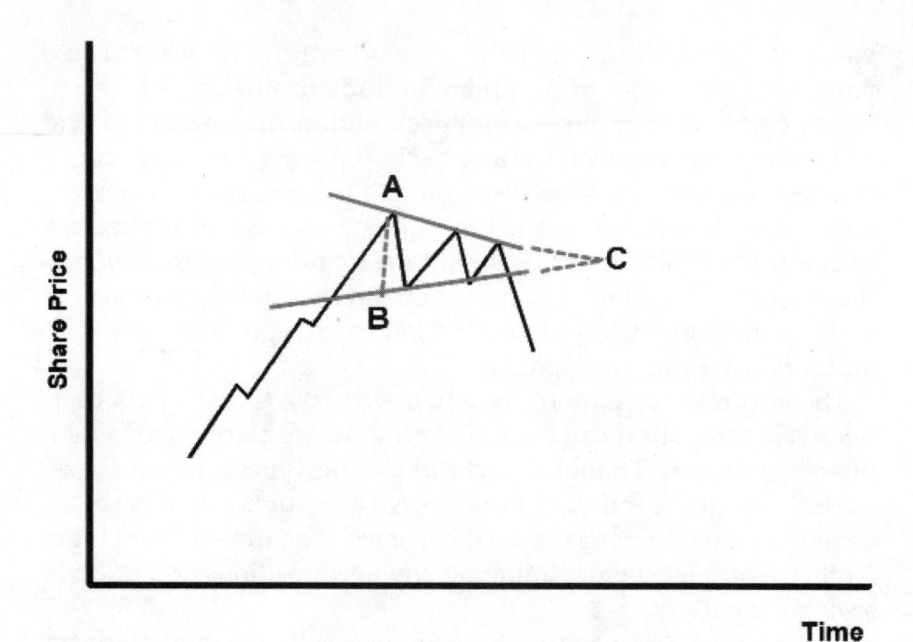

Figure 2-11. Symmetrical triangle topping formation.

direction of the breakout ensues. Typically, the predictive value of the triangle pattern is determined by the vertical size of the triangle. In the case of Figure 2-11, the move downward from the break of the upward trendline (the line from B to C) will be equal to the vertical distance from point A to point B.

Also in Figure 2-11, the trendlines have been extended to meet at the apex, marked by point C. If a breakout has not occurred by the time the price action meets point C, the triangle pattern should be assumed to have expired without any effect and you should move on in your search for tradable patterns. This places a time limit on how long you will wait for a tradable move to occur when seeing what appears to be a triangle starting to form. Examining volume, or the pace of trades, is useful when trading triangle patterns. You should expect to see pace slow as the price action progresses toward the apex and pick up significantly when the price action breaks one of the trendlines. The highest-probability trade to make with triangles is to wait for the trendline break, then wait further until a pullback in the newly established trend occurs. This will yield smaller profits than trading immediately in the direction of the trend break, but increases the likelihood of profits rather than losses. Moreover, this will protect you more from the occasional false breakout from a triangle pattern that does occur.

The descending triangle, as seen in Figure 2-12, is generally a continuation pattern, but it can form a reversal, which ends up looking a lot like a double- or triple-bottom. Again, discipline is necessary to let the pattern complete before initiating any positions.

In this figure, a downtrend is in effect and the triangle is formed by a horizontal lower line and the downward trendline shown. In this case, the bulls win and the bearish down trendline is broken. While the triangle was still being formed, the probability was just as strong that the bears would win and the horizontal support line would be broken, which just emphasizes the need to be patient when trading these patterns.

The ascending triangle is the inverse of the descending triangle, as illustrated in Figure 2-13.

In this figure, the bearish line is the horizontal resistance line and the bulls have the upward trendline. Figure 2-13 shows the ascending triangle in its more familiar role as a continuation pattern, but this pattern can also become a reversal pattern, depending on whether the bulls or the bears have their trendline broken.

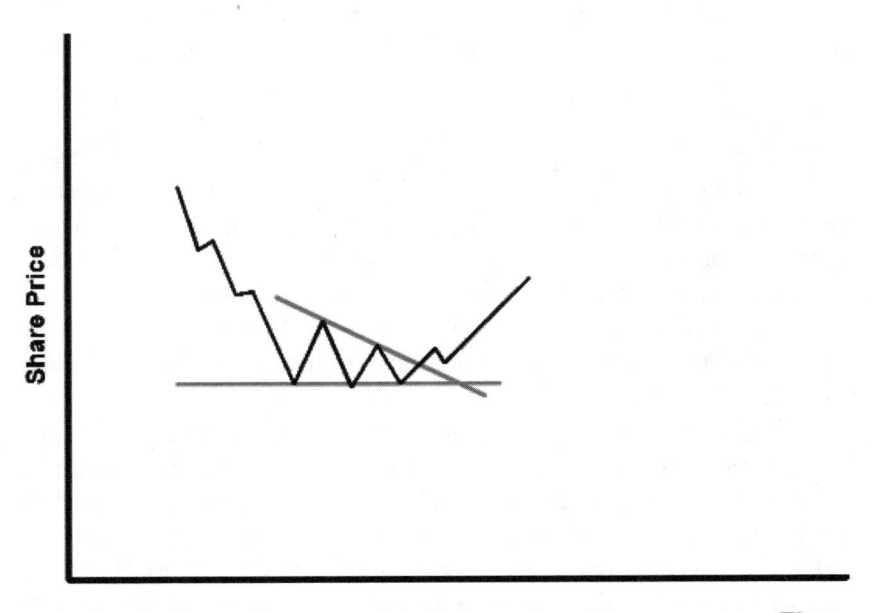

Figure 2-12. A descending triangle as bottom reversal.

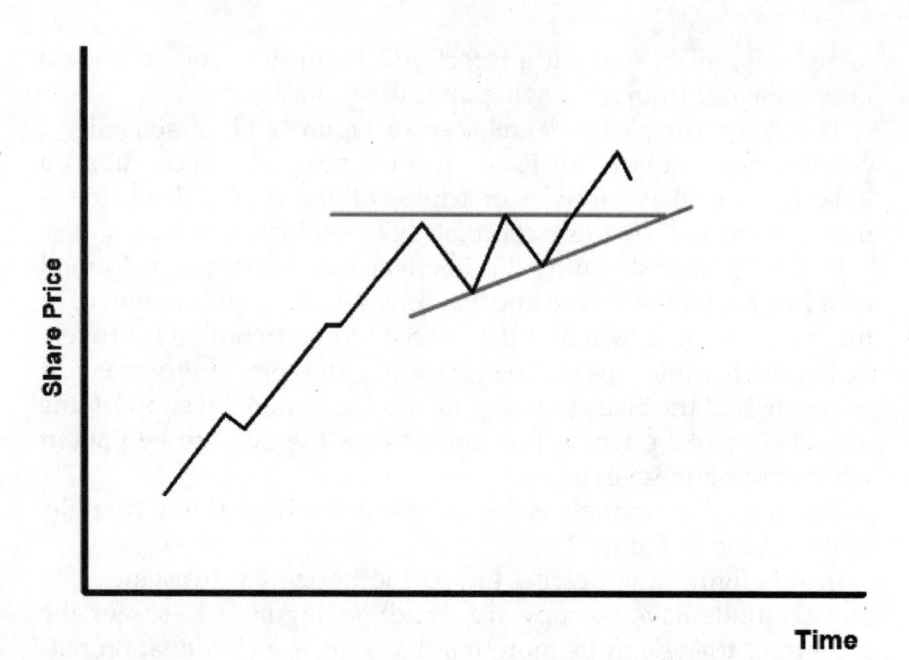

Figure 2-13. The ascending triangle formation as a reversal pattern.

Examining these patterns, you may well question the value of identifying triangles, since the trading actions could also have been determined by simply looking at support or resistance levels, trendline breaks, or looking for multiple tops or bottoms. In many instances, good trading decisions are signaled purely by these means. Nevertheless, triangles are still worth looking for because they bring two lines into the decision-making process, both a bullish and a bearish line. As such, they offer more predictive value than the analysis of support, resistance, or a single trendline.

The final triangle pattern is very rare and does not offer very high trading probability. The broadening formation is illustrated in Figure 2-14.

Again, the broadening formation can be either a reversal or continuation pattern, depending on the direction of the breakout. In the previous constricting triangle patterns, volume decreased as the pattern progressed from left to right toward the apex; that is, until a breakout occurred. With the broadening formation, the opposite happens. Volume increases as the swings get bigger and bigger. Unlike the other triangle patterns, which more commonly are continuation patterns, the broadening formation, when it does

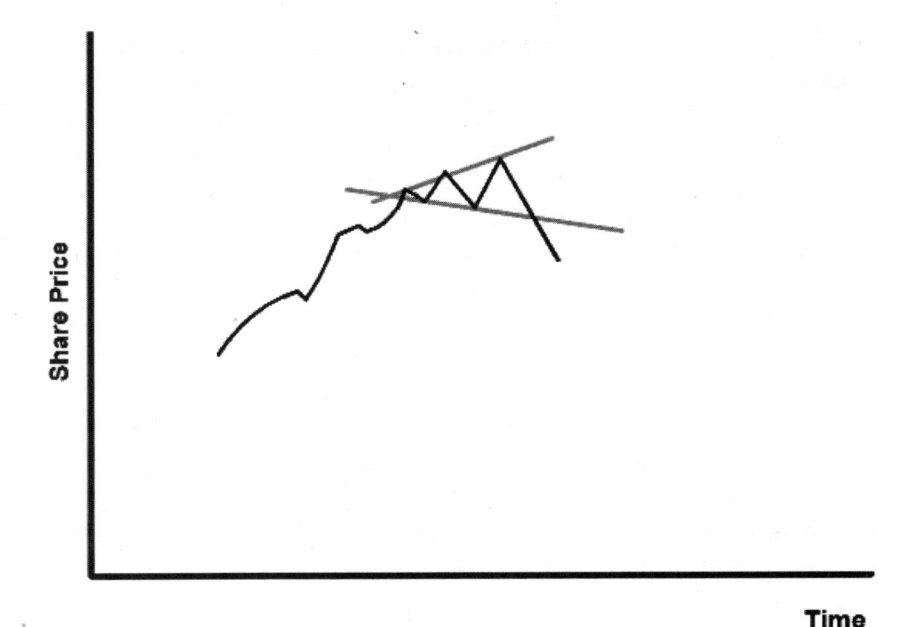

Figure 2-14. A typical broadening formation.

exist, is most often a reversal pattern at the top of a bull run. The reason for this is that market action that swings wildly is indicative of a market that is out of control, one where the emotion of the market participants is all-consuming. Typically, this only occurs when the only people left in the market are the weak hands. It is best to keep clear of broadening formations unless they appear at the end of a prolonged and sharp bull run, in which case this formation can signal a top quite nicely.

Now for the most common reversal pattern, the head and shoulders. As previously mentioned, the head-and-shoulders pattern is not as common in intraday charting as it is with charts in which each point represents a day's worth of activity (referred to as a daily chart). However, the market dynamics of a reversal (outside of Phase 1 market activity), with regard to the shifts in supply and demand, are the same for intraday as for daily charts. What does change is that in intraday charting, the pattern tends not to take such a classic head-and-shoulders form. In fact, with all reversal patterns, you should concentrate more on identifying their characteristics than worrying about classifying each one as head and shoulders, triangle, or whatever. In all charting, and intraday charting, in particular, the patterns rarely fit exactly with the textbook description, so a distorted head and shoulders, for example, can look similar to a triangle reversal, a swing failure, and so on. So concentrate more on the market dynamics during a reversal, which we will now cover with respect to a classic head-and-shoulders reversal, as depicted in Figure 2-15.

In this figure, we see a defined upward trend with consistently higher highs and higher lows. Points A, B, and C represent occasions when the upward trendline has been respected and provided support. The first sign of trouble for the upward trend appears at point D, when the trendline is broken. Further evidence of concern arrives when the next high fails to be higher than the previous high. The head and shoulders is complete at point F, when what is referred to as the *neckline* is broken. The normal market action is for the neckline to be retested, or at least an approach made toward the level of the neckline, prior to a downward trendline being established.

The head-and-shoulders pattern itself is shaded in Figure 2-15. The left shoulder appears to the left of point C; the head is the

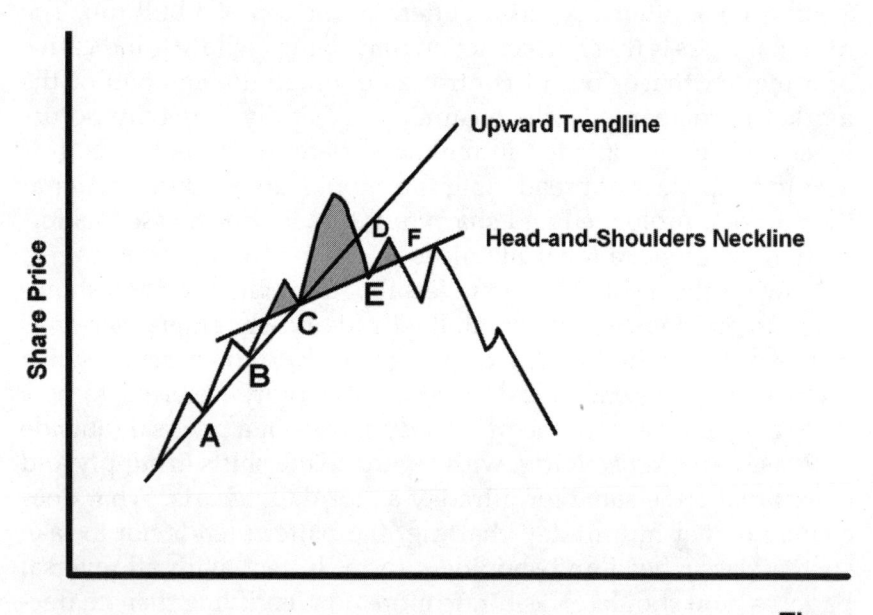

Figure 2-15. A classic head-and-shoulders reversal.

main section of the pattern, between points C and E; and the right shoulder appears between points E and F.

Use of the head-and-shoulders pattern will depend upon your position in the market at the time. Let's say you were long in the security in Figure 2-15 during the initial upward trend. You would become concerned at point D and maybe exit there. If you have a higher tolerance for risk, you might see the bounce at point C, but you would definitely exit after the failure to make a new high with the right shoulder. If you had no position in the security, the break of the upward trendline might attract your interest and cause you to look at the security more closely. The failure to make a new high should alert you to look for shorting opportunities. You would not actually enter a short position, however, until the head-and-shoulders pattern was complete and the expected return toward the neckline had occurred.

As you can see, several different concepts we've discussed come together to generate trading actions in this case. It is feasible that a trader with a high tolerance for risk might enter a short position after the right shoulder has peaked, noting that the trendline has been broken and a new high has not been made, thus making the head-and-shoulders pattern redundant to his thinking. This is okay if it fits your risk profile. What is important here is that you register the breaking of support and the establishment of resistance.

I have purposely illustrated the neckline in Figure 2-15 at a slant. In textbooks, the head-and-shoulders pattern is most commonly drawn on the level, but that is not the most common scenario. The most common slant for a head-and-shoulders pattern that is reversing an upward trend is as depicted in Figure 2-15. Less frequently, the neckline will be horizontal, and in rare cases it will slope down from left to right.

If you suspect that a head-and-shoulders pattern is being formed, looking at the pace of trading (the volume of trades) can give additional insight. Typically, volume increases in the direction of the trend, and it decreases as the price action moves in the opposite direction of the prevailing trend. With reference to Figure 2-15, you would expect to see trade pace increase as the price appreciates up until the middle of the head in the formation. Past that point, upward moves in the price action would see decreasing volume, and downward moves would see increases in volume. If volume does not confirm the head-and-shoulders formation, you should be less convinced of the formation's predictive capability.

The head-and-shoulders pattern also works inversely, that is, when it marks the reversal of a downward trend. It is essentially a mirror image of the formation shown in Figure 2-15. All the discussion on when to liquidate longs and initiate shorts is reversed when considering the inverse formation. If an inverse head-and-shoulders appears at the end of a downward trend, the break of the downward trendline should cause concern for existing short positions, and new long positions would be initiated upon completion of the formation and the return move.

So let's summarize the main points when considering all of the reversal patterns discussed. First, and most important, a reversal pattern only has significance if it is preceded by a trend. Preferably, you will be able to identify the three stages of the prior trend: the early move from the previous reversal, the main move, and then the weak hands pushing the trend to exhaustion. Second, all reversal patterns incorporate a break of a major trendline, which should immediately alert you to a possible trend reversal.

The next points are less significant than the first two. Usually, the larger the pattern is, the bigger the subsequent move. This is in line with the predictive qualities we discussed for each pattern, such as the expected move upon the completion of a triangle usually being equal to the base of the triangle. Volume should confirm the movement of price action. This is particularly important for bottom formations, since prices can fall on light volume, but it always takes strong volume to push up a security.

It would be nice if these reversal patterns worked 100 percent of the time, but that simply is not the case. When attempting to use any of these patterns to make trading decisions, it is your discipline that will determine your financial success. As an example, if you are using the breakout from the side of a triangle as a trigger to initiate a position, you must liquidate that position if the price action moves back over the triangle's side line. Essentially, if the price action does not move in the way you anticipated when you entered the position, you need to get out immediately. This is one of the most difficult things to do when trading your own money. It is much easier for most people to hope that the price action will come around to favoring their position than to take a small loss and move on. However, that is exactly what is necessary for long-term survival in day trading. These patterns are reliable enough that over time, your gains will outweigh your losses—as long as you keep discipline.

Discipline is required for all trades initiated by technical indicators. One feature, though, that is particularly true with reversal patterns is that most traders tend to enter a position too early. The psychology is probably the desire to be a hero, to be the first in on the new trend. This may lead to a few spectacular wins, but it will invariably lead to many more failures. It is a fact that every reversal pattern that is not complete resembles a continuation pattern. Not until the reversal is completely formed is it distinguishable as a reversal. The goal should be to see reversal patterns as a way of alerting you to new trends and trading in the direction of these new trends, not trying to anticipate new moves.

You must also consider the time of day at which you are operating. This type of pattern analysis is most suitable to the Phase 2 or Phase 3 types of market activity. Phase 1 is characterized by wild swings; no intraday trends have had the time to establish themselves. Therefore, it is best to take profits at the first sign of the price action reversing from the direction you bought into.

Common Continuation Patterns

Continuation patterns are the bread and butter of the technical analyst. Trading continuation patterns does not provide the same glory as correctly identifying a reversal pattern and calling the change in sentiment in the market, but it does lead to surer profits. What we said about reversal patterns looking like continuation patterns until the pattern is completed is true in reverse of continuation patterns. The beginning of a continuation pattern will look a lot like a reversal pattern until it has completed, and you need patience to see the formation complete and to wait for the best entry point.

The classic continuation pattern represents a pause in the main trend, a consolidation of what has just happened, often as a result of a stock accelerating rapidly in the direction of the overall trend. The continuation patterns that you will look for in Phase 2 trading are as follows:

- Flags
- Rectangle formation
- Head-and-shoulders
- Triangles and wedges

All of these patterns have the same characteristics in that they represent a pause in the major trend. Since real-world patterns rarely match the textbook examples exactly, it can be difficult to distinguish a flag from a pennant or a triangle from a wedge. What is important is the dynamics of price action during these periods. By examining each formation in turn, you should get a feel for what is happening in the market as each pattern forms.

Flags

The flag formation is characterized by narrow oscillations contained within two bands that form a channel. Typically, the channel is either in the direction of the trend or against it. The pattern has a higher degree of predictive capability if the channel is in the opposite direction to the main trend. These two options are illustrated in Figure 2-16.

The pattern is complete upon the break of the upper line that marks the boundary of the channel. The number of oscillations in

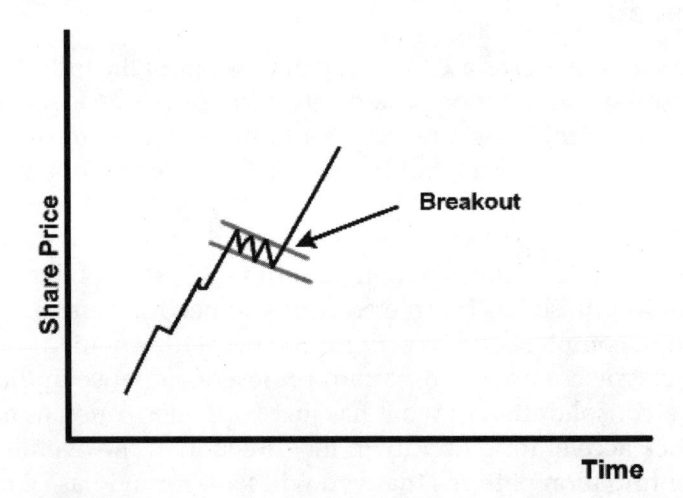

Figure 2-16a. Flag formed counter to trend.

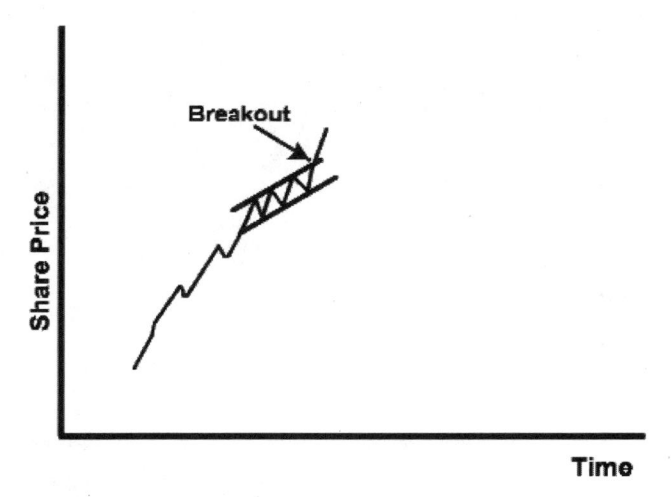

Figure 2-16b. Flag formed in direction of trend.

the flag is not important. That will vary depending on the time horizon of the chart you are using. I traded a continuation pattern recently that looked quite different on a one-minute chart from how it appeared on a five-minute chart, both of which are shown in Figure 2-17.

In this instance, the stock had fallen in premarket activity on weak bad news and staged a strong recovery in the Phase 1 mar-

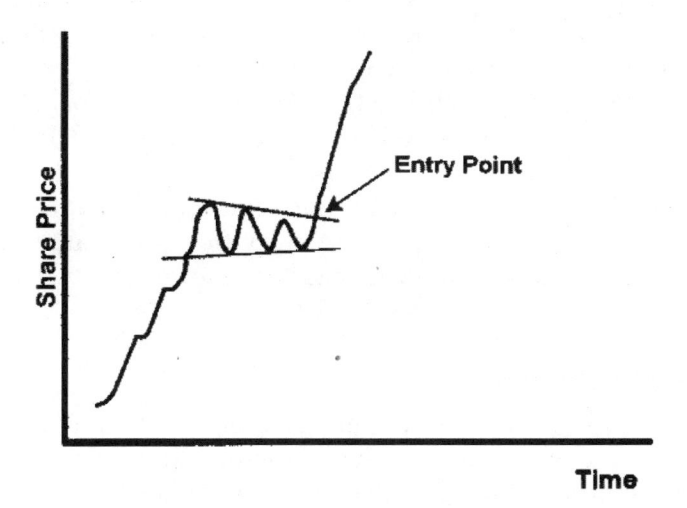

Figure 2-17a. One-minute representation of a continuation pattern.

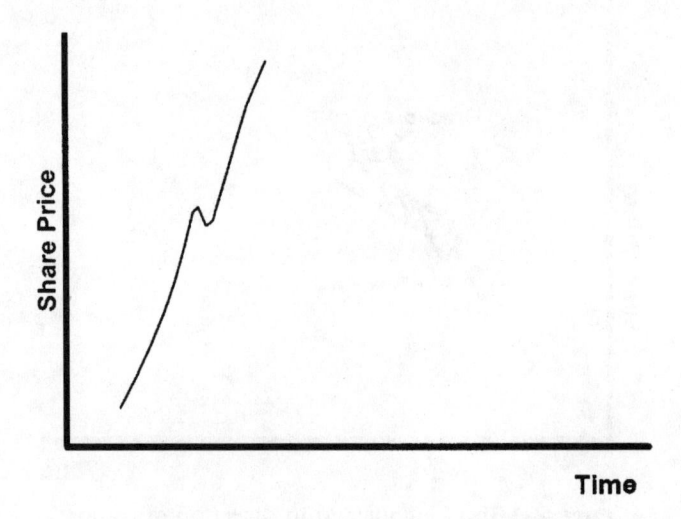

Figure 2-17b. Five-minute representation of the same continuation pattern.

ket period. As no trends have been formed this early in the market, any trades that I enter are usually either the result of the first move in the opposite direction of the premarket gap, or of continuation patterns if I miss the first move. In this case, I missed the first move against the gap and took a long position as close to the entry point as I could get. In this situation the trade worked out well, and I exited the position when the upward move positioned the flag at halfway in the trend. Typically, a consolidation flag will appear halfway within a move, which has led to the expression: "Technical flags fly at half mast." What actually happened in this case was that the stock moved appreciably higher than the point at which I exited. On a technical basis, however, holding the position beyond what was predicted by the continuation pattern would have moved me into the hope and away from the reality column. Over time, that most likely will lead to diminished returns.

Rectangle Formations

The sideways continuation pattern that forms a rectangle illustrated in Figure 2-18 is a special case of the flag. It essentially has the flag on the horizontal rather than at any slant.

This pattern can easily be confused with a triple-top or triple-bottom formation, which again reinforces the point that you need

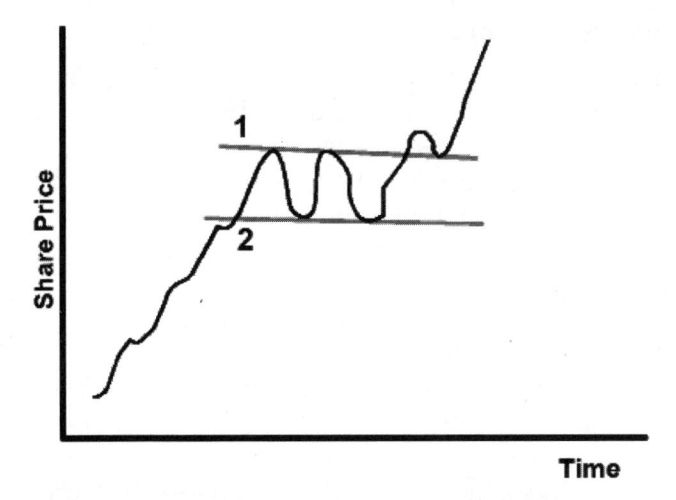

Figure 2-18a. Bullish continuation rectangle.

to wait for the pattern to complete before you initiate a position as a result of seeing a formation. Typically, the horizontal flag (that we call a rectangle) will experience a retest of the channel lines prior to resuming the trend, and it is here that the best entry point occurs. When this pattern occurs, the predictive value is restricted to a move equal to the vertical size of the rectangle itself, which in Figure 2-18 is between points 1 and 2.

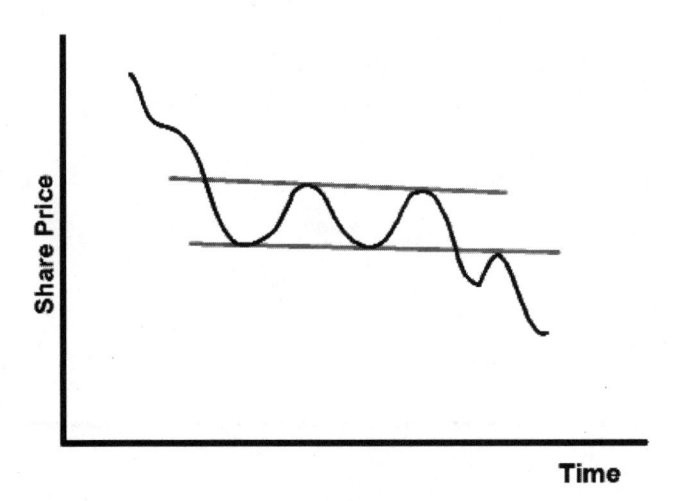

Figure 2-18b. Bearish continuation rectangle.

Head and Shoulders

The venerable head-and-shoulders pattern can reappear as a continuation pattern, as shown in Figure 2-19.

In this figure, the head-and-shoulders pattern starts at point 2, where a failure to make a new high occurs. For those long the security at this point, the high-percentage trade is to exit as quickly as possible and take profits. Additional concern regarding the continuing validity of the prior uptrend becomes apparent at point 3, where the next low is lower than the previous low. This is not enough evidence to initiate shorts (for those who believe a reversal of the uptrend is beginning), so the astute technical trader will wait for the pattern to complete. The pattern completes at point 5 with a break of the neckline. New long positions can safely be entered on the retest of the neckline. Clearly, those who saw the failure to make new highs and the establishment of lower lows as evidence for considering shorts will be glad they watched the formation complete. Again, this reinforces the need for patience on the part of the technical trader. There is a difference between the evidence needed to liquidate existing positions and the near proof needed to initiate

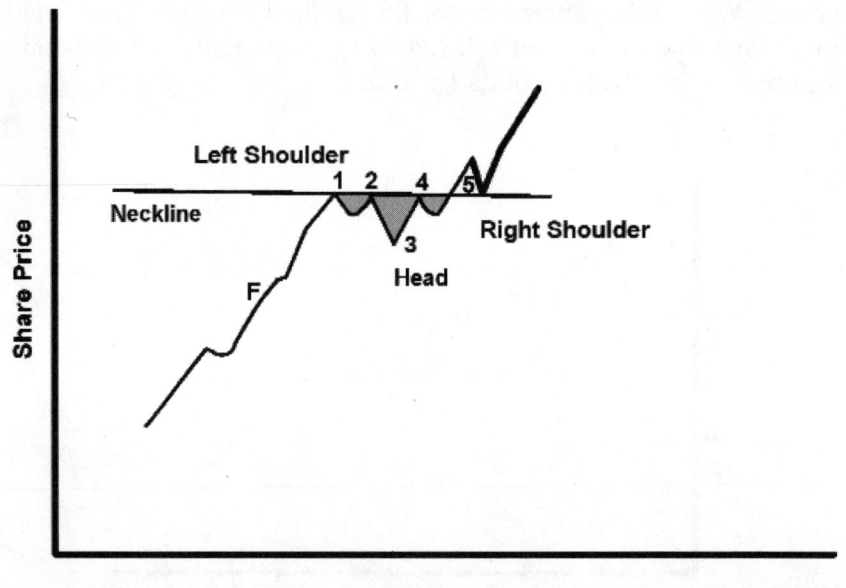

Figure 2-19. Classic head-and-shoulders continuation pattern.

new ones. In this instance, the head-and-shoulders is upside down. The key point, however, is that the expected move is in the opposite direction of that to which the head points, and it is equal to the distance between the neckline and the apex of the head.

Triangles

Triangles can also be continuation patterns, as illustrated in Figure 2-20.

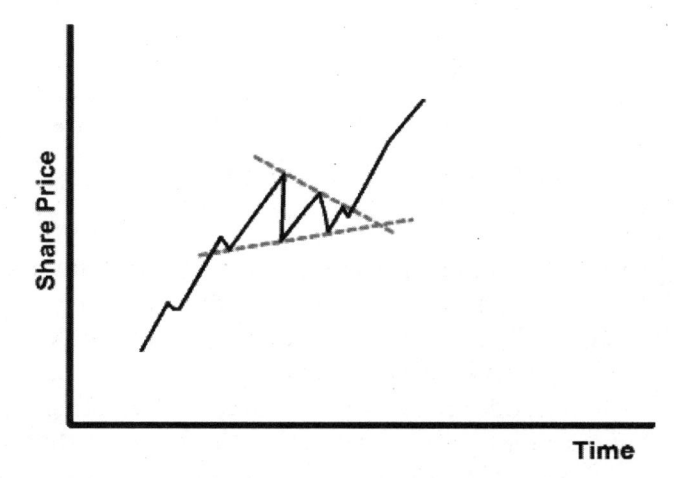

Figure 2-20a. Symmetrical triangle continuation.

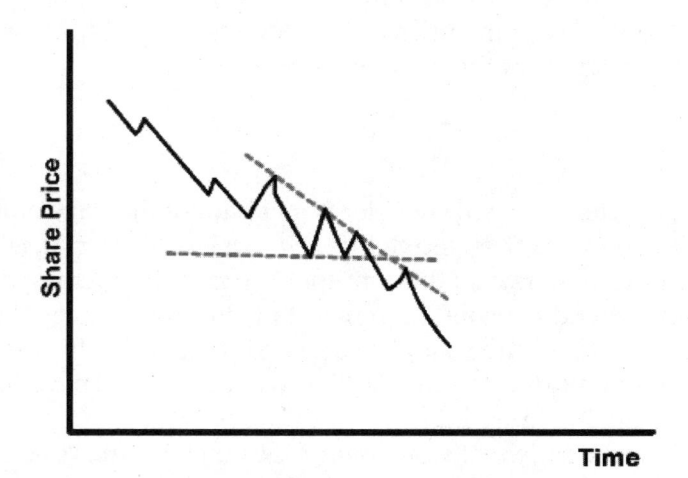

Figure 2-20b. Descending triangle continuation.

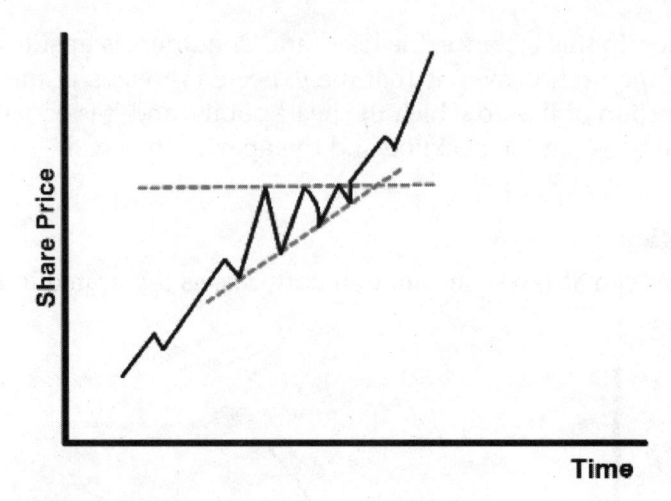

Figure 2-20c. Ascending triangle continuation.

Here we see the familiar triangle patterns, the symmetrical, ascending, and descending triangles, and the respective breakout points that signal the appropriate points to start to look for entry positions into the trend continuation. The most powerful patterns are when the ascending triangle continues an existing upward trend and when a descending triangle continues an existing downward trend. Again, the usual triangle predictive qualities exist, i.e., the predicted move is equal to the size of the triangle base, and the price action must break out of the triangular constriction prior to reaching the apex. If the price action extends beyond the apex, it is likely that a tailoff in the price will occur.

Wedges

The final pattern we will consider is a variant of the flag combined with the triangle. It is termed a *wedge*. Here, again, it is more important to understand the concept of what is happening during a period of trend consolidation than to get hung up over classifying a pattern as a pure triangle, wedge, or flag. Nevertheless, I am showing you a typical bullish falling wedge and a typical bearish rising wedge in Figure 2-21.

These wedges are really symmetrical triangles that are angled in the opposite direction of the main trend. Each wedge supplies a signal to initiate positions in the direction of the breakout.

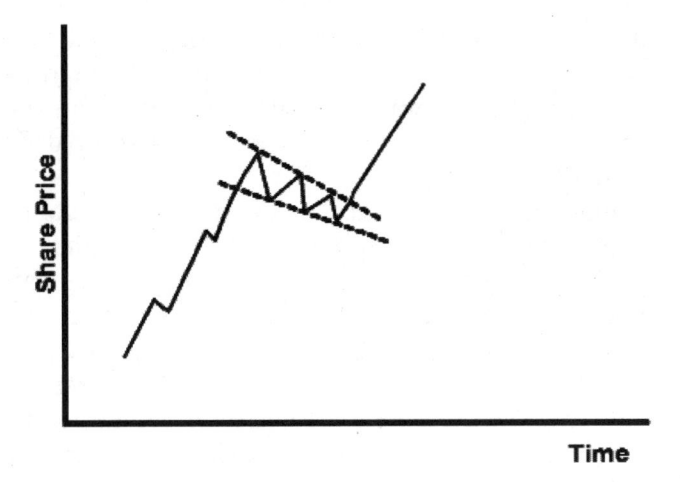

Figure 2-21a. Bullish falling wedge.

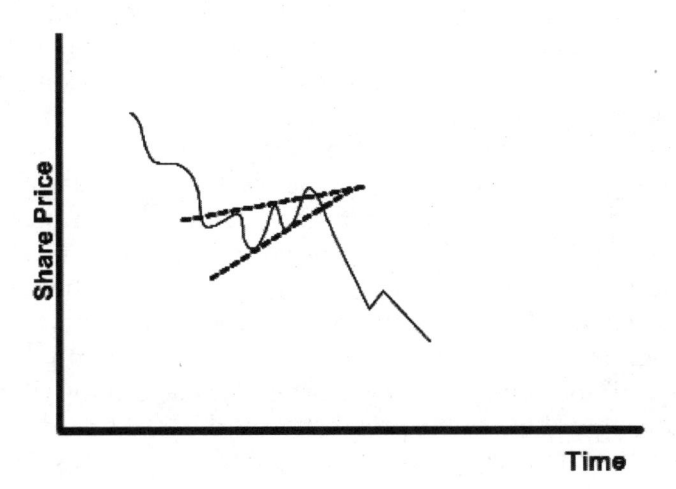

Figure 2-21b. Bearish rising wedge.

Interpreting Continuation Patterns

As these formations are in progress, it is easy for the overeager trader to think that the new series of lows and highs is forming a new trend in the opposite direction of the prior trend and to initiate a position in the direction of the wedge. This, however, is a mistake. Wait for the patterns to complete and for the trends to become established before initiating positions.

By trading with discipline and waiting for completion of these patterns, you will likely miss the chance to execute on many of the opportunities that you identify, but this is part of the business, and is necessary for long-term success. Remember, your goal should be an ever-higher level of capital.

The continuation pattern should be the bread and butter of what you do. The whole essence of technical trading is to identify trends and trade in harmony with them. Continuation patterns present the perfect opportunity for that. Continuation patterns are necessary for a trend to persist and be tradable, even though they present a temporary reversal in the direction of the price action. Temporary breathers are necessary to allow profit taking. Otherwise, a trend tends to stagnate, since everyone who might take a position in the direction of the trend already has. Temporary pullbacks that the trend can survive allow those trading the trend to initiate new positions as the trend continues and give it more strength. In fact, if a continuation pattern exists in the direction of the trend, I am wary of trading it. That can often imply hope and no fresh positions. The time horizon for a continuation pattern will vary, depending most notably on how long the trend leading up to the continuation pattern has existed. In general, a pattern length of between 5 and 15 minutes on an intraday chart is all you should expect for Phase 1 trading. If the pattern persists any longer than that, you should become suspicious and think about liquidating existing positions or gathering evidence for a trend reversal and looking to initiate positions in the direction of the new trend.

The tendency of continuation patterns to be in the opposite direction of the prevailing trend brings us back to the dogs-on-a-leash analogy. Think of the price action as the tracks made by a dog being led by its owner. For whatever reason, the dog tries temporarily to head in the opposite direction and for a short period of time is allowed to do so by the elasticity of the leash. Inevitably, though, the dog is drawn back into line by its owner. Those who operate in countertrend trading practices (in day trading, typically those who trade off news stories that are commonly broadcast after the effects of their content have already been discounted into the price action) are behaving like the dog in the analogy. They may have their way for a brief time, but the strength of the trend will pull them back into line. In Chapter 6, you will see that even though we may trade in the opposite direction of premarket gaps, it is only when that premarket movement indicates that a support or resistance level has been met by the price action.

Trading Concepts That Have Stood the Test of Time **87**

The best practice for identifying continuation patterns is to print a whole series of intraday charts and see how long trends tend to persist and how the price action differed in the formation of continuation patterns and reversal patterns over the course of the day. It is only by practice that you will learn how to judge the difference between continuations and real reversals.

The most common continuation pattern, and the one that the technical day trader will use most in initiating positions, is the simple pullback in a trend. It is like a slingshot, but it requires correct timing and a favorable overall market. This was illustrated in Figure 2-17, which showed how different time scales for the chart could affect the pattern formed.

The other consideration for determining trading actions from continuation patterns, or reversal patterns for that matter, is the size of the pattern relative to the prior trend. When we first discussed trends, we discussed the three time periods: major, secondary, and tertiary trends. As a matter of caution, if you correctly identify a continuation or reversal pattern in, say, the tertiary trend, it is advisable to only hold that position within the tertiary trend. If you use the guidelines given for the predictive qualities of each pattern, you should be able to keep out of trouble. To reinforce this point, look at Figure 2-22.

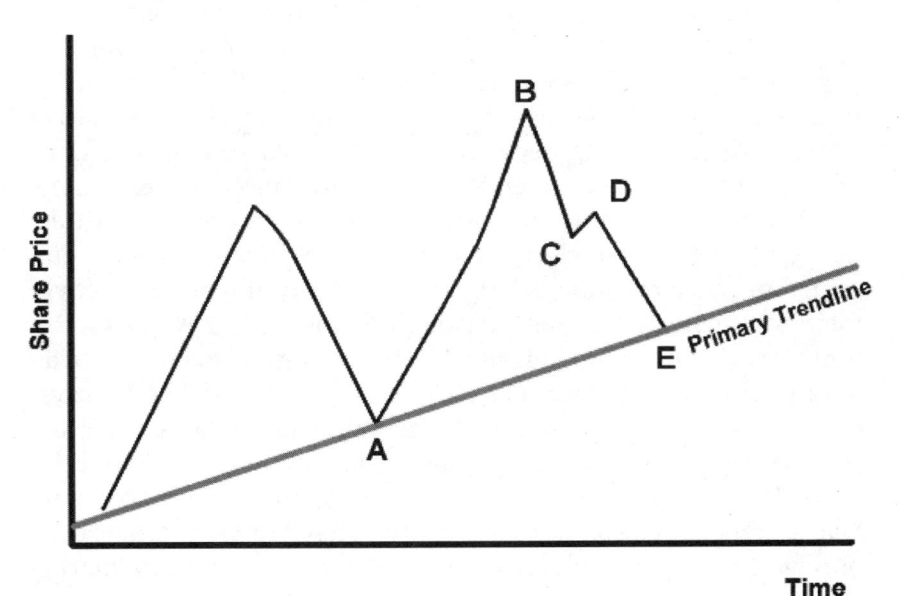

Figure 2-22. A tertiary trend correction within a secondary trend.

Here, the primary trend is up, and the price action between points B and C represents a pullback within that trend and can be classified as a secondary trend. From point C onward, the secondary trend reverses into a tertiary trend, which is in harmony with the primary trend, until point D. There we get a secondary trend resumption to point E. In this case, we can only use the tertiary move from C to D to indicate a continuation of the secondary trend to point E, and no further.

Breakouts

Breakouts are typically among the patterns least traded by day traders. The characteristics of a breakout are that the price action will stagnate within a fairly narrow price range until that range is broken out of. Once the price range has been breached, the move away from the area of congestion is often quite dramatic. Breakouts within the trading day usually occur toward the end of the day for securities that have not moved significantly during Phase 2 trading. There can be many reasons for this type of price action, the most common of which is referred to as a *short squeeze*, which we will now discuss.

It sometimes happens that traders see a security fall during Phase 1 trading. They believe this security is moving lower that day and take a short position but it does not fall any further. At some point in the trading day, most commonly near to market close, those short of the security will start to cover their positions by buying the security. Given that the security has not been falling, this buying starts to push the price up. This buying can also attract new buyers of the stock, which pushes the price up further and brings in the remaining short holders to buy the stock to cover their now losing positions. Although this is quite a neat description of market behavior, it is not a terribly common event. The way to catch these happenings is to set alerts on your market data system that will give off audio and, preferably, visual alerts should a security move out of an area of congestion.

A different type of breakout, a gap, is useful in Phase 1 trading. Gaps rarely appear on intraday charts. They typically can be seen only on daily charts, which show the movement from one market period to the next. Moreover, gaps only appear on bar charts, because line charts connect the close of each time period in one continuous line.

Price gaps occur when the price for a given security opens sharply higher or lower than the previous close. During Phase 1 trading, if an opportunity presents itself, we seek these movements and look to trade in the opposite direction. This is contrary to the traditional way to trade gaps, so let's review the traditional way that gaps are traded.

There are three types of gap, and each one indicates a high degree of price volatility, which is what attracts us as day traders. The *breakaway gap* occurs at the beginning of a new trend, often completing a major reversal or continuation pattern in the daily chart. A characteristic of these gaps is that the price action moves quickly away from the prior area of congestion (that was within the reversal or continuation pattern) and the gap does not get filled. This means that the price action does not move back to the level it was at prior to the gap until the newly formed trend has expired, which is typically weeks, months, or more. Now, suppose you see a security that has moved up significantly in premarket activity. The smart thing to do is look at the daily chart for that security and attempt to determine what type of gap that move represents. Those that look like they might be breakaway gaps are to be avoided for typical Phase 1 trading because the price is likely to continue in the direction of the gap. Trying to take intraday positions in the direction of breakaway gaps does not yield consistent enough profits for this to be a regular activity. It tends to lead to some spectacular gains but many more losses.

The second type of gap is referred to as a *runaway*, or *measuring*, *gap* and typically appears about halfway through an existing trend. This type of gap is partially filled. It is not, however, the type of gap we search for when operating in Phase 1 trading. The third type of gap, the *exhaustion gap,* is really worth searching for. The exhaustion gap appears near the end of a trend that has run its course. It signifies price action that has run out of momentum. These gaps are always filled by the price action. The exhaustion gap typically is characterized by opening at or near what turns out to be the high at least for Phase 1 trading, and often for the whole day.

When we consider the trading week in Chapter 6, we will look for early gappers, quickly determine the stage of the trend at which these gaps are appearing, and then look for confirmed opportunities to take positions in the anticipated direction of the price action. In addition to exhaustion gaps, we will look for gaps that bring the price action close to a support or resistance area. The three types of gap are illustrated in Figure 2-23.

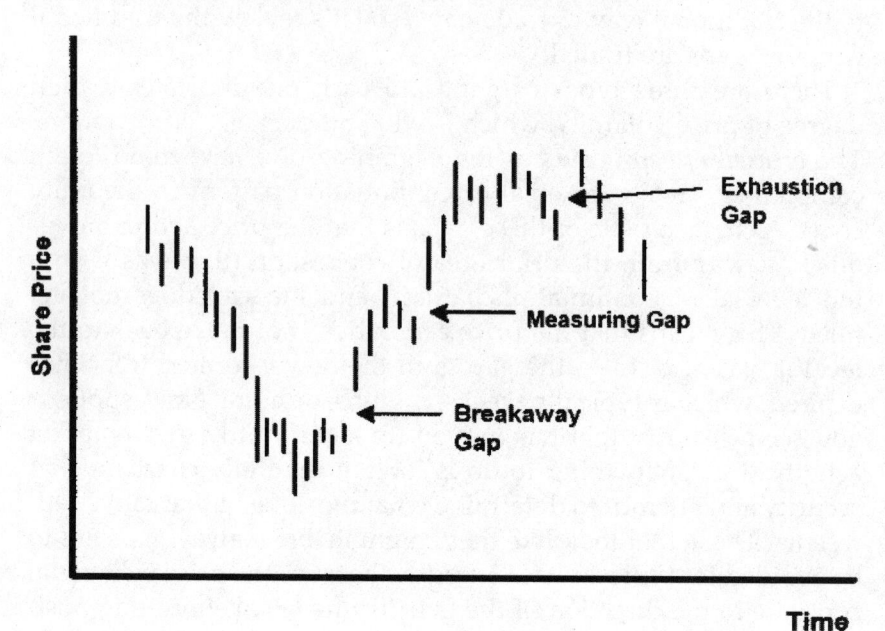

Figure 2-23. A bar chart illustrating the three different types of gaps.

3
Activities to Avoid

In this chapter, I'll take you through some of the methods and strategies that I have tried over the course of my trading career and which I have found do not live up to their hype. The people who have promoted the techniques covered in this section by one means or another tended to benefit from traders following the techniques. Many former, or failed, traders have found that by moving to the brokerage side and using their talents to motivate people to trade, or by running seminars or chatrooms on the Internet, they can enjoy as much potential for gain as they would trading—without the rigors and risks that trading involves.

The issue here is credentials and whose advice you can trust. If a person is really successful at trading, why would she or he devote (or indeed, how would it be possible to devote) a full working day to running seminars, chatrooms, or a brokerage business? The answer is that they don't. They have turned to these alternative activities to make an easier living. In other words, they are not successful traders. And if a person is *not* really successful at day trading, how reliable can their advice be? The longer you trade, the more you will realize that making consistent profits over the course of years of trading activity is a very difficult thing. It takes focus, enthusiasm, and discipline every day for years.

Here, then, is my list of the top things to avoid.

Derivatives

Among the most alluring instruments in all financial markets are options and futures. They allow you to go long, short, or hedge your position and enter all kinds of markets with terrific leverage. As a day trader, don't touch them with a 10-foot pole. In fact, any type of investor should avoid derivatives. I say this as an experienced options trader who was once convinced that this was the only way to get superior returns from the market. I was convinced because I was getting good returns from trading options. Over the course of years, however, I came to realize that the derivatives game has too much in it that stacks the deck in favor of the option writing firms.

First of all, consider this: Unlike the stock market, where lasting wealth is created by the appreciation of securities, and which gives all participants the opportunity to gain, derivatives truly are a zero sum game. Derivatives are manufactured out of thin air and only exist for a predetermined amount of time, so at the end of that time, someone has to pay. Either the person who bought the option loses, or the options writing firm loses. Understandably, the options writing firms are not in the game for altruistic reasons, and the ones you will find to deal with generally price their derivatives correctly, and on average, they end up winning. Certainly, if the options writer were not competent, bankruptcy would soon result.

Of course, we've all heard the stories about some guy who bought 10 contracts of an option priced at $2 (which cost him $2000; each contract represents a count of 100), the option went to $10 in a week, and the guy netted $8000 profit for a $2000 stake. I've had returns like that, but not many, and they have been outweighed by lots of purchases that went from $2 to $1.

Think about it: Companies whose sole business it is to price options devote lots of bright people and computer power to getting it right, or they will go out of business. Is anyone really going to catch them out on a consistent basis for years? Certainly, not decades. If you're still not convinced, let's delve into the world of derivatives a bit further to see why this is the case.

First, let's look at options, since they are the most common derivative vehicles for those trading in the equity markets. Futures are more common in the commodity markets, and even there, it is becoming more common to trade options on futures contracts rather than the underlying futures themselves. We'll only discuss the American style options here, as there is no benefit to trading the less flexible European style options.

Options are of two types, puts and calls. A *call* gives you the option to buy a predetermined amount of a specific security at a specific time in the future. A *put* gives you the option to sell a given amount of a security at a given price at a specific time in the future. Both types of option can be traded by anyone authorized to do so at any time up until the expiration of that option. The key concept here is that you have the choice, i.e., the option, to enter a transaction, and you are not committing to it when you purchase the option. When you enter a futures transaction, you *are* committing to the transaction at the time of contract purchase.

Let's look at a real-world example; in this case AOL. For the sake of argument, let's say that AOL has just come out with tremendous earnings and you think it will appreciate significantly. AOL is priced at $120. You do not have $120,000 available to buy a thousand shares, but you would like to do that. You turn to options as a means of leveraging your money, so that you can effectively own 1000 shares for a set period of time. If today is October 21, referring to an options pricing service, you determine it will cost you $7500 to buy the right to purchase 1000 shares of AOL at $120 on the third Friday in November. Options contracts always expire on the third Friday of the month. So, AOL has to appreciate to $127$1/2$ before you can make a penny, and that doesn't include commission fees. Not only that, it has to do this prior to the option expiry date.

The price of $7$1/2$ for the option has been calculated by the options writer to take into account the trend of AOL, its volatility, and the probability that AOL will exceed the $127$1/2$ level within this time frame. AOL's share price had been oscillating at the time of writing. If AOL was in a strong uptrend, the price of the option would have been higher, requiring even greater appreciation in the share price before you could break even.

So what happens if AOL goes to $125 in the week or so after you buy your option? Do you make any money on it? Probably not. Options prices are made up of two parts, the intrinsic value and the time value. In the case we have just described, the intrinsic value is zero, because the exercise price is equal to the current price of the security. This is called an *at the money* option. If we had purchased an option with an exercise price of $115, it would have been priced at about $10^1/_2$, the extra three dollars representing the intrinsic value of being able to buy AOL at $115 in the future when it is currently $120 in price. This is called an *in the money* option. Similarly, there is an *out of the money* option at $125, priced at $5^1/_2$ for November.

The time value decreases as each day goes by, so if AOL stays at $120 for the next month, the value of the option you purchased would gradually diminish from $7^1/_2$ to zero on the day of expiry. So, in effect, AOL could go to $125 and the value of the option would never go above the $7^1/_2$ paid for it. This illustrates how you can get the direction and timing of a move correct with options and still never make money.

But the bad news does not stop there. Say something dramatic happens in the market that moves AOL significantly. Do you think you would be able to trade your option during the first 10 to 20 minutes of the equity market opening? Most likely not. Options firms do not have to open their quotes right at market open if they don't want to, so they can let the equity market stabilize and then price the options at a level that is advantageous to them. Lots of options firms might offer good reasons for all of this, but the fact is that they stay in business by taking option premiums out of the pockets of those willing to buy them.

So, if this options writing thing is such a good deal, why don't you write options yourself? I was once enamored of the idea of writing covered calls on securities I owned, although this did not do severe damage to my trading capital, it is an activity that I now avoid. The idea behind covered call writing is that you want to get the premium yourself rather than paying a premium to an options company. The process is this: You purchase a security you believe will appreciate in value at some time and then sell a call at the bid price for that option to the options market. Here's an example. We will look at AOL again, which is now trading at $124. We expect AOL to appreciate, but we're not sure when that will occur. If it goes to $130 by the third Friday of November, I will be happy to get paid $133^7/_8$ and close out my position. If AOL does not go to $130 by this time, I will be happy to hold my stock and take $3^7/_8$ per share from the options traders. You get these figures by looking at the bid price of the November $130 calls on AOL, which happen to be $3^7/_8$, which is what the options firm is willing to pay for these calls.

This all sounds fine and dandy. You immediately get some cash back from the security you have purchased, and if it does well, you are forced to take your profits. There are, however, downsides to all this. If AOL gains slightly, or holds its value, this strategy is a good one. But if AOL should start to fall, the tendency is to hold the security, since you have a commitment on the call option that is against the stock you hold. In addition, the premium you collect for volatile stocks like AOL is significant because they can run up very fast. If AOL does run up past $130, let's say to $150, all you will get is $133⅞, and your AOL stock will be delivered to the option holder at $130.

Writing calls against stock you own is a way of selling the security. Options are not as liquid as the underlying security, primarily because of the delay in opening options quotes and because trade volume is significantly less. Writing calls does limit your upside potential, and provides only minimal protection on the downside. Again, the options firms tend to price these derivatives accurately, or they would go out of business, so your chances of winning against them in the long run are not that great. If you get into the game of trying to spot mispriced options, you are basically betting that your computer model is more accurate than their computer model. That means you better fully believe in the person who wrote the software you use.

What it boils down to is that using derivatives gives you great leverage if you buy a call or put to go long or short a security. However, the time value in the option price is always ticking against you, so you are really betting not on the price of the security but on the pricing of the option as defined by the options company you are dealing with. Sure, the security's price is a big determinant, but volatility, time to expiration, and other factors will determine the price of the option itself.

The price you pay for the leverage is the additional risk that all these factors bring to the price of the asset you hold. As a zero sum game, derivatives really do favor the big guys over time. Interestingly, the best analysis of the success of derivatives trading comes from the commodity markets, and year in, year out, it is those who are hedging positions in real commodities who make the best bets in the derivatives markets. The reason for mentioning this is that some day traders reference the put-to-call ratio in a security to gauge whether that security is likely to rise or fall in the future. The thinking is that if lots of calls are being purchased, the security is likely to go up; if more puts are being purchased, the price is likely to go down.

This technique has not been anywhere near accurate enough a predictor for me to commit my own money based on its direction. What we can infer from the research in the commodity markets is that those who own and operate cotton fields, import cocoa beans, and the like tend to get the future direction of commodity-driven derivatives prices correct, whereas those speculating in the markets do not. This does not mean that speculators cannot get the direction of commodity prices right, just that the extra hurdle of paying for the derivative's time value and always having to pay the spread between bid and ask is too much for the majority of traders.

Trading individual securities, in which you can eliminate the spread on at least one side of the transaction (either the buy or sell) and avoid paying for time value, significantly increases your opportunity to make profitable trades. And, as we shall see in Chapter 6, the opportunity to trade right at the open yields the lowest risk and the most profitable day trades.

Avoiding derivatives will, over the long term, lead to greater trading capital for the vast majority of traders.

Overreliance on Complex Chart Analysis

The most successful technical traders use either bar or line charts as their primary sources for short-term trading decisions. All other forms of analysis are secondary indicators. That is not to say that these secondary forms are not referred to. In fact, it is good practice to have secondary indicators confirm your analysis, but it is a mistake to have these secondary indicators drive your trading decisions. I go into these tools in this section strictly because I want to stress that they should not be primary factors in your trading decisions.

Many of the more complex chart forms are heading toward what are referred to as black box trading systems, in which the system gives you trading actions that you execute without really understanding why the trading call came about. With black box trading systems, you are putting your faith blindly in your belief that the system will be correct.

As an example of this, consider what is probably the most common form of complex or advanced charting technique, oscillators.

Stochastic oscillators are best used as secondary indicators in range-bound markets. I say secondary because the oscillator behaves differently for a range-bound market than for a trending market, so you need to know what type of market you are in before you try to understand what the oscillator is telling you. The reason I specify range-bound rather than trending markets for stochastics is that the classic buy or sell signal from an oscillator is more accurate within a range-bound market than when the market is trending. In fact, there is a term for the misleading signals that stochastic oscillators give you in trending markets: *stochastic creep*. We'll look at this more closely when we examine the stochastic form of oscillator in more detail later in this section.

Oscillators are designed to give easy-to-read signals, based on whether the oscillator sees the object of study as overbought or oversold at the time. Most commonly, the oscillator has a y axis which ranges between -1 and $+1$, or between 0 and 100. As we progress through the analysis of each oscillator, we will see that classically, signals can be given by any of the following:

- Crossing the midpoint line (commonly 0 or 50)
- Pullbacks from extreme readings
- Divergence of two lines within the oscillator
- Classic trendline breaks and patterns within the oscillator

Moreover, oscillators tend to fall into one of three categories: momentum, rate of change, or moving average oscillators.

Momentum Oscillators

Momentum and rate of change oscillators have similar uses for finding short-term changes in direction. They are essentially the same tool, except that rate of change oscillators give readings in percentage form, whereas momentum oscillators give readings in point form. Moving average oscillators are best for trading with a trend.

A momentum oscillator measures the acceleration or deceleration of price rather than the actual price level. For example, a five-period momentum oscillator will calculate the difference between the current period's closing price and one five periods ago (whether the period is a day, a minute, or a week). At the end of each time period, the resulting figure is plotted on a graph, and the resulting graph will tend to oscillate around zero. With a simple momentum oscillator like this, there are no upper or lower boundaries as there are with rate of change oscillators. In the example just given, a time period of five would yield a more sensitive oscillator than the more standard 10-period graph. Conversely, a time period of 20 would give a less sensitive graph.

The basic idea behind a momentum oscillator is that for a security to reverse direction, it must decelerate in its current direction and reach zero velocity before picking up momentum in a new direction. Think of this in the same way as throwing a ball up in the air. The vertical velocity has to slow to zero before the ball can change vertical direction and start heading down again. Of course, unless you have a ball with its own way of generating thrust, the ball *must* head down after reaching zero vertical velocity. This is not necessarily true of a security. It may reach zero on the oscillator, but it can get a new injection of thrust from a news story or some other market action. Bearing that in mind, an oscillator is not as sure a bet as gravity working on a ball, but it can be a useful secondary indicator on occasion.

An example of a momentum oscillator is shown in Figure 3-1. This one uses the equation $M = P - Px$, where M is the value plotted on the oscillator, P is the current period closing price, and Px is the closing price x number of periods ago.

In this case, we can see that during the opening 20 minutes, this security gained momentum. At around 9:55 a.m., the momentum leveled off, and close to 10:00 a.m., the momentum started to head down. It is imperative to remember that the momentum line is measuring the difference between price at two time intervals. In order for this oscillator to gain in value, the difference in closing price between the two periods being studied must be getting greater. Essentially, if this type of oscillator is flat, it means that a stable trend is in effect and the price increases (or decreases) are constant. Any reading above the zero line means that prices are increasing. Any reading below the oscillator zero line means that prices are falling.

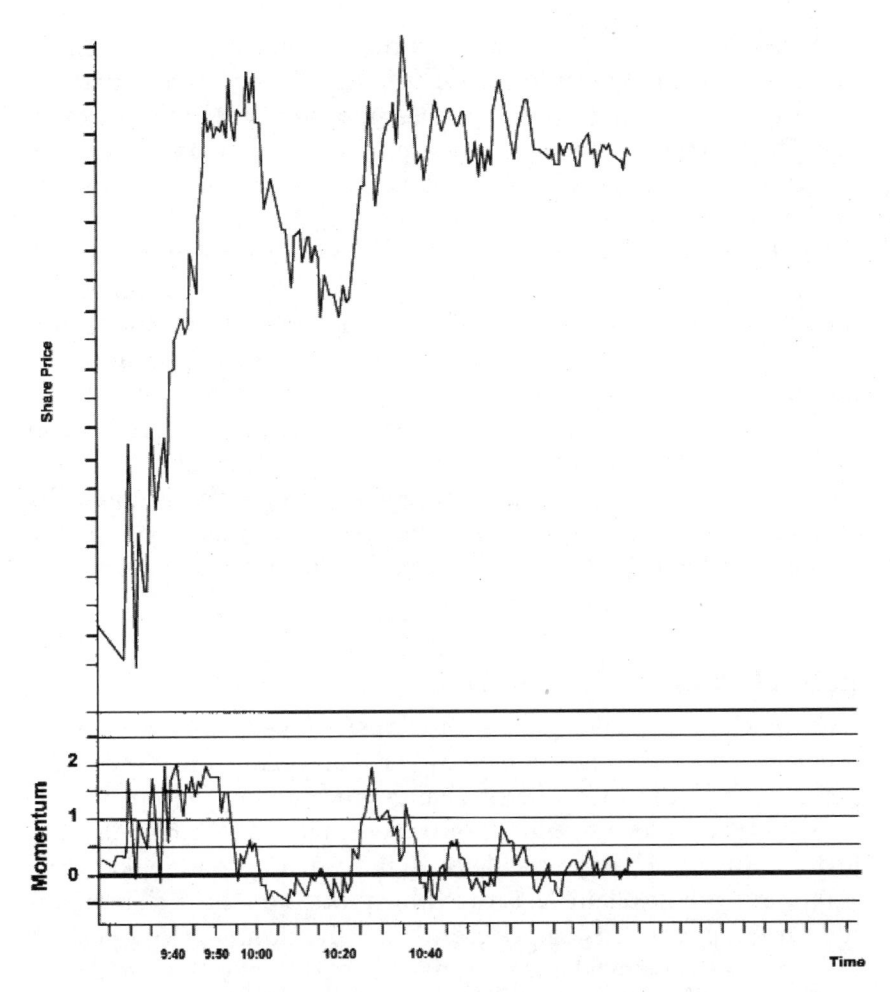

Figure 3-1. Example of a momentum oscillator.

Given the significance of the zero line for this type of oscillator, a crossing of this line is often used to generate trading signals. Following these crossings of the zero line is, however, a bad thing to do without further knowledge.

If a security is trending up, only crossings from negative to positive territory should be used as buying signals, and you would ignore the sell signals from a cross from positive to negative territory. This is a good tactic for when you are looking to find appropriate entry points for getting in on a trend, because it will make you wait until the security has pulled back to an area of support and has started to appreciate in value again before initiating a position. Note, however, that you first have to have identified the trend using basic charting principles in order for this to be of any use. The reverse is true, of course, for a security in a downtrend. In that case, crosses from above to below the zero line are used to confirm entry points.

In the Figure 3-1 example, the broad interpretation of the momentum graph is as follows. During Phase 1 trading, the momentum is positive and gaining, so long positions are appropriate. Any longs should be liquidated by 9:55 a.m., because the momentum has leveled off. By 10:00 a.m. the trader should be looking for shorts, since the momentum is negative. At around 10:25 a.m. the momentum is starting to reverse up, so shorts should be liquidated. Toward the end of the graph, at noon, the momentum is stuck around zero, and you would move on to look for another security that is either trending or has momentum.

Rate of Change Oscillators

Rate of change oscillators, as previously stated, are momentum oscillators quoted in percentage rather than point form. To get to a percentage reading for rate of change, the present period close is divided by the close x number of periods ago. To put this into context, a rate of change oscillator will use a formula like $M = 100(P/Px)$, where again, M is the value plotted on the oscillator, P is the current period closing price, and Px is the closing price x periods ago. In this case, the 50 line becomes the midpoint of the oscillator.

You will see that when you plot a rate of change oscillator and a momentum oscillator side by side, they look very similar. In fact, all of the discussion on how to interpret a momentum oscillator applies equally to a rate of change oscillator.

Moving Average Oscillators

The third type of oscillator revolves around using two moving averages and plotting the divergence between them. To understand these oscillators, a small detour to look at moving averages is appropriate.

A moving average is calculated by averaging the closing price over the previous x periods. For example, a simple moving average of closing price over eight days is the sum of the closing price of those last eight days divided by eight. So, to get one point on an eight-day moving average, you need eight data points. A simple moving average is shown in Figure 3-2.

A single moving average is of limited use. All it comprises is a lagging average of what has gone on before. Lagging means the price action itself will have changed direction before the moving average. In some instances, a moving average performs a similar function to a trendline on a chart in that it will act as a line of support in upward moves and a line of resistance in downward moves. As such, the crossing of a single moving average can signal a change in trend. There is much more that can be done with moving averages, though.

When you combine two moving averages, you get clearer signals. Essentially, you pick a short-term moving average and a long-term moving average and take your trading signals from when they cross each other. The two most significant patterns formed by the crossing of two moving averages are the golden cross and the dead cross.

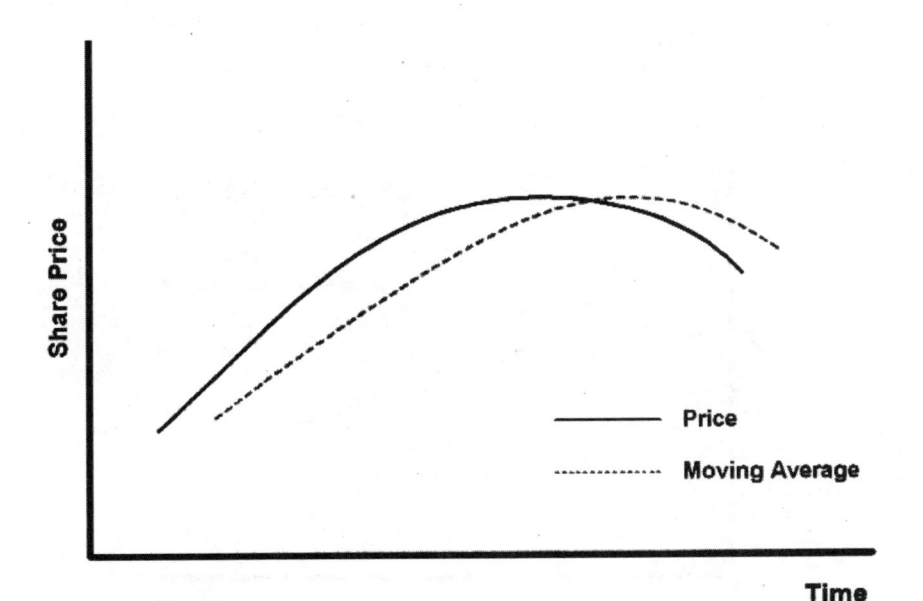

Figure 3-2. A simple moving average.

The Golden Cross and the Dead Cross The golden cross is formed as the shorter-term moving average crosses from below to above the longer-term moving average. The dead cross is formed as the shorter-term moving average crosses below the longer-term moving average. Both crossing formations are illustrated in Figure 3-3.

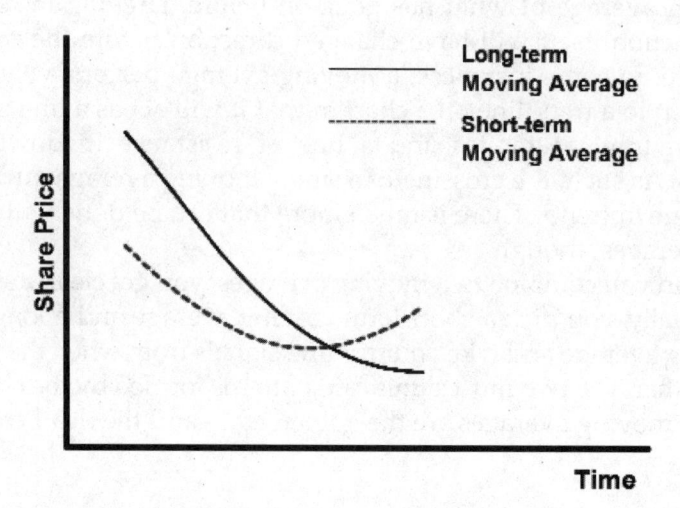

Figure 3-3a. The golden cross formation.

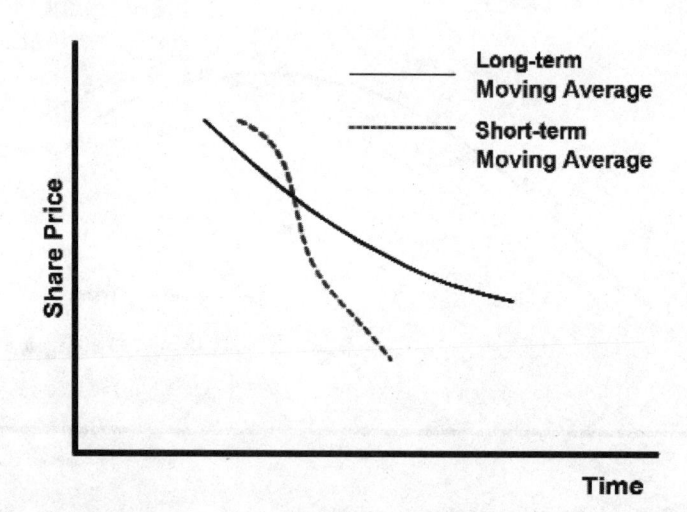

Figure 3-3b. The dead cross formation.

The golden cross is, of course, a buy signal, whereas the dead cross is a sell signal. The most difficult thing in the use of moving averages is the selection of a long-term and short-term averaging value. Do you set the short term for 5 periods and the long term to 20 periods, or something else? Selecting different values will change the point of crossing for a dead or golden cross and, hence, time the buy or sell signal differently. There is no easy answer to this one. You have to take every graph on a case-by-case basis and judge it with respect to the overall trend of the security in question. To make this general statement of more use, I'll discuss what I typically do using two moving averages.

Basics of Fibonacci The Fibonacci sequence is a sequence of numbers that appears in many places in nature and technical analysis. I tend to use Fibonacci numbers as my moving averages. In this sequence each successive number represents the sum of the previous two, such as:

1, 2, 3, 5, 8, 13, 21, 34, 55, 89, 144, etc.

I have no reason to justify their use other than that these numbers have worked for me in the past. More than I do in individual day trades, I use moving average analysis of this form when assessing the likely continuance of an existing trend in a security, market sector, or the market in general. When I am looking for evidence of potential reversals, I experiment with combinations of Fibonacci numbers and see which one yields the best indications for previous changes in trend, and I use that combination when looking for the next change. My starting point is generally 34 for the long-term average and 13 for the shorter-term average. Each can be moved in isolation to see the effects of changing the value, and you then select the combination that best matches the object of your study.

Weighting Before moving back to look at moving average oscillators, the final point to note about basic moving averages is that these moving averages are often weighted. The idea behind weighting is to give more significance to the most recent price action. For example, instead of just summing the previous five closing period values and dividing by five to get the next point on the moving average, you multiply the most recent closing price by five, the previous one by four, the one previous to that by three, the one before that by two, and finally, the fifth most recent one by one. This figure is summed and the total is divided by 15 (the sum of 1, 2, 3, 4, and 5). However, this still only takes into account the last five values for a five-period moving average. The exponentially smoothed weighted average extends the concept one step further by gradually assigning a diminishing weighting to all data points back to the beginning of the study.

The Concept of Divergence and MACD When viewed on daily or weekly charts, moving averages are at best a secondary indicator when assessing the overall trend strength of a security. For the intraday charting used in day trading, the oscillators we will discuss next are better at showing moving average divergence.

As we saw with the golden and dead crosses, a shorter-term moving average crossing over a longer-term moving average can generate buy and sell signals. This crossing process is called *divergence*, because the short-term and long-term moving averages diverge from a common point. When you are looking at intraday charts and using tools to make day-trading decisions, the speed at which you can assimilate information is critical. Using an oscillator can be beneficial in identifying moving averages that cross over, and telling when the short-term average extends too far from the long-term one.

The simplest oscillator approach that utilizes these principles is a line that graphs the difference in value between a long-term and short-term moving average, as illustrated in Figure 3-4.

Gerald Appel of Signalert Corporation has refined this method into a more useful oscillator, which is called the Moving Average Convergence Divergence (MACD) method. What MACD does is produce two exponentially smoothed moving averages of the difference between a short-term and a long-term moving average of the price action in a security. This may seem strange at first, since we are going from two moving averages to a single value and then creating two moving averages from it. You might wonder what has been gained. Figure 3-5 shows a daily chart of Microsoft as an example. The moving averages on the chart are set to 13 and 34, which give a confirmed buy signal on 6/18 and sell signals on 4/28 and 8/03. The MACD oscillator, however, gave signals for the

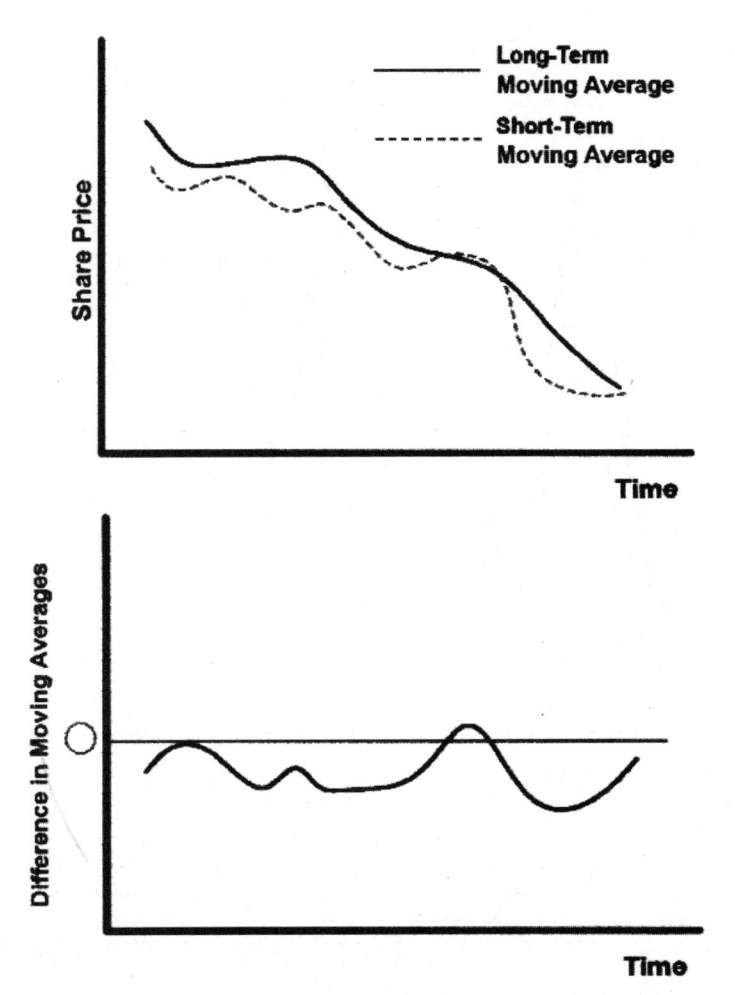

Figure 3-4. Graphing the difference between two moving averages.

same moves much earlier: on 5/26 for the buy signal when the faster line crosses above the slower line, and on 4/01 and 7/21 for the sell signals when the faster line crosses below the slower line. So what you are getting is an earlier notification of a divergence in shorter-term and longer-term averages. I chose the Microsoft daily chart at random. You will find that this setup works for just about any actively traded security you choose on a daily chart. This indicator is less useful on intraday charts; therefore I tend to use it more for assessing the overall trend direction of the security than making actual day-trading decisions.

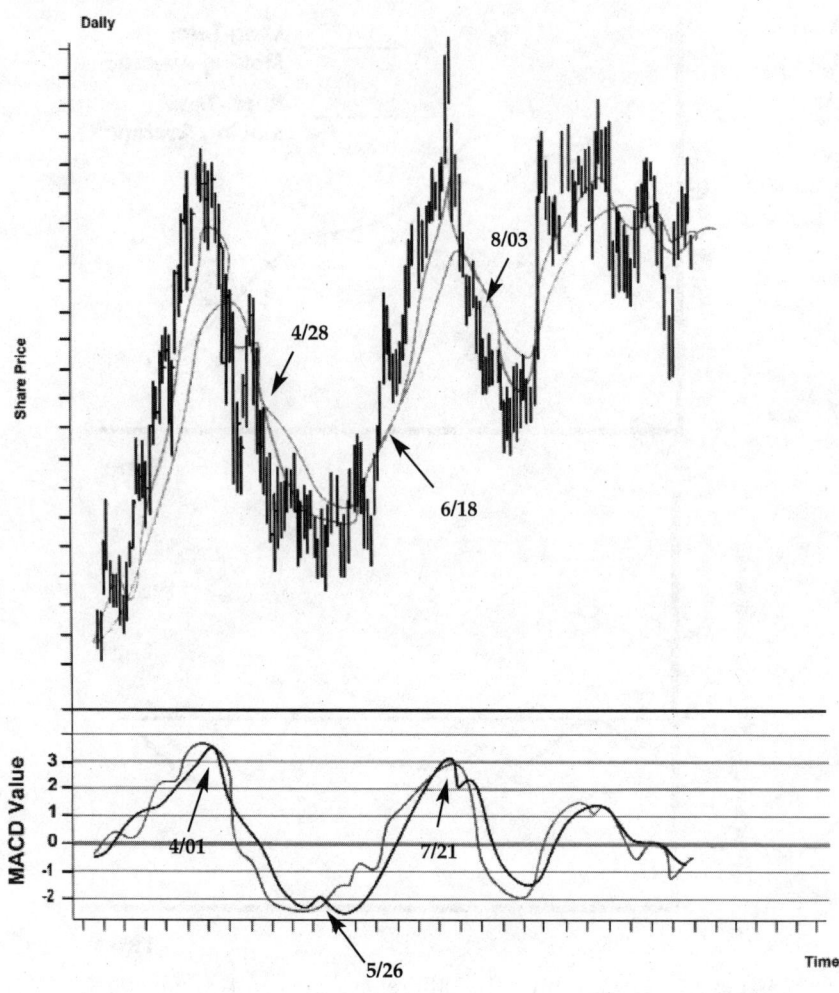

Figure 3-5. The MACD method of determining divergence.

Let's review the signals that these basic types of oscillators give before moving on to two oscillators that you may want to use in intraday charting as secondary indicators.

My advice is always this: Never use just an oscillator to generate a trading decision; use them only to confirm decisions once you understand the trend or trading range of the security being studied. The key to success in technical trading is to use the right tool at the right time, and you can only select the right tool if you understand the basics of trending and can decide which tool is appropriate for range-bound securities, those in a trend, or those attempting to reverse trend.

How to Properly Use Oscillators

So what's involved in interpreting the oscillators covered so far? We first looked at momentum oscillators. The best time to use a momentum oscillator is when a security is trending and you are looking for a safe place to enter an existing trend. The key points are as follows:

- Crossing the zero line generates the signal; from negative to positive is a buy signal, from positive to negative is a sell signal.
- When a security is in an uptrend, only use buy signals from the oscillators to initiate positions. When a security is trending strongly upward, there will be many false sell signals.
- When a security is in a downtrend, only use sell signals to initiate positions. Likewise, there will be many false buy signals that should be ignored.

The rate of change oscillator is just another form of momentum oscillator and is interpreted in the same way. Regarding moving average oscillators, we would use the crossing of the faster over the slower line in an MACD oscillator to signal a reversal of trend. This crossing of two averages in an oscillator is the second type of signal we can take from oscillators and is best used to confirm a suspected change in trend.

The third type of signal, taken from RSI (Relative Strength Index) and stochastic oscillators (both of which are discussed next), uses *edge band analysis*. This means the oscillator will have upper and lower bands that will identify the security as either in overbought or oversold territory. Again, it is essential to know the overall trend of the security before considering that either of these oscillators is providing a trading signal. The aforementioned stochastic creep will show a security in overbought territory consistently if the security is in a sustainable uptrend, so those avoiding a strongly trending security on the basis of a stochastic oscillator classifying the security as overbought will miss out. Even worse, should a security form a continuation pattern in its overall uptrend, it is likely that the oscillator will temporarily dip below the overbought band line (typically a value of 80), causing anyone initiating a short position as a result of that dip to make a loss. Classically, RSI and stochastics are good for confirming reversals when a security is trading within a specific range. As always, you must apply the right tool for the job at hand, and you only know what that job is if you can read the basics of trend in the price action.

The Most Commonly Used Oscillators

Relative Strength Index The most commonly used oscillators are the RSI and stochastic oscillators. RSI is the brainchild of J. Welles Wilder, Jr., who introduced it in his 1978 book called *New Concepts in Technical Trading Systems*. The worst thing about RSI is what the acronym stands for, Relative Strength Index. The reason this is bad is that relative strength was already in use in trading terminology, and RSI is actually quite different. Relative strength is something we will revisit when we come to assess market sector and individual security health in Chapter 7. To save confusion, I will only refer to RSI as an acronym, and I recommend you forget what it stands for.

The RSI oscillator was constructed to address two of the main criticisms of simple momentum oscillators. The first is that a sudden step change in security price, as is seen when a gap occurs, can distort the oscillator. Suppose a security is trading at $50, then gaps up to $60 on some outstanding news. If we are using a 10-day oscillator, the effects of this $10 change will still be seen 10 days from now in the oscillator, even if price moves after that are minimal. To stop this effect, some sort of smoothing is necessary, and RSI supplies that. Second, RSI is also helpful in measuring things on a scale from 0 to 100. Regular momentum oscillators have no fixed scale. The RSI oscillator is able to achieve this because it uses a formula that guarantees a reading of between 0 and 100. The exact formula for calculating each point on the RSI oscillator is given below, where RS equals the average of N periods up closes divided by the average of N periods down closes.

$$RSI = 100 - \frac{(100)}{(1 + RS)}$$

Here's an example of how the average up value is calculated. Let's say we are looking at a 10-period oscillator. To calculate the average up value for 10 periods, first look at all the periods in which the security appreciated in value for the 10 most recent periods. Then add the total number of points moved up. Once you have this number, divide it by 10 (the time period chosen for this oscillator), and you have the average up value for the last 10 days. For the average down value, do the same: Add together the total number of points moved down during each of the down periods and divide by 10.

The key factor when using the RSI oscillator is choosing the number of periods you want to use in calculating each point value. Essentially, the bigger the number you choose, the smoother the oscillator appears, and the fewer signals the oscillator gives. The smaller the number of periods chosen, the more sensitive the oscillator becomes and the more signals it generates. When using one-minute or five-minute intervals for day trading, I use 10 periods in the RSI calculation. That has served me most effectively in the past when using RSI as a secondary indicator.

There is widespread misinterpretation of both RSI and stochastics. Correct interpretation of RSI is based on two things: (1) divergence of price action from oscillator trend and (2) the Dow principles of failure swings. The reason for all the misinterpretation is because the band above 80 on the RSI is called overbought and the band below 20 is called oversold. Most people think that this is all they need to know about this oscillator. That simply is not the case. If you want to use this oscillator, even as a secondary indicator, reading Wilder's original text is a good idea.

When viewing the RSI oscillator, your primary goal should be to identify trends and failure swings in the trend to determine trading signals. A failure swing occurs in an uptrend when the zig-zag motion of the oscillator in a trend fails to make a new high, and then the next low is lower than the previous low. This formation has the most significance when it occurs above the 80 level in an uptrend. For a downtrend, the failure to make a new low, followed by the next high being higher than the previous high, is a strong signal, given that the formation occurs below the 20 value line. These formations were discussed fully in Chapter 2 and were illustrated in Figures 2-2 and 2-3. The essential point is that you should be looking for reversal formations within the overbought and oversold areas, not just at the fact that the oscillator has reached these levels. As you should know by now, a security that is trending strongly upward will stay in the overbought region for some time. If you are interested in looking at these charts, you can go to www.bigcharts.com or www.prophetfinance.com for free charts of this type.

The second use of RSI comes in the form of divergence analysis, meaning divergence in the trend of the oscillator and the underlying price action. This warrants its own illustration and is shown in Figure 3-6.

Here we see a security that was previously in a downtrend bottoming and forming a new uptrend. In the price action, the line drawn between points 1 and 2 is sloping downward, whereas a line drawn on the oscillator between the same two points in time shows an uptrend. We therefore have a divergence in the trend between the price action and the oscillator. This formation typically does not occur within the edge bands above 80 or below 20 on the RSI. Divergence is, however, in the opinion of Wilder himself, the single most valuable indication given by an RSI oscillator. Again, those who only focus on edge band analysis when using the RSI oscillator are missing out on some of its most valuable qualities.

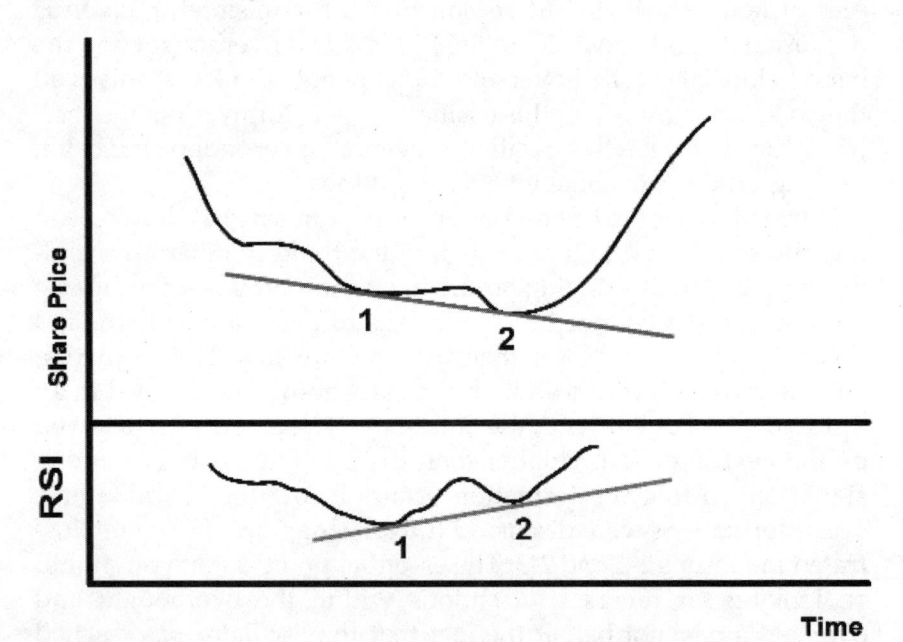

Figure 3-6. The difference between a security's price action and its RSI oscillator trend.

Activities to Avoid

Stochastic Oscillators The second oscillator that is commonly used in day trading, and which also is widely misunderstood, is the stochastic oscillator. This oscillator is attributed to George Lane of Investment Educators, Inc. Stochastics are oscillators that can range from 0 to 100 in value. The objective of stochastics is to help you visualize when a trend is running out of steam. This arises out of the fact that when a security is trending upward, the price tends to close near the upper limit of the price variation for that period. To clarify, let's look at an example of a daily oscillator. Suppose a security has a daily range of $52 to $54 during one day. If the security is in an upward trend, the price will tend to close nearer $54 than $52. If the security is in a downtrend, the reverse is true; the security is more likely to close nearer to $52. So with stochastic oscillators, we try to get a measure of how near to the top or bottom of the trading range the security closes for the time period we are looking at. The implication for an upward trend is that as soon as the price starts to fall away from closing at, or close to, the high for the period under study, that upward trend is losing strength.

The stochastic oscillator differs from most other oscillators in that it uses two lines instead of one. The first is the %K line, which is calculated as follows:

$$\%K = 100\ [(C - Lx) / (Hx - Lx)]$$

In this formula, C is the most recent closing price, Lx is the lowest low for the last x periods and Hx is the highest high for the last x periods. The second line is termed the %D line and is just a smoothed-out version of the %K line. It is calculated as:

$$\%D = 100\ (Ty/By)$$

Here, Ty is a summation of the $(C - Lx)$ values for y number of periods, and By is a summation of $(Hx - Lx)$ values for y number of periods. The actual formulas are not all that important. The stochastic oscillator is all computerized these days, and the computer performs all the tedious calculations required to generate the %K and %D lines. However, the values that you choose in the %K and %D calculations are important. I have achieved the best results by using 13 periods for %K (the x value in the first calculations) and 3 periods for %D (the y value in the second calculation). Some calculations also smooth both the %K line and the %D line to make them easier to read. In this instance, I use eight-period smoothing for %K and exponential smoothing for %D.

In many articles on stochastics, the most important signals are described as divergences between oscillator trend when in an edge band, followed by a crossing of the faster K line over the slower D line. This is shown for a downward trend in Figure 3-7.

In this figure, it can be seen that the stochastic reverses trend, as indicated by a failure to make a new low before the price action actually bottoms out. The signal is actually given when the faster K line crosses over the slower D line as the oscillator turns upward.

The stochastic oscillator has different uses depending on the time of day in which it is used. During Phase 1 trading, where we see quick reversals, seeing both the %K and %D lines head out of an edge band area is generally all we are looking for as confirmation of a reversal. The values I use for calculating %K and %D prevent me from using anything more sophisticated than the edge band breakout during Phase 1. During Phase 2, there is generally more time for reversals in trend to occur, and I can utilize the more traditional form of stochastics analysis described above.

Incidentally, I see many recommendations in chat rooms and on day-trading sites that suggest much faster settings for stochastic

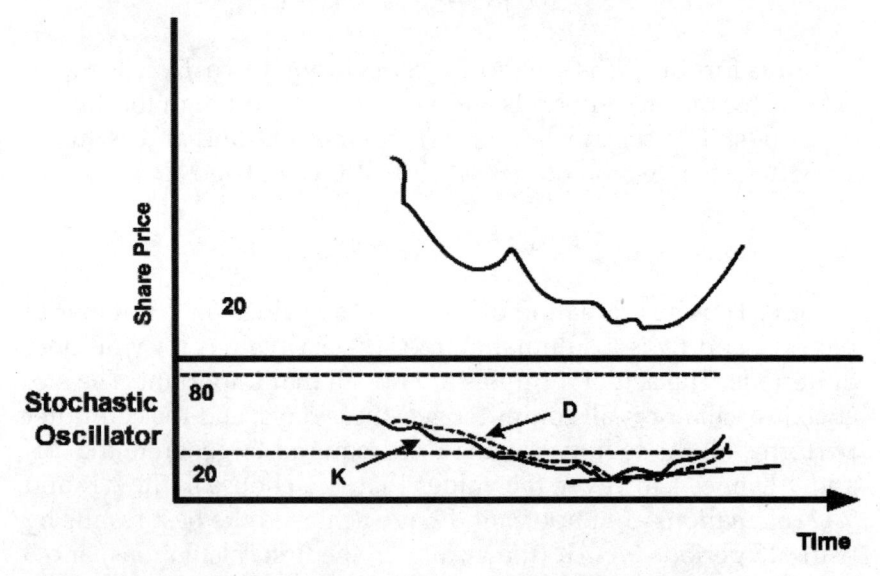

Figure 3-7. Bullish divergence in the stochastic oscillator.

oscillators. This is a mistake. Generating your buy and sell signals purely from a Level II screen and a stochastic oscillator with fast settings (such as 3 periods instead of 13 for %K and 8 for %D) is a dangerous game. As we will see in Chapter 6, the Level II screen gives many signals to either take or close a position, and it is not in the interest of the day trader to act on every one of them throughout the trading day. The same is true of stochastics with fast settings. A fast oscillator will give many more signals, if you interpret a signal as crossing out of an edge band area, either 20 or 80. The reason some experts suggest these tactics is that they are using hindsight to point out how this method gave a good signal when a trend reversal actually did take place. That may be so, but it will also give you a lot of false signals that look just as convincing when you don't have the benefit of hindsight. The way we will deal with this when we approach the markets for real in Chapter 6 is to be aware of the trend and market position of the security and have an idea of the behavior we are looking for in that security. When we suspect a security is behaving as we anticipated, we can use things like oscillators for confirmation.

Having covered oscillators and how they can be useful as secondary or confirming indicators (as long as you know which oscillator to use for the trend and market position of the security being studied), let's look at some advanced techniques that day traders should avoid like the plague. Gann analysis and Elliot wave analysis are too complex to be of any use in day trading. In fact, they are so complicated that few people can ascertain whether they even have validity in trading securities. The reason they are presented here is so you will know about them and not be tempted to explore them further and make trading decisions based on them.

Gann Analysis

W. D. Gann lived from 1878 to 1955. During the latter half of his career, he devoted his time to writing about his extremely complex mathematical techniques and delivering seminars about their use. The seductive thing about these and other similarly complex techniques is that they offer the practitioner the illusion of being able to see into the future. This speaks to the essence of trading as opposed to investing. A trader looks for a repetitive patterns in behavior to start to occur and then takes a position in the market in harmony with the way the market is behaving at that time. It is not possible to have any hard-and-fast idea of where the stock really will end up 10, 30, or 120 minutes from the point of taking a position. What you can do is hold positions for as long as market conditions support that position being held.

When you start to take action based on complex mathematical techniques, you are putting yourself in the hands of the person who devised the formula, and you lose control over what you are doing. You are merely acting out what is prescribed by the formula. Einstein said it best by stating that elegance is for tailors. The message being that just because some theory has some mathematical beauty, it is not necessarily correct. It is my philosophy that you cannot say that a stock will move a half dollar, a dollar, or more in any given direction at any given time. All you can do is take a position when the trend suggests that you will win and stay with that trend until your judgment tells you that the trend you bought into shows signs of weakening. Anyway, let's look at what Gann had to say.

As with most of the truly seductive schemes, there is a liberal spattering of truth and value in what Gann did. To portray him as a person without a grasp of the markets would be unfair and inaccurate. It must be said, however, that many people have suspected he made more money out of seminars and writing than actually trading his techniques. One of the key concepts that can be attributed to Gann comes from his belief in the significance of historic highs and lows. Gann correctly identified the market behavior that respects these figures as areas of future resistance and support and noted that should those levels be breached, their roles as support or resistance reverse. We have already discussed this idea in the analysis of trend. Once Gann gets away from the simpler concepts, however, the day trader has to say good-bye to him. Gann used sophisticated formulas to attempt to predict future levels of support and resistance, and he coupled that with placing fan lines on a chart, which predicted future trendlines. Although books that promote this technique can come up with examples of securities that follow Gann's predictions to the letter, I can come up with just as many that don't. In fact, I can come up with a study that shows certain stocks gained in value each day this week that I turned left rather than right at the bottom of my road on my way to get a bagel. That doesn't mean that next week the behavior will be the same. This is the crux of technical analysis. Chart reading is based on human behavior, not mathematical formula. Chart readings give only general indications of expected movements, not exact predictions. In addition, as already stressed, you do not take positions in securities unless a common pattern has been completed and the security is behaving as you expect. The goal of trading, especially day trading, is to get yourself in the position to react to market events, not to predict them. Predicting market events is for investors.

Let's at least cover the basics of Mr. Gann's method, so you know why to avoid these techniques. The first of Gann's popular techniques is to predict future areas of support and resistance by what is known as the *cardinal square method.* This method calls for you to place a security's all-time low price in the center of a piece of paper. Then, starting with a position immediately to the left of this value, write in the value of the all-time low plus $2. Continue this in a clockwise fashion until you fill out the square, as Figure 3-8 shows for a stock whose all-time low value is $20.

44	46	48	50	52
42	24	26	28	54
40	22	20	30	56
38	36	34	32	58
	66	64	62	60

Channel Containing the Likely Values of Support and Resistance

Direction of Value Placement

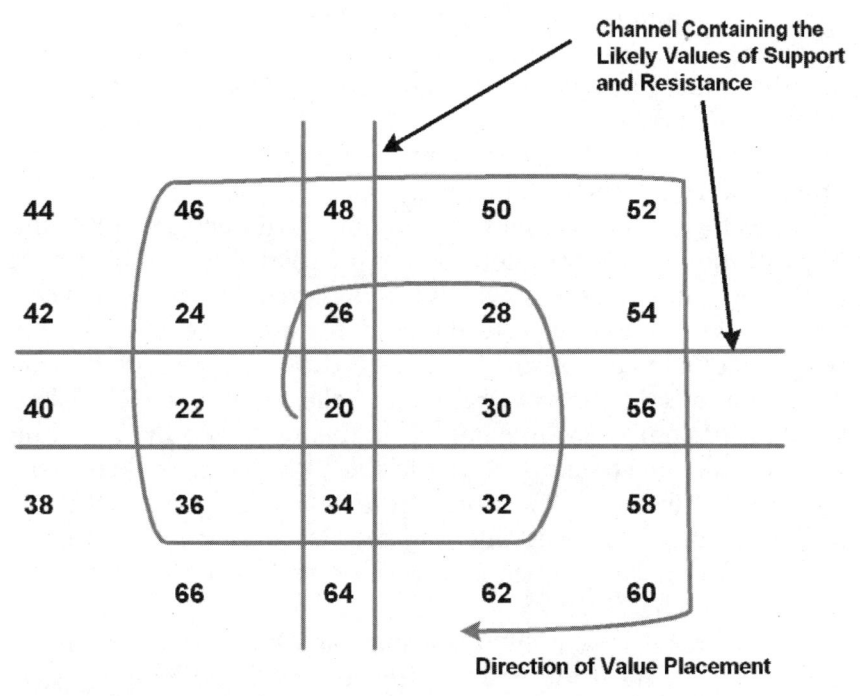

Figure 3-8. Illustration of Gann's Cardinal Square Rule.

Clearly, the question is why $2 as an increment? Since there is no easy answer to that, one just selects a value that has best fit with historic areas of congestion and uses that to predict future areas of support and resistance. Conceptually, this is not too different from the idea of using a trendline to suggest a support or resistance level. However, trendlines are simple to draw and are, therefore, quickly interpreted, which is what you want.

Gann also placed significance on using the important angles in a circle to identify the number of days it would take a future market turn to appear, such as 90, 180, 360, etc. In addition, Gann would use the price of a security, when it reached a big round number, to predict the time going forward for the security to change direction. For argument's sake, let's say a security reaches $100 in value today. Gann would say that 100 days from now, that security will reverse.

What has probably gained more widespread use these days are the Gann angles which can be drawn with most of the computer-based technical analysis trading tools currently available. I think the Gann angles have gained popularity more because they look nice and computers are adept at drawing them, not for any real predictive value they possess. The idea behind Gann's angles is that they attempt to predict the next trendline that will act as support or resistance, depending on whether you are analyzing an upward trend or downward trend. For simplicity, let's assume an upward trend, as shown in Figure 3-9.

In this figure, the origin of the fan lines is drawn at point A, the scene of the last recent bottom in the price action. From this point, a 45-degree line is drawn, which is a diagonal line that spans one horizontal box and one vertical box on the graph. In addition, the two horizontal to one vertical box line is drawn, along with the one horizontal to two vertical line. Gann believed that the 1×2 line would contain upward movements in the trend, and the 2×1 line would be an area of support should the 1×1 line be broken.

Like most technical techniques, it is best to get confirmation of signals from more than one source. Gann supplied a second method, based on retrenchment levels, that can be used in conjunction with his fan lines.

Retrenchment is actually a concept that Dow referred to in his editorials. The most important retrenchment value is the 50 percent retrenchment line, where it is believed significant support will

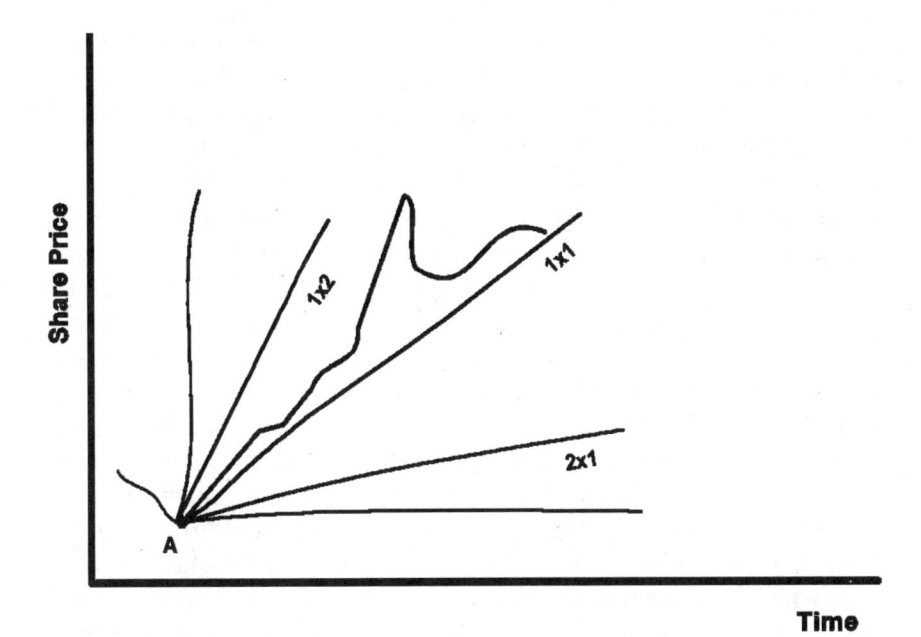

Figure 3-9. Example of Gann's fan lines for an upward trend.

be found if a security's price action retrenches 50 percent of the upward move from a major low point. So, if you drew Gann's fan lines and retrenchment lines, then the price action pulled back to a point where the 1×1 and the 50 percent retrenchment lines crossed, you would expect strong support there.

This is all a bit too much to swallow. There is not enough evidence to support its validity, particularly on the intraday charts used by day traders.

Elliott Wave Analysis

So much for W. D. Gann. Now for Elliott wave analysis, probably the most complicated of all technical methods. Those who follow Elliott wave analysis tend to make very bold predictions. Based upon the principles Elliott set out at the end of the 1930s, Elliottitians, as they are known, use wave analysis to predict the point a market will reach.

As with many highly complex techniques, the Elliott wave theory has its roots in something that is simple and familiar to most people, the motion of the sea on the shore. Elliott was an accountant who contracted a serious illness in South America and underwent a protracted convalescence in a beach house. During this time, Elliott observed the crashing of the waves on the shore and noted how the waves increased in amplitude and then subsided. With lots of free time on his hands, Elliott started to look at the stock market and noticed that the prices there seemed to move in waves also. From this realization, Elliott became a little overambitious and came to believe that his theory of wave motion guided not only stock prices but just about everything else that people do. Does he have a point? Are biorhythms, for example, a part of Elliott's master wave theory? I don't know and do not much care. The basic points of wave theory are reasonable, and they do actually relate to the way markets move. It's just when you start to use them to make far-off predictions that things come a little unstuck. Elliott wave analysis is all based around a count of highs and lows, and when an Elliottitian gets one of the grand predictions—which the theory constantly suggests—wrong, the defense is always that the analyst got the count wrong but the prediction was correct. In defense of Elliott, his analysis led him to predict the start of the long bull run that began after the crash of 1929. Many market gurus, it seems, get one major prediction right, then milk it for all it's worth.

Elliott's analysis led him to believe that markets and individual securities move in a five-leg formation up, followed by a three-leg formation down, which is illustrated in Figure 3-10.

This figure shows a full market cycle. The five-leg bull formation is designated by numbered waves (one through five), whereas the bear formation is designated by waves A, B, and C. Legs that are in the direction of the trend are known as *impulse waves*, and those against the main trend are termed *corrective waves*. Elliottitians will see these formations in all stages of a market cycle. Essentially, this means that the eight-leg formation of Figure 3-10 may appear as one impulse wave in a larger formation. If ever you hear Elliottitians talk about the fifth wave of a fifth wave, you know that they are anticipating a major market correction.

Trying to fit this model to any real charts of price action is not an easy task. Elliott did, however, devise a number of rules to assist in identifying which parts of market price action correspond to which leg of the eight-leg model.

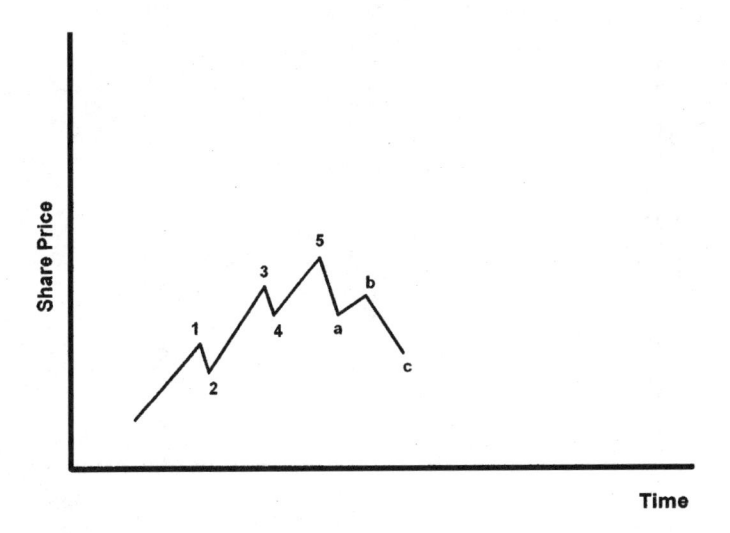

Figure 3-10. A typical Elliott wave formation.

First, Elliott stated that markets move in the eight-leg formation described, five up and three down. He then went on to be more specific about the ratio of the legs that make up this pattern. Wave three is never the shortest wave, and wave four should never extend lower than the top of wave one. If you start a count and your wave four does extend below the top of wave one, you must recount; it means that you are still in the wave-one phase. Elliott was comfortable with this type of recounting. He saw that price action moves in a zig-zag formation, so he did not mind each wave consisting of several zig-zags in themselves.

If this hasn't put you off Elliott and his theories yet, let's look at some of the formations Elliott mapped out, beginning with the three types of correction, zig-zag, flat, and triangle. These correction patterns have different counts, and we will look at each one in turn.

The zig-zag correction has a count of 5-3-5, as shown in Figure 3-11. In this figure, the Elliott zig-zag correction corrects an existing downtrend, and the 5-3-5 formation constitutes the corrective upward trend prior to a new downward trend beginning. As you can see, the A wave consists of a five-leg pattern, the B wave of a three-leg countermove, which is followed by the five-leg C wave. A flat correction identifies a time during which the price action remains fairly constant and is identified with a 3-3-5 count. The triangular correction is identified by the extremes of waves one

120 Chapter 3

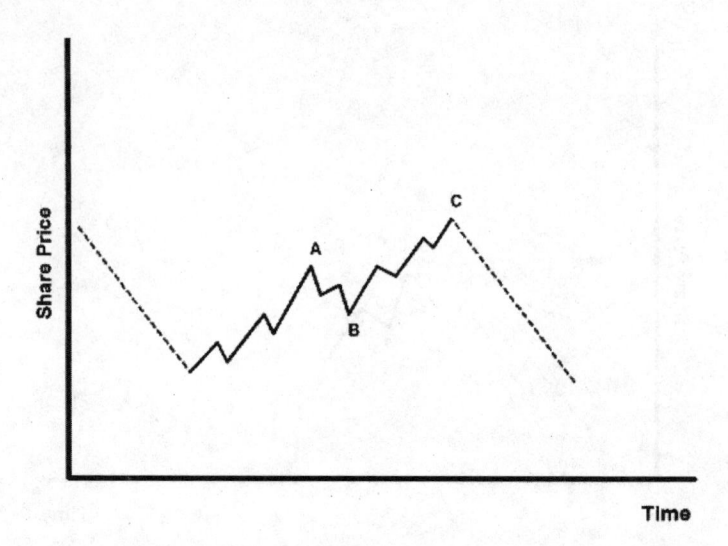

Figure 3-11. The Elliott zig-zag correction of a downward trend.

through five being contained within a triangular boundary, much like the ones we drew when we looked at triangles in a security's price action.

So, given that we know that the market will not always follow the perfect five-wave upward and three-wave downward formation, how are we going to use these more complex forms? Well, I don't know. If you're still not put off, let's look at one more segment of the Elliottitians' armory of possibilities, Elliott wave extensions. As I said, there always seems to be an escape clause for those practicing Elliott wave theory. When the grand prediction does not work out, there is always a justification for a recount of where the waves really are.

Elliott himself stated that impulse waves, those that form in the direction of the prevailing trend, can be extended. Corrective waves cannot. He also said that only one of the three impulse waves in the basic five-wave formation can be extended, either wave one, wave three, or wave five. Elliott made this refinement to his theory because at times, strong buying in an upward trend will overcome areas of resistance without a substantial pullback. Essentially, the rationale behind extensions is that a wave may consist of several zig-zag legs, as illustrated in Figure 3-12, which shows a wave-three extension, so there are nine legs in the five-wave formation.

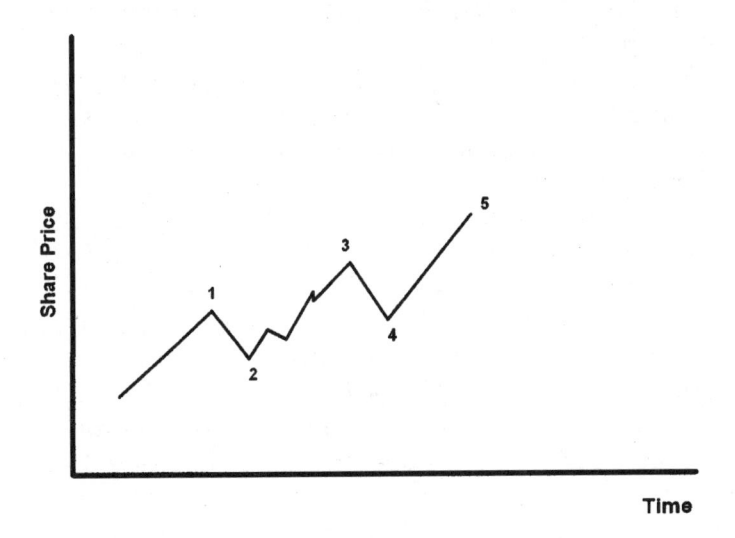

Figure 3-12. A wave-three extension.

When Elliott made his post-1929 predictions, he was alone in believing them. Most analysts were still nervous about future prospects. Likewise, if you read an Elliott wave-based prediction, treat it with caution, and do not let it impact what your more basic chart pattern analysis tells you.

Although I have come across several analysts who promote the use of the Gann and Elliott forms of analysis, they tended to make their money writing newsletters about the technique or selling systems that use the technique, rather than successfully trading it. You can see how the complexity of these techniques might make them worthy subjects for ongoing newsletters. There is always something there that can be interpreted—and argued—as relevant to current market conditions.

Overtrading

Compared to the last section, this one is short and simple. Among the people I have found to be successful on an ongoing basis in trading, there is one striking similarity. They all tend to focus on their strengths and avoid their weaknesses. For example, some might find, over time, that they are more successful during one particular phase of market activity than the other two, so they concentrate their efforts where they are successful.

Given a little thought, this is not unusual. The three phases of trading offer three very different types of market behavior, and at the beginning of this book, I advised you to trade using a method that seems natural, makes sense, and feels comfortable to you. This holds true as well for time of day and the types of trades. If you feel comfortable looking for reversals to overreactions (as I do), or holding positions for very short periods of time, you should focus on trading during Phase 1. If you like to follow trends, are more comfortable holding positions longer, and have more tolerance for seeing the value of your holdings fluctuate, Phase 2 should be your home. If you are the trigger-happy trader, who looks for very fast-paced moves, then the breakouts that occur in Phase 3 should be your focus.

When you stray away from your home base, the likelihood that you will make ill-advised trades grows exponentially. Another advantage of restricting the majority of your activity to one phase of the day's trading is that it gives you more time to follow other pursuits and hobbies. Sitting alone in front of a trading screen all day is a lonely and, at times, boring activity, even though day trading is often promoted as a glamorous profession. The truth is that the longer you sit in front of the screen without making a trade, the more likely you are to convince yourself that you see a tradable pattern emerging, when, in fact, one does not exist. To trade profitably requires 100 percent focus and concentration, and I have known very few, if any, individuals who can maintain that for the entire trading day. As you will see in Chapter 6, the techniques I use to produce profits, and shown in this book, can deliver a comfortable living wage from $20,000 capital. They will not require you to spend more than two hours per day in front of the screen, more commonly less than one. I am most happy when I make one profitable trade during Phase 1 and can turn off my screen, having made a reasonable profit for the day. What happens to most people who try to trade throughout the day is that they trade away their profits. Don't do it. There's more to life than trading!

Trying to Assimilate Too Many Variables

This is possibly my favorite activity to avoid. So many other market gurus would have you attempt to consider too many market variables in your trading. Ultimately, it becomes too confusing. Day trading requires focus, discipline, and adherence to your own trading rules. What drives your decisions to buy or sell an individual security has more to do with its own level of supply and demand than the condition of the market. Of course, the overall health of the market is important too, but in a down market, you will see some stocks going up, and in an up market you will see some stocks going down. The condition of the overall market places a bias on your actions, but it is not the driver of your decisions to buy or sell any individual security.

The first misinformation pitfall here involves the usual treatment of S&P futures. Many day-trading books go into elaborate detail on how money managers use the S&P futures as the most efficient way to access the market, that they put their money in these instruments in preference to stocks, and that the futures are therefore a leading indicator of where the market is going. This is a neat explanation if your goal is to persuade novice traders to sign up for an expensive day-trading course, where the promise of revealing further market secrets like this is enough to lure them into the classroom. The fact is that almost nothing in day trading is as simple as that.

Now, I know I said you can find examples from market charts to prove or disprove just about any point. However, to make my point here, I'm using some real market charts. My defense is that the deductions drawn from these charts are true practically any day in the market, which is a rare and powerful statement.

Figure 3-13 shows a graph of the S&P futures charted against the NASDAQ Composite. For both the initial market bottom just before 10:00 a.m. and the initial market top just after 10:00 a.m., you can see that the futures turned several minutes before the composite, and this holds true during the early part of market trading almost every day. I am using the NASDAQ Composite index as a proxy for the overall market, since as day traders, we are only going to trade NASDAQ securities. As the day progresses, the

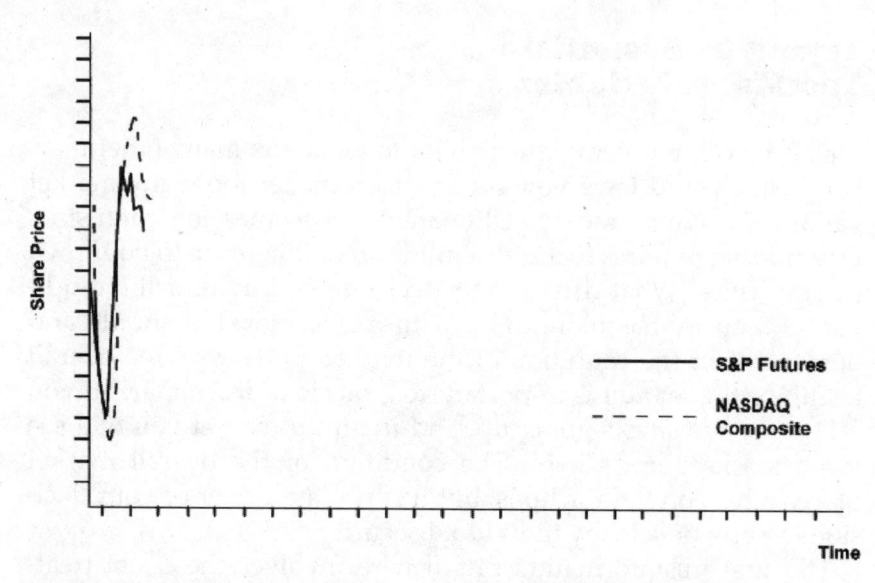

Figure 3-13. The S&P Futures as graphed against the NASDAQ Composite.

time difference for how much the futures lead the composite decreases, and usually they will trade in step with one another. So far, it seems I am arguing a convincing case against myself. But, if you look a little deeper, you see the folly of using the S&P futures as a leading indicator. For reasons already discussed, one does not day-trade derivatives. You would not want to trade the S&P futures because they seem to lead the Composite, so you might conclude that all you have to do is wait for the futures to turn, then buy an index option to catch the move. Options are very risky choices for day-trading instruments. Or you might think that a stock like Microsoft is probably the most influential stock in the Composite, so if the S&P futures turn, the Composite will turn. Why then, not trade Microsoft? Just look at Figure 3-14.

Here you see that Microsoft leads the future by about the same amount of time that the futures lead the Composite. In fact, on any given day (unless something dramatic is happening with Microsoft), you will see the S&P futures lag the price action of Microsoft. So, watching the S&P futures does not really help you too much in timing trades in individual securities.

In addition, there is so much talk of the S&P futures being either up or down in the premarket, indicating that the market will open higher or lower, respectively. By itself, this is true, but what value

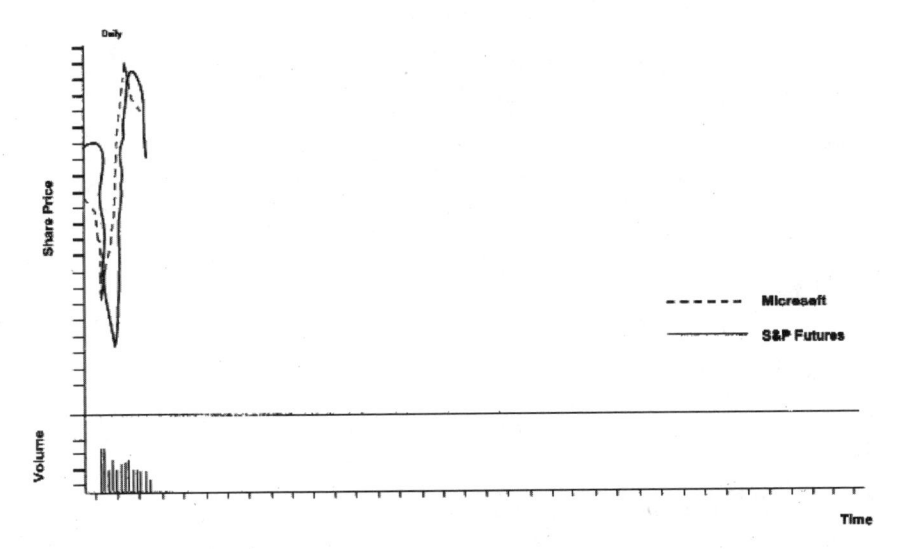

Figure 3-14. Watching the S&P Futures does not help time trades in individual securities.

does it have in deciding which stock to buy or to short on any given day? When the market opens, you cannot buy or sell securities at yesterday's closing prices, so does the knowledge that a security will gap necessarily mean that you know what trade to make? I don't think so. A discrete value, either up or down, is meaningless. It is only the trend of an instrument that actually gives you useful information.

The charts we used to look at how the S&P futures lead the Composite were graphed on October 14, 1999. On the fifteenth, I decided to look at how a premarket move of the S&P affects trading activity and how news stories might influence trading. The statistical relevance of samples notwithstanding, the market behavior we are about to discuss happens every day. So I don't feel any need to pore over years' worth of data. Listen to the news; look at the premarket activity and see what happens to the stocks you are considering trading that day.

On October 15, a Friday, the S&P was down about 25 points, a big move. So, what do you do? Short some stocks? Trade in the premarket on Instinet, Island, or some other ECN? Well, let's take a look at what happened that day in the Internet sector, a favorite haunt for day traders. Inktomi (INKT) followed the sector pretty well that day, and I will use that as my example. It's illustrated in Figure 3-15.

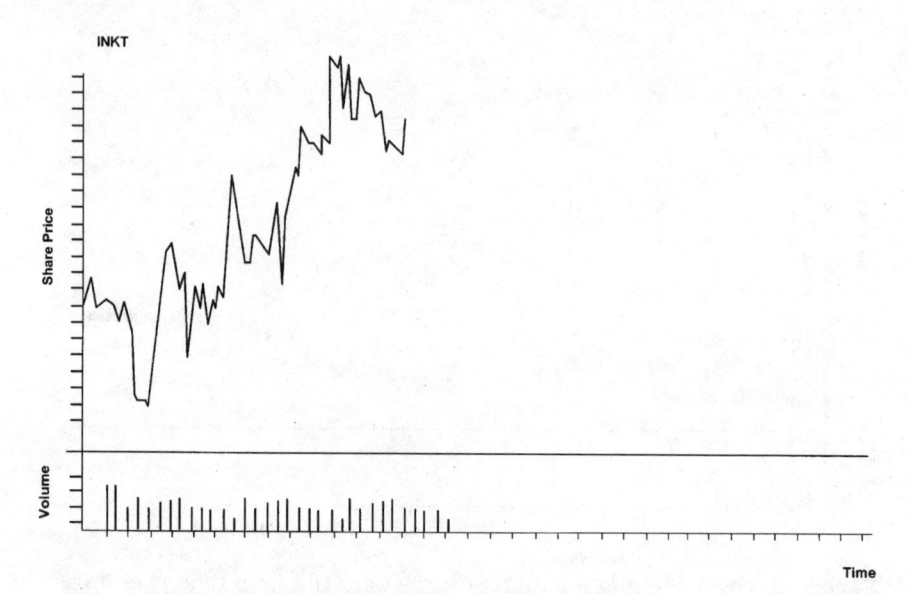

Figure 3-15. Watch the charts, not the news hype.

INKT opened $3 lower, along with just about all the other Internets, as we would expect from the S&P futures level. Figure 3-15 shows a strong performance from INKT and, indeed, almost all the securities in that sector during the first half of the day's trading. This is typical. After big moves in the premarket, the probability is that those sectors or securities that have pulled back to areas of support on the daily charts will experience at least temporary gains. Just before 10:40 a.m., a news story came across all the newswires, the essence of which was something like:

> Stocks tumble. Greenspan spooks investors with a troublesome inflation report and negative comments. Bond prices strengthen and the dollar slides. The Dow and NASDAQ Composite fall sharply, as the September inflation figures are higher than expected and investors pull out of securities and rush to bonds.

The timing of this story is laughable. The move down was before the market opened. After the market opened, stocks in general made solid gains from their opening prices.

How does one reconcile this premarket futures action and the news story with the price action of INKT and the other Internets? The answer is that premarket action tends to be an overreaction. This is not always the case. It is not something that you can follow

Activities to Avoid   **127**

blindly, but it tends to be the case. Look at Figure 3-16, and you will start to see how to improve your chances of knowing when the overreaction is real and when it is not.

Here we see a daily chart of the NASDAQ Composite. On October 15, the index was headed back toward the upward trendline. It does not reach the trendline on this pullback, but it is getting in the vicinity. Given that the upward trend is still in effect, since no signal is evident that the trend has reversed, Dow theory tells us that we should be looking at pullbacks as opportunities to go long. The high-percentage play in these circumstances is to go long when the market reverses up when nearing support.

It is by placing that day's premarket action in the context of the longer-term chart that we get our signals for what to do in the market. When we come to select individual securities for trading, during Phase 1 trading we will look for gaps, determine what type of gaps they are, and make a trading decision based on whether the price action is more likely to head in the direction of or away from the gap.

Beyond the simple level of the S&P futures, some market analysts recommend looking at fair value, the commodities markets, and bond yields. All of these things may have their uses, but you

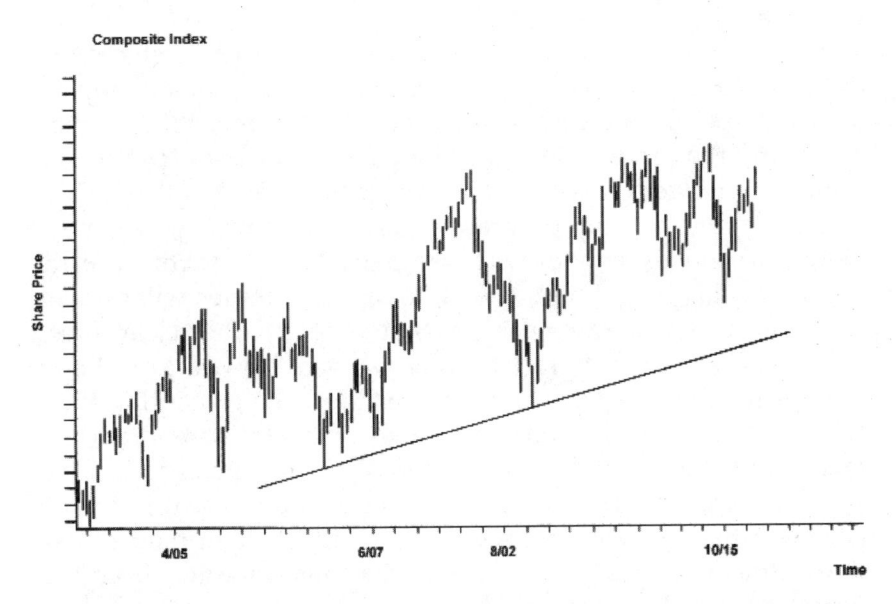

Figure 3-16. An example of how to determine when market overreaction is real and when it's not.

should not be analyzing them on a minute-by-minute basis when you want to make your trading decisions.

The issue of fair value provides market commentators plenty of material for sounding knowledgeable and giving student traders the notion that by mastering the concepts of fair value, the doors to riches will open. Sadly, this does not pan out in the real world. Loosely speaking, fair value equates to the mathematical difference between the cash constituents of the S&P Index and the S&P futures. The concept of time value is always inherent in a live derivatives contract, making it worth more than the equivalent cash instrument. Analysis of fair value seeks to identify whether or not this premium is valid. Fair value is calculated every day and advertised on CNBC and Dow Jones news stories. It is possible to have a real-time spreadsheet monitor the spread between the cash and futures index and alert you when the two get out of line. Here is an example to clarify.

Say the fair value is 5.0 today. If the spread between the futures and cash indexes is at six, it is likely that the futures will be sold and the cash index bought, so the differential closes. If the spread gets down to 4.0, the reverse is true. Stocks will be sold and futures bought. This is done in practice by program trades, normally by large institutions. A program trade either buys or sells a large number of securities that are aligned with the index—automatically, without human intervention.

As we know, it is the presence or lack of demand for stocks that drives prices either up or down. Some people think that if they can anticipate program trades, it is possible to be either long or short as the program trades move the market and take a safe profit. Few things, if any, work this neatly in day trading. First of all, on NYSE there are rules that stop program trades from being executed if the Dow Jones moves up or down more than 50 points. In this case, the fair value may be saying buy, but no program trades will be coming in to back up your position. Moreover, it is not clear which stock to buy when program trading kicks in. Do you just blindly buy Microsoft when fair value says so? More than worrying about fair value, I would be concerned with Microsoft's trend and the level of purchasing at the ask and selling on bids that is occurring. If you look at how the cash and futures indexes vary through the course of the day, you will see that the difference in their respective values is almost constant, and that any variation from that constant is quickly corrected.

When we progress into the real world of day trading in Chapter 6, we will see that the most difficult thing is being in the right place at the right time to take advantage of a move in a security. If you are using fair value, the commodities, or bond markets, it is too long a trek from there to deciding which stock to buy or sell and at what price. It may be that some of these factors do have key influences on certain securities, but the point is that studying these broader market indicators does not give you clues as to what to buy and sell. The techniques we will use in Chapter 6 are all about putting you right where the action is each and every day. The only things we as day traders need to be interested in are price movement and volume. We want price movement because, obviously, we are looking to buy for less than we sell. Volume is just as important, because it shows that there are others to trade with. Without either one, no security is a candidate for trading. As I have stated previously, technical analysis can be a shortcut in analytical terms. You can look at fair value, commodities, bonds, news stories, upgrades, downgrades, etc., and try to figure out which stocks are likely to move. The simpler choice, however, is to look at the technical picture by getting a program that tells you which stocks have volume and are moving in price. Chapter 6 covers this in more detail.

As well as looking at these broad market indicators, some teachers of day-trading techniques focus your attention on stock splits, earnings reports, or earnings upgrades and downgrades. I have religiously tracked all of these things and attempted to identify profitable day trades from them. Sometimes the effects of a split, better-than-expected earnings, or an analyst upgrade are as expected, and sometimes they are not. Often, this is because the news has already been anticipated correctly by the market and factored into the price. However, on too many occasions to number, the same headline coming out on company A will have a totally different effect coming out on company B. An example is Wit Capital, which jumped (very temporarily) when it was announced that it would acquire Soundview Research in a stock deal. The day that happened, demand for WIT soared, the typical overreaction, allowing a safe short to be entered. On other days, the announcement that a company is buying another will lead to an almost immediate depreciation in the purchaser's stock price and no tradable moves. The reason I saw this move by Wit and was able to trade it profitably was that I use a system that alerts me to stocks moving in value with good volume. I will give plenty more hard evidence of when I have put my own money on the line for the techniques I support, but just for completeness, here is my trade report from trading Wit Capital.

```
Terra Nova Trading, LLC DAILY TRADE LIST Page 1
STCS 4.4.65 (SWST) 11/1/99 15:10:18
Account: XXXXYYYYY
```

Tick	#Typ	Symbol	B/S	Shares	Price	Price (Loss)	Comm	SystemTime	By
2902	3	WITC	Shor	200	$23^7/_8$	4,775.00	ISLD	09:47:	ISLD
2903	3	WITC	Shor	200	$23^7/_8$	4,775.00	ISLD	09:47:	ISLD
2904	3	WITC	Shor	200	$23^7/_8$	4,775.00	ISLD	09:47:	ISLD
2905	3	WITC	Shor	200	$23^7/_8$	4,775.00	ISLD	09:47:	ISLD
2906	3	WITC	Shor	100	$23^{13}/_{16}$	2,381.25	ISLD	09:47:	ISLD
2907	3	WITC	Shor	100	$23^{13}/_{16}$	2,381.25	ISLD	09:47:	ISLD
3928	3	WITC	Buy	100	$23^3/_{16}$	2,318.75	ISLD	09:55:	ISLD
3929	3	WITC	Buy	200	$23^3/_{16}$	4,637.50	ISLD	09:55:	ISLD
3931	3	WITC	Buy	300	$23^3/_{16}$	6,956.25	ISLD	09:55:	ISLD
3932	3	WITC	Buy	100	$23^3/_{16}$	2,318.75	ISLD	09:55:	ISLD
3933	3	WITC	Buy	200	$23^{15}/_{64}$	4,646.87	ISLD	09:55:	ISLD
3934	3	WITC	Buy	100	$23^1/_4$	2,325.00	ISLD	09:56:	ISLD

```
Total Gain 659.37
Total Net Gain 613.47
Commission 45.90
```

This shows me entering a short for 1000 Wit Capital at 9:47 a.m. and covering it at 9:55 a.m. for a gain of just over $600. This was a very conservative trade, because I exited my position at the first signs of strength in Wit returning. As it turns out, Wit went down further, and I could have made far more if I had held. Again, though experience has taught me that making regular small profits and just as important, taking those profits while I can leads to a less stressful life and healthier capital balance in the long run. One point of interest before we move on is that you can see how the order I put in on Island was hit by lots of other traders with smaller sizes. Even though this led to many trades for me to get my 1000 shares, I only got charged the one commission.

Another area that you will be directed to by educators of day-trading techniques is to look for companies whose securities are going to split. This tends to happen to securities that are in an uptrend, and the price tends to move up after the split. This is true as far as it goes, but it does not mean that you should use a list of splits as a main source for finding potential trades. If a security exhibits price movement and increased volume after a split, then so be it, the security has become eligible for trading. I cannot stress this enough: Price movement and volume are the only worthwhile indicators for looking at securities to trade. Combine that with analysis of the daily chart and you will have just about all you need to come to decisions regarding day-trading individual securities.

Using the Wrong Tool at the Wrong Time

This is another favorite of mine. Most market gurus are so enamored of a particular tool, they promote its use for everything. We have already covered when the various types of oscillators are useful and when they are not. We have also covered the difficulties in relying too heavily on charts of any type during the opening 10 minutes, since trade reporting can legitimately lag by up to 90 seconds during this period.

A technical point of interest is that the NASDAQ has more than one feed of data that it supplies to quote vendors; NASDAQ supplies both the NTDS feed and the NQDS feed. The NTDS feed carries the last trade information. NTDS can introduce its own delays into the data you see on your screen. During times of heavy market volume, this feed can introduce another minute's delay in the time it takes for a trade to be executed and the NASDAQ reporting it to the quote vendor. The NQDS feed, however, is treated a little differently. This feed carries the quote information, the quotes that populate the Level II screens. This feed rarely, if ever, gets behind. So what does this mean for what you see on your screen? Well, if you take worst-case scenarios where you are attracted to a heavily traded security during the opening 10 minutes of a high volume day, you should expect the following results.

First of all, the last trade price reported will tend to be $1 or more away from the best bid and ask quoted. Typically, this is because trade reports are behind prices currently being quoted. I have read in a Level II handbook that market makers in order to mislead traders tend to advertise prices away from where current trades are taking place. This is incorrect. If a market maker advertises at the best bid or ask, he is likely to be hit and traded via SOES. The reason that last trade prices do not match bid or ask prices has more to do with the speed of trade report dissemination than anything else.

Beyond the last trade not matching the bid or ask, real-time tick charts tend to give a misleading picture. Since tick charts are usually driven off the last trade price, any inaccuracies in the last trade price feed directly into the chart display. At best, the tick chart is a time-delayed version of what is happening in the market. What happens in most cases is something much worse. With trades delayed by the 90-second rule and system backups, trades that took place minutes apart will appear consecutively in the NTDS feed. This gives an inaccurate impression of volatility in the price of the security. Clearly, this will have a detrimental effect on the accuracy of any oscillators used during this time. The faster the oscillator settings (the lower the numbers used for %K, etc.), the more these trade price discrepancies will adversely affect the oscillator. Oscillators with slower settings are displayed with more smoothing, which tends to lessen these effects.

In many guides for spotting early reversals in the market, I have seen mention made of looking for a trade to be reported somewhere in between the bid and ask as a primary indicator of a reversal. This is no longer appropriate. The goal of looking for a trade in between the bid and ask is to see whether there are trades being executed on Selectnet that indicates market makers willing to pay better than the best bid, but trying to hold out for lower prices. As you can see, there are lots of reasons why the trades being reported may not match the price of trades being executed during the market opening period, or, for that matter, at any time where there is heavy market activity. If your market data system has the option to chart bid rather than last prices for charts, that would be a good option to select during periods of heavy market volume. This makes use of the different types of feeds delivered by the NASDAQ and gets around the trade reporting delay allowed during the opening 10 minutes.

The tool that needs to be used during the opening period is the Level II screen, which is the subject of the next chapter.

A Potpourri of Helpful Hints

In this section, I will just give an overview of some other activities that I recommend you approach with caution. Especially for those relatively new to day trading, I recommend avoiding Internet securities. These securities do exhibit many of the qualities of ideal day-trading stocks, but there is one huge problem. These stocks can move so quickly that any mental stop you have placed on a position can be blown by, and you can find yourself facing a far greater loss than you were prepared to take. In every trade it makes sense to set a level above which you will not let your losses extend. The problem of blowing your stops is not one to be taken lightly. As I have stressed throughout this text, maintaining discipline is the highest goal one can have as a day trader. By not cutting your losses at stop points, you are losing discipline, and it is a slippery road downhill once that happens. Getting your stops blown on a regular basis will tend to make you act on hope rather than the reality of price movement. Remember, what you consciously do one day as a day trader will become part of your trading reactions the next day. Do not get used to watching your stops get blown and acting on hope thereafter.

This is a difficult recommendation to make, as I have made some of my most profitable trades in Internet securities. Unfortunately, however, I have also sustained my biggest losses in them. If you are going to commit yourself to the discipline of a technical approach to day trading, you should only consider Internet securities when their behavior meets your criteria for selecting a security to trade. Furthermore, due to their nature in current market conditions, you should get out of a position in them as soon as any trouble appears, whether your position is winning or losing at the time.

The same is true for IPOs, which, again, have provided me with some of my best gains, but only at higher risk. IPOs have no history for you to fall back on to analyze support and resistance. With IPO trading, you are flying a bit blind, and so treat IPOs with extreme caution. Currently, day trading IPOs is popular. This book is about practicing techniques that will stand the test of time, not jumping on the latest fad, which may be short-lived.

Regardless of what securities I am trading, it is very rare, if ever, that I make use of premarket trading. Your main concern should be that the premarket does not indicate any mandatory execution paths. At best, you could perhaps advertise an attractive price if you wished to close out a position and hope that someone would decide to take it.

Finally, as we shall see in Chapter 7, a key part of trading with discipline is to generate your own set of trading rules that you live by. It does not stop when you have your list, however. That list requires daily reading and reinforcement. Just because you know what to do and what not to do does not mean that you will do the right thing and avoid known pitfalls. This is one of the fascinating challenges of trading: At any point, any action is open to you, and it is completely within your control to decide what you do next. You cannot control what the market does, but you have complete control over how you react to its movements. For many, this is a difficult proposition, and the freedom to act can lend to overactivity and trading away profits. Whatever you decide to make a rule, live that rule by reinforcement.

I myself find listening to CNBC radio and scrutinizing news reports a distraction. The actual content of news in over 90 percent of cases is unimportant. The expectations of traders and their positions prior to the news coming out are important. At times, apparently good news will come out on a security and it will decline. At other times, similar good news will come out and the security will appreciate significantly. It is difficult to tell what will happen based just on the news itself. For these reasons and a host of others, it is best just to analyze volume and price movement, and not a company's news and research of market reports, at least from a day trader's perspective. Most market-moving stories happen outside of market hours and cause gaps to occur when they are out of line with expectations. It is these gaps and the subsequent reactions that are worth trading, not the news behind them.

4

The NASDAQ Level II Screen

Correct use of the Level II screen is one of the essential skills for an aspiring day trader to acquire. The skills discussed in this chapter have a different focus than in the majority of texts on this subject. Most other books focus on identifying the Axe market maker and attempting to follow that market maker's actions. The Axe market maker is perceived as the one that has the large orders to execute and drives the price of the security. It is unrealistic for the individual day trader to try to think and act like a market maker. The day trader does not have the capital or order flow advantages of a market maker, and to attempt to emulate their actions can be disastrous.

As with all technical tools, interpretation of the Level II screen is useless unless placed in the context of the trend and recent price movement of the security being studied. The Level II screen will give many signals to buy or sell, and it requires discipline and knowledge of a security's market position to act only on the ones that will lead to a profitable position.

The Components of the Level II Screen

A standard Level II screen is shown in Figure 4-1. An explanation of its components is necessary before we can proceed. The top of the display contains what we refer to as *Level 1 data*. Essentially, this tells you what the inside market is in terms of the best bid and ask prices

136   Chapter 4

EBAY	147 1/16 ↓ -5 3/16	100	Ot	10:57			
High 150 5/8	Low 147		Acc. Vol. 1044500				
Bid ↑ 147 1/16	Ask 147 3/16	Close	152 1/4				

Name	Bid	Size	Time	Name	Ask	Size	Time
MASH	147 1/16	100	10:57	ISLAND	147 47/256	400	10:57
REDI	147	100	10:56	ISLAND	147 3/16	100	10:57
NFSC	147	900	10:56	ISLD	147 3/16	500	10:57
FLTT	147	200	10:56	CWCO	147 5/16	100	10:56
HRZG	147	300	10:56	ISLAND	147 3/8	500	10:56
ISLAND	147	800	10:57	COST	147 3/8	100	10:57
PERT	147	1100	10:57				
ISLD	147	800	10:57				
MLCO	146 3/4	100	10:56				

Figure 4-1. A standard Level II screen. (Used with permission of Townsend Analytics, Ltd.)

currently being advertised by anyone in the market. The top line of the display shows a box containing the security code for which information is displayed, followed by the price of the last trade reported, then the change on the day, last trade volume, and the time of that trade. The second line shows the high and low trade prices for the day and the total volume of shares traded in the security that day. The third line tells us the current best bid (the highest price someone is willing to pay) and ask (the lowest prices at which someone is willing to sell) prices, along with the value of yesterday's closing price.

Underneath these first three lines of information is the multicolored bar that attempts to show the overall buying or selling pressure in the security. It is here that we start to see the importance of color in this display. It is the convention for each band of prices, either at the bid or ask, to be on a different colored background. The bar that we are looking at shows the depth of each price level. This depth shows the number of market makers or ECNs, electronic communication networks, at each price level rather than the number of shares they are offering. This is just a quick way of seeing how the overall positions—bids and asks—are lined up.

The bottom window of the Level II display is where the real information that we are interested in is kept. Different systems will display different amounts of information. This discussion is based on the Townsend Analytics Real Tick™ system display. To understand this window, it is essential to understand the abbreviated names for the market participants used and how it is possible to trade with each participant. The upcoming section provides an overview of the participants listed in this window and the order routes available to deal with them.

Level II Participants, the Market Makers and the ECNs

All market makers have their own four-letter ID. Examples are GSCO for Goldman Sachs, NITE for Knight Securities, MLCO for Merrill Lynch, and so on. There are lots of them, many of which you probably will never see, but it is important to know the most common ones. Generally, it is possible to trade via SOES with any market maker you see on the screen whose price has reached the inside market. SOES stands for small order execution system. We will discuss use of SOES more fully in the next chapter. SOES is a mandatory execution system, but if no market maker is at the best bid or ask (meaning one of the ECNs or the Mid-West Stock Exchange), SOES is not a valid route.

The second category of market participants is comprised of the ECNs. These are typified by Instinet (INCA), Island (ISLD), Archipelago (ARCA), and more recently Bloomberg Trade (BTRD), Spear Leeds's REDI system (REDI), and others. In many Level II displays, it is up to you to know the participants displayed and whether the participant is a market maker or something else. Some systems are a bit more helpful and will place an indicator beside the four-letter ID to signify whether it's a market maker or ECN.

With either of these categories of participants, it is possible for you to electronically execute a trade for the security at the price and quantity they are advertising. When you get a direct access trading system, the order entry screen has an order route for SOES and each of the ECNs it supports. Typically, each route has its own button to click on for sending orders. There is a third type of participant that is a little more tricky. MWSE, the Mid-West Stock Exchange, can quote prices and will often hold the best bid or ask, taking many trades while holding the price constant, but you cannot trade with it by SOES, nor is it an ECN. The only way to access the price offered by MWSE is to enter a preferred Selectnet order to MWSE, and if MWSE feels like it, your order will be executed. The point is that there is no mandatory route for trading with MWSE, only the Selectnet request-to-trade route (which we will explain more fully in Chapter 5).

Within the main window of the Level II display, let's first consider the left-hand pane, which contains the bid information. You can see listed the market participants offering a price to buy the security. These participants are listed first by the price at which they are willing to buy, with those willing to pay the highest price at the top. If there are multiple bidders at the same price, those offering the largest size will be higher in the list. The right-hand pane lists the ask side, those quoting a price at which they will sell the security. This is organized with those offering the lowest sale price at the top, and again, those offering stock at the same price are listed by size.

In addition to the price and size being offered, the time that the quote was placed on the Level II screen is shown. When a security's price is moving quickly, the time of the quote in the display is usually of little value, because it will always be the current time. When a security is reversing in direction, however, say, finishing an upward trend and entering a downward trend, quoted prices will tend to stay longer. For example, in a topping formation, prices at the best ask will be taken out quite quickly as the security moves up in price. Once the peak has been reached, the buying pressure subsides, there are no more purchasers, and the ask prices will tend to stay. This is a signal for the next movement to be down. Typically, if the person offering to sell stock at the best ask is not getting a buyer, that person will lower the price in order to attract buyers.

Within the Figure 4-1 display, you see several quotes attributed to ISLAND and a single quote attributed to ISLD. This is a feature of the Real Tick™ system that shows the Island order book meshed with individual market maker quotes. At this point, it is worth discussing the difference between a quote-driven market and an order-driven market in the NASDAQ realm.

The NASDAQ is considered a quote-driven market. By that, it is meant that the best bid and ask prices are determined by the prices the market makers are willing to quote. Competition between market makers for orders is generally effective at keeping the spread between the bid and ask low. The NYSE is a specialist system, wherein orders are placed with the specialist for each security, who matches buyers and sellers or may choose to fill orders out of his own inventory. This is an example of an order-driven market. Order-driven markets are very popular in Europe, which has no market makers, just a publicly viewable book of all orders to either buy or sell a security. In this type of market, a trade occurs when an order to buy matches the price for an order to sell. These types of markets can experience high spreads, particularly at market open and close, because there is no mandatory requirement for any one person to maintain a market as there is on the NYSE. If no one wants to place an order to sell a security, there will be no asking price.

These European-style order-driven markets are essentially the way that ECNs work. An ECN allows participants to place orders to buy or sell and matches those orders it is possible to match. The best bid price that cannot be matched becomes an ECN's best bid price, which appears on the Level II screen, as does the best unmatched ask price. It is by this mechanism that an individual who has order entry capability to an ECN can place offers to sell at the ask price and offers to buy at the bid price, and if hit by another trader, avoid spread costs.

So the NASDAQ quote-driven market is no longer purely a quote-driven market. Those trading on the ECNs are operating in an order-driven market. In the classic Level II display, you will just see the bids and asks advertised by the market makers, along with a single entry from each ECN, showing its best unmatched bid or ask order. In the display we are using we also get a feel for the order book of Archipelago as well as that of Island, since at times you will see several quotes attributed to ARCHIP, a summary quote to ARCA, and the Island detail. Initially, this makes the display more complicated to read. The advantage is that you have in one place all the information available on the quotes and orders in the marketplace you are interested in.

Another potentially confusing thing about this display is that there can be bids in the Level II window that are better than the best bid. These orders are typically orders preferenced through Selectnet to a market maker by Archipelago users. Selectnet is really just an electronic form of the telephone. Preferencing an order to a particular market maker on Selectnet is like calling them on the phone and asking them if they want to trade at a given price.

A good reason these Archipelago users try this route is because the SOES queue is sometimes backed up and their orders are not getting executed in a timely fashion through SOES. In Chapter 6 we will see that placing an executable order through SOES does not guarantee instantaneous execution. As you can imagine, it is very important to know whether it is a market maker or ECN offering the best price in the market, because that will affect which order route you use to place your trade.

That covers the basic information of what the display contains. The real value in the Level II display, however, is in being able to determine whether there is an excess of demand or of supply in the market, or equilibrium between bull and bear forces.

Look at the Flow Rather Than the Snapshot

There is very little information on Level II display interpretation that has any value at all. Let's just review the most common descriptions first, and then discuss how to make best use of the Level II screen.

Approaches to Avoid

One of the prevailing descriptions in the available literature tells you that if Level II display prices are moving in a clockwise direction, the security is falling in value, and that if they are moving counterclockwise, the security is appreciating. This description refers to the two columns, bid and ask, in the bottom pane of the Level II display. A clockwise price movement describes a price that is currently the best bid becoming the best ask. This leaves room for the bid price that previously was second best to become the best bid, essentially moving up the left-hand pane of bids. This movement of prices up the column of bids and down the column of asks gives the impression of a clockwise motion.

This analysis turns what is a very simple process into something that is difficult to understand. You do not need to determine a clockwise or counterclockwise motion of prices in the Level II display to know whether the best bids and asks are moving up or down. Just looking at the best bid and ask tells you that.

Another common description of how to use the Level II display centers around analyzing the number of shares offered at the best bid or ask and the price levels immediately supporting those prices. The idea is that if you see a total of 10,000 at the best ask and only 1000 at the best bid, there is selling pressure in the market and the price is likely to go down. The reverse is said to be true if there are 10,000 at the best bid and 1000 at the best ask. That would signify buying pressure. This is an overly simplistic description, and is potentially very dangerous to your capital if you follow it blindly. There is much more to the analysis of the screen to determine likely future price movements than just the number of shares offered at particular price levels. To get the most information from the screen, you have to know the trend that the security is in, both on its intraday and its daily chart. You also need to get a feel for whether market makers are taking multiple lots at the prices they are advertising or just taking one lot and refreshing their prices to a different level. This is important. As we discussed in Chapter 1, you should view the market as consisting of two segments. The first segment offers to buy or sell at a given level (market makers or those at the best bid or ask on ECNs). The second segment accepts those prices and transacts against them.

What the Level II Screen Can Show You

When you look at a Level II display, it should be your goal to determine the following:

- Which side of the display is being transacted against?
- Is that side seeing an increasing or decreasing number of shares at its best level?
- Are participants on the other side chasing the price action?

These points are best described with an example, starting with the display in Figure 4-2.

This figure shows the NASDAQ test security TESTA and uses fictitious values for the purposes of discussion. As is convention, this fictitious Level II display shows the bids of individual market makers and ECNs in the left-hand pane and the offers in the right-hand pane. Just bringing up this display without knowledge of the daily chart trend and the intraday trends could well lead to inaccurate analysis of the information in the display. Traditionally, the material available on Level II interpretation will tell you that there are more shares on the bid than the ask and that there seems to be

Security	TESTA						
mm	Bid	Size		mm	Ask	Size	
GSCO	17	10		ISLD	17 1/16	2	
MSCO	17	10		NITE	17 1/8	1	
MWSE	17	30		SHWD	17 3/8	2	
ISLD	16 3/4	35		PIPR	17 5/8	3	
BTRD	16 5/8	5		MRZG	18	5	
BRUT	16 1/4	8		MASH	18 1/2	5	
REDI	16 1/16	9		COWN	18 3/4	5	

Figure 4-2. An example of what the Level II screen can tell you.

strong support at 17, so the next move is likely to be upward. This is one possible outcome, if the previous price action supports that hypothesis, but a single snapshot of a Level II display is not enough evidence to initiate a position.

What we have to determine is which side of the screen is receiving attention from those initiating trades in the market. Outside of the opening 10 minutes of trading, this is normally a straightforward affair. What one does is look at a dynamic time-of-sales display to see the trades being executed at that time and see whether they are going off at the best bid or best ask price.

Let's look at how different circumstances could lead to the Level II display in Figure 4-2, first of all leading to a fall in the bid price, then to an increase in the bid price.

If we look at the dynamic time-of-sales screen and see that all the trades are going off at $17, we can determine that the segment of the market that initiates trades (usually individual traders) is selling out of long positions in this security. If this is occurring, the first analysis needed is to see whether the market makers bidding for stock at $17 stay or withdraw their bids. If a market maker is on the inside market, he is free to refresh the price and take more trades at that price level, or to change his quoted price level to something new. Should the market makers move to a lower bid, a downtrend is in effect. To judge how long that downward trend will be in effect, you need to observe the pace of trades going off at the bid and how quickly market makers move off the best bid. Remember, market makers have to offer a two-way market in securities, so even if they do not want to buy a security, they have to offer a price. Those who offer the best prices get the most order flow and earn the most commissions.. As soon as you see the pace of trades slow down, the prices at the bid will tend to stay longer, and you will see that the downward trend has started to run out of steam.

In this situation, you should not just be looking at the bid column. The ask column also has useful information. If you see market makers and ECNs follow the bid price down rapidly, consistently offering stock at a price $1/16$ higher than the best bid, you can deduce that the downward trend has some strength. Activity of this type in the ask column is indicative of market participants attempting to initiate short positions in a security. We will discuss initiating short positions more fully later, but the essential point here is that if a security is falling in value, the only way to initiate a short is by offering stock at $1/16$ above the current best bid price.

Another situation that could lead to the Figure 4-2 scenario producing a downward bid price is if the security has already fallen several levels of bid price and the $17 level has been set by bid prices that have been outstanding for some time. Market makers will often leave bid prices (or ask prices, for that matter) active for long periods of time. This may result from one of their customers placing an order to buy only when the price has pulled back to a given level. If the bids at $17 have been there for some time, they will not indicate as much support for the $17 price level as if they had just been posted. The reason for this is that if the bids are old, they tend to represent one order. When new bids are being placed at the best bid, it tends to indicate market maker interest in the security, and the market makers will then tend to take several hits at this best bid price, if they can get it.

What is important in all this is to see which side of the inside market is being transacted against, either the best bid or best ask. Once you can determine that, you must see how the market makers are positioning themselves in response to those transactions. If the majority of transactions are going off at the best bid and market makers are not refreshing their quotes at that level (which will be indicated by a shrinking number of market makers on the inside bid), the price is headed down. If the transactions are against the best bid, but the market makers are refreshing their prices, or more market makers are joining the best bid, then there is real support at that level and an uptick can be expected.

A comparable situation is true if transactions are going off at the best ask. This means that traders have an appetite for that security. If the market makers try to get out of their way by reducing their numbers on the best ask, you can bet the stock is going up. If the market makers stay and refresh their prices, you can say the buying pressure will likely subside and the price will fall.

The analysis you should perform regarding the Level II screen is not just to look at it at any one point in time and see that there are more market makers on one side than the other. It is the flow and how the market makers react to transactions that gives you information.

Games Market Makers Play

Market makers know that traders use this information in their trading decision process and can use that to their advantage. There are occasions when a market maker may want to buy, but will post a large size on the ask side of the market to scare purchasers away, or shake out holders of the security. Market makers have anonymous routes, like Instinet (INCA), as well as the ECNs, like Island and Archipelago, with which to disguise their intentions.

There is one time of day, though, that the market makers do not tend to play so many games with the prices they advertise, and that is at market open. During this time, there is so much volume being transacted that advertising fake bids or asks to move the activity in the market is too dangerous. During the high volume open, the prices advertised by market makers tend to give a true indication of their intentions. For this reason, the Level II display is the best tool to use during the market open. Although it is difficult to get a feel from the time-of-sales screen for whether the bids or asks are getting transacted against, you can take the market maker actions as information enough to make trading decisions. Past the market open, the volume subsides and the games really begin.

There are manuals available that show examples of market makers using Instinet to hide their actions, and that urge you to try to spot market makers hiding their intentions so that you can take positions in harmony with them. This is a fine goal, but it is not realistic. Think about it. Market makers are given orders by large institutions to get the best price. If a market maker shows his hand consistently enough for traders in the market to observe his actions and take advantage of them, he is moving the market against the interests of his client. Ultimately, this will lead to the market maker going out of business, because he will not get orders from the better institutions. If he is not in business, he is not there for you to follow his actions. This means that the only market makers left out there are the good ones who can fill an order without adversely affecting the market.

A popular description of the "chief" market maker in a security is the Axe. The Axe market maker is the one who gets all the big orders from institutions and drives the price of the security either up or down—or so perceived wisdom would suggest. It is not a difficult thing to look up trading data on the www.nasdaqtrader.com Web site and see which market maker transacts the most volume for a security that you are interested in. Those who try to follow the Axe believe that a trend will start when a large order from an institution is placed with that market maker. The trader's goal is then to spot the Axe accumulating stock and follow his actions. If you attempt to do this, you are likely to overtrade and take many losing positions. To balance their positions (and from which to take the spread), market makers have the benefit of orders coming in to them. They have enormous capital and higher leverage available than the individual trader. If you try to play their game with them, the most likely outcome is that they will win and you will lose.

Fading the Trend To crystallize this point, let's look at a couple of the more popular strategies that manuals on Level II interpretation cover and see how inconclusive the information from the Level II screen, by itself, can be. The first is described as a market maker *fading* the trend. The idea here is that during a quiet time of trading, the market maker will attempt to push a security lower in the hope of accumulating stock cheaply. One reason to do this is to add cheap stock to the market maker's own account. Another, more likely one, is to fill a customer order to purchase the security at a cheaper price than when the order was placed. To do this, the market maker must sit on the inside ask with a large size and absorb all comers who want to take stock from him. If the stock has been moving up, this may amount to a large short position by the market maker. What the market maker is hoping to do is absorb all the appetite for the security in the market and panic others into selling. If the market maker is successful at this, those who are long the security will start to sell, believing that the upward trend has finished and wanting to take their profits. As stock is sold to bidders, these bids are not refreshed and the bid moves lower, at which point the market maker fading the trend moves to a lower bid price. At some point, the market maker fading the trend has to start accumulating stock, and he may do that via one of the ECNs to hide his intention. Ultimately, this buying has to cover the shorts generated when pushing the stock down. It must also provide enough to accumulate the required amount to fill the customer order or fill the market maker's own account. This is an immensely risky thing for any market maker to do and requires large amounts of capital. In practice, there is no way for a trader to distinguish this behavior from the behavior of a market maker who simply has a large sell order from a client. In either case, the market maker will sit on the inside ask and drive the price lower. The reason a trader might try to identify whether a market maker is a real seller or just fading the trend is if the trader is long and has to decide whether the move is temporary, in which case he will hold the stock, or the start of a new trend, at which point he should sell the stock. I do not believe that analysis of just the Level II screen can determine this. Analysis of chart trend, support, and resistance is far more likely to tell you the direction in which a security is headed and whether pullbacks are temporary or the start of a new trend.

The Head Fake A similar, but shorter-term, move is called a *head fake*. Here, in an attempt to shake traders out of their positions, a market maker will temporarily drive the price down by sitting on the inside ask, and then step off the ask and let the security continue its upward trend. To try to use the Level II screen in this instance to try to determine whether a market maker is serious about buying or selling is dangerous. Market makers can hide their intentions through INCA, ISLD, and the other ECNs and make stock accumulation look like stock disbursement. What does not lie is the price action of the security. If an upward trend is broken, the succession of higher highs and higher lows will be broken. In addition, the time-of-sales screen will tell you on which side the transactions are taking place, bid or ask, and that tells you where the interest in the security is at that time.

Key Points for Getting the Right Focus

The key to using the Level II screen to improve your trading is not to look at individual market maker behavior, but at the group behavior, and then to try to trade in harmony with the crowd. In Chapter 6 we will use the Level II screen to identify entry and exit points for trades during the market open period. We do not, however, select which stocks to trade by analyzing the Level II display for all possible securities, because that would be too inefficient. The two things day traders need to make money are price movement and volume. So when we look for securities, we use a program that searches for those two things.

In the next sections, we will look at successive snapshots of Level II screens at sample points during the price action of a security that is moving in price. The key points to gain from these observations are to see how the flow of movement by market makers on the Level II display is driven by the trades that are executed against them and displayed in the time-of-sales window. As you watch the ebb and flow of supply (excess supply is generally seen as trades going off against the bid) and demand (excess demand is seen as trades predominantly going off against the ask), you will see how the concepts of trend, support, and resistance come into play.

The Level II Screen at the Break of an Upward Trend

I did not have to search very far to find this example. In fact, I just looked for a trending security that is moving in price. You, too, can analyze these movements on a daily basis, and I encourage you to do so to practice your chart-reading and Level II interpretation. The first stock we will look at is Qualcomm, which has been in an upward trend since January 1999.

Figure 4-3 shows what appears to be an even distribution of those willing to buy and those willing to sell QCOM. This is the danger of viewing Level II as a snapshot. What we do is look at the dynamic time-of-sales window to the right of the Level II display to see that trades are mainly going off at 343, the bid price. The tick chart is already pointing down, so we think the direction is going to be down, at least for the moment.

If we move on a few moments, we see the classic Level II depiction of excess supply, as shown in Figure 4-4. In the ask column, we see both market makers and ECNs jumping on the lowest available asking price of $342^{13}/_{16}$. The trade reporting for QCOM is still showing 343 and is therefore slow. At this point, we have difficulty in interpreting where the transactions are taking place. This is a fact of life when using the NASDAQ system and using market data sys-

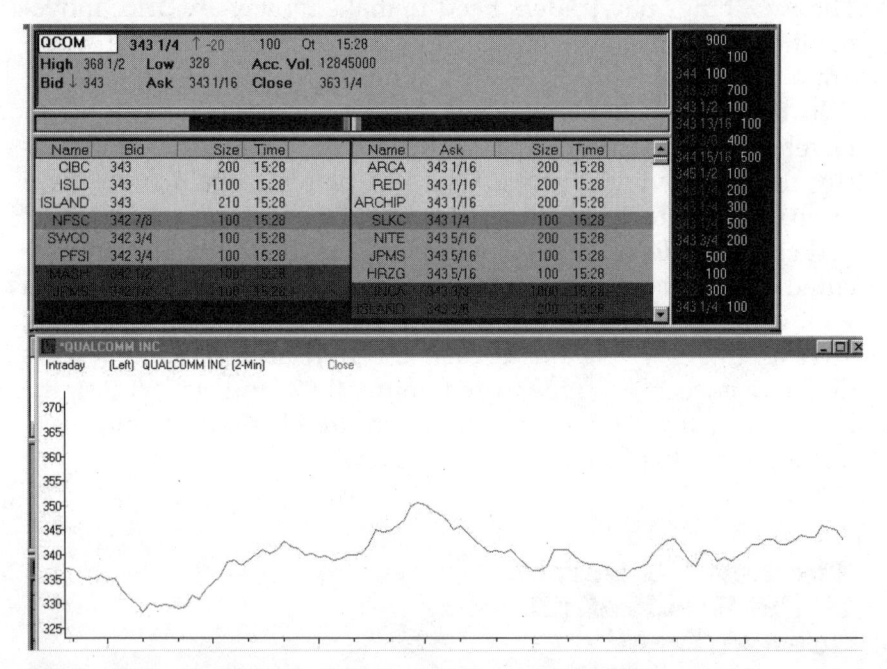

Figure 4-3. The danger of looking at the Level II screen out of context. (Used with permission of Townsend Analytics, Ltd.)

The NASDAQ Level II Screen   **149**

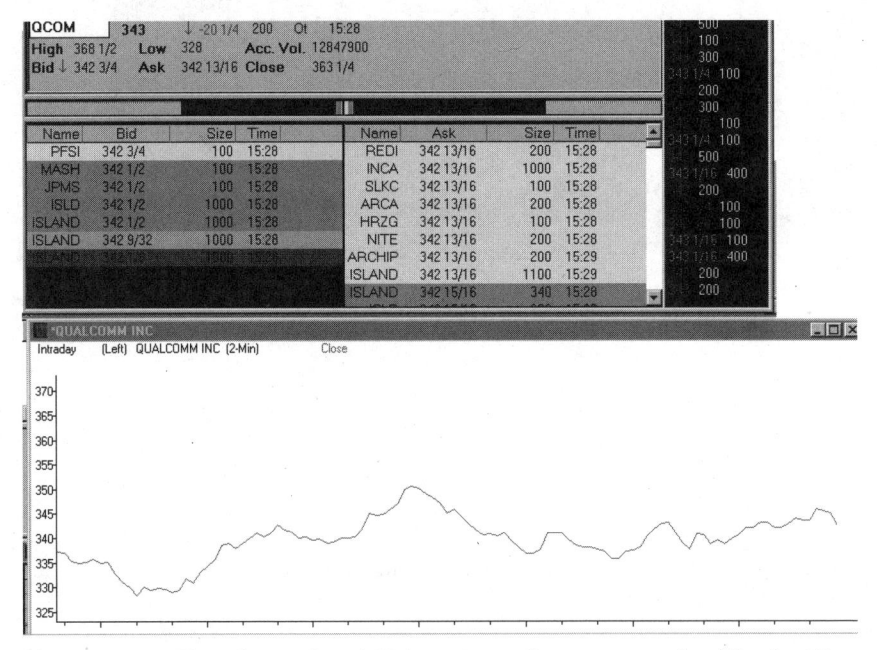

QCOM	343	↓ -20 1/4	200	Qt	15:28			
High 368 1/2	Low 328	Acc. Vol. 12847900						
Bid ↓ 342 3/4	Ask 342 13/16	Close 363 1/4						

Name	Bid	Size	Time	Name	Ask	Size	Time
PFSI	342 3/4	100	15:28	REDI	342 13/16	200	15:28
MASH	342 1/2	100	15:28	INCA	342 13/16	1000	15:28
JPMS	342 1/2	100	15:28	SLKC	342 13/16	100	15:28
ISLD	342 1/2	1000	15:28	ARCA	342 13/16	200	15:28
ISLAND	342 1/2	1000	15:28	HRZG	342 13/16	100	15:28
ISLAND	342 9/32	1000	15:28	NITE	342 13/16	200	15:28
				ARCHIP	342 13/16	200	15:29
				ISLAND	342 13/16	1100	15:29
				ISLAND	342 15/16	340	15:28

Figure 4-4. The classic Level II depiction of excess supply. (Used with permission of Townsend Analytics, Ltd.)

tems delivered over the Internet. This process of the bid lowering and being taken out by traders executing against these bids continues until the price reaches 341^3/$_4$, which is shown in Figure 4-5.

Here we see that bids are starting to build up at the best bid level, and trades are starting to go off at the best ask. This is not enough information to determine that a reversal has occurred, but it does tell us that at least a pause in the current downward movement has occurred. Just a few moments later, though, selling onto the bids resumes and the familiar pattern of bids being taken out, exposing lower bids as the best, and market participants lowering their ask prices continues.

Moving on to Figure 4-6, we see the bid has fallen to 338, and the tick chart is starting to show that the downward trend may be running out of steam. At this stage, the Level II screen by itself is still indicating an excess of supply: There are more market makers at the best ask than at the best bid. Looking at time of sales, however, shows that transactions are now going off at the best ask, and the price starts to move up.

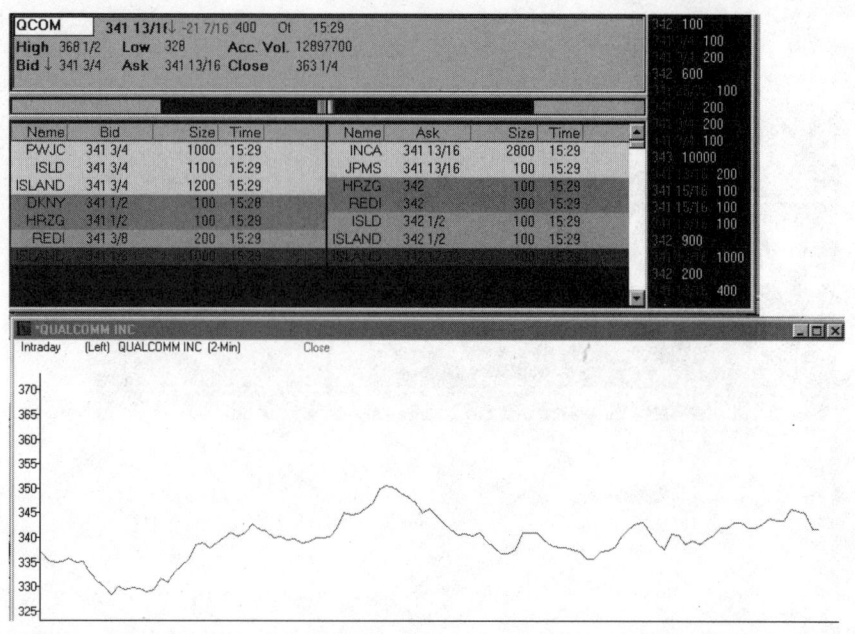

Figure 4-5. A pause in the downward movement of QCOM. (Used with permission of Townsend Analytics, Ltd.)

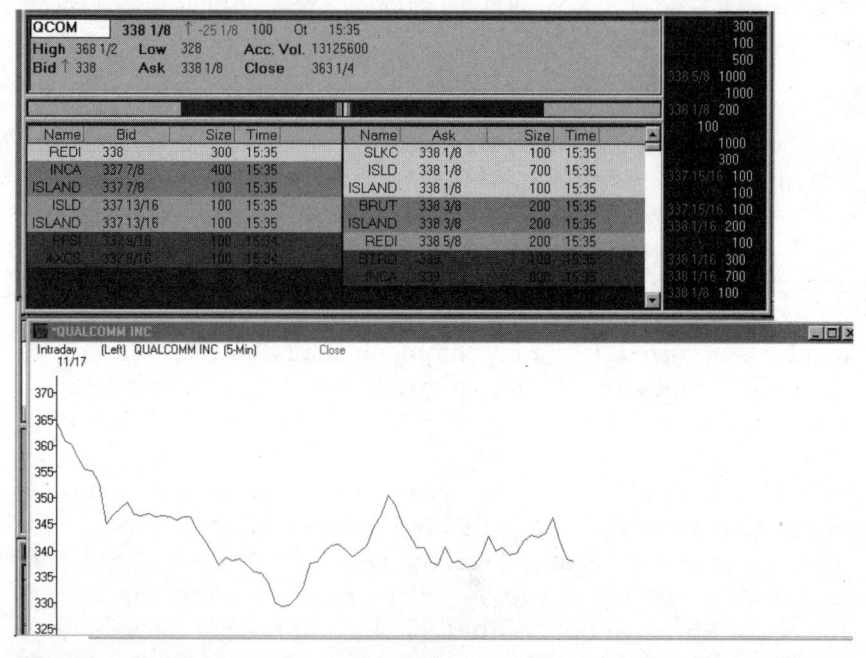

Figure 4-6. Time-of-sales window shows price starting to move up. (Used with permission of Townsend Analytics, Ltd.)

150

The NASDAQ Level II Screen 151

Figure 4-7 shows that the tables have turned again. There are no more trades going off at the ask. There are trades going off at the bid, and no one is queuing up at the bid to take them, which will lead to a price fall. From here, we jump forward to Figure 4-8, where we conclude our look at QCOM with a hint on how to interpret these movements. Here we see that the bid has fallen to 339 and transactions are going off against this level. The downward move is still in effect.

What makes this more readable is that I have drawn in a trendline on the tick chart, which starts to make sense of all this price movement. As you can see, the upward trendline was respected three times before being broken with the downward move we observed. When the initial downward move expired, the price rose to the trendline and fell, illustrating the prior support now becoming resistance. We can also use the dog-on-a-leash analogy here. The dog's path is represented by the price action, whereas the trendline corresponds to the path of the dog owner.

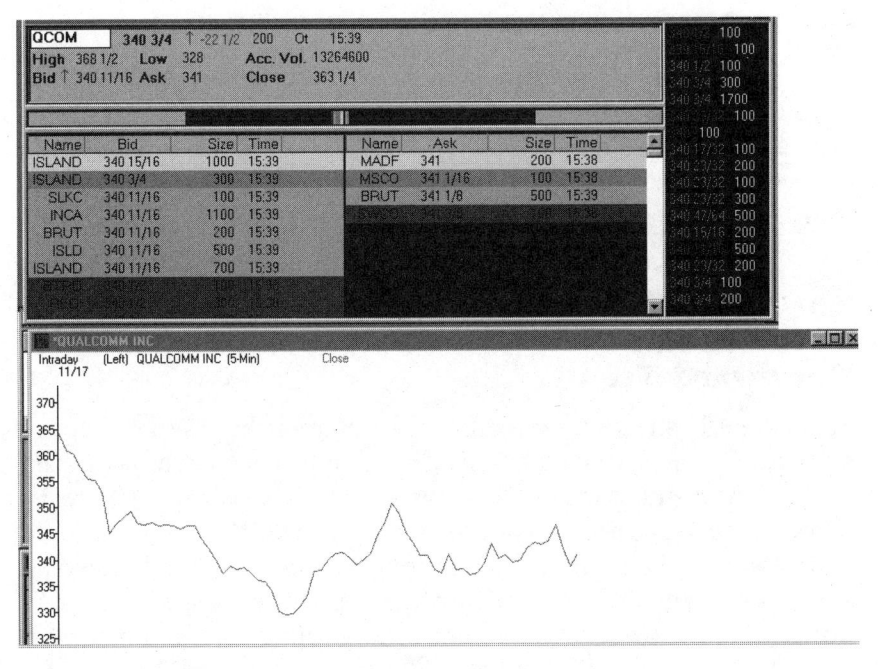

Figure 4-7. The price falls again. (Used with permission of Townsend Analytics, Ltd.)

152 Chapter 4

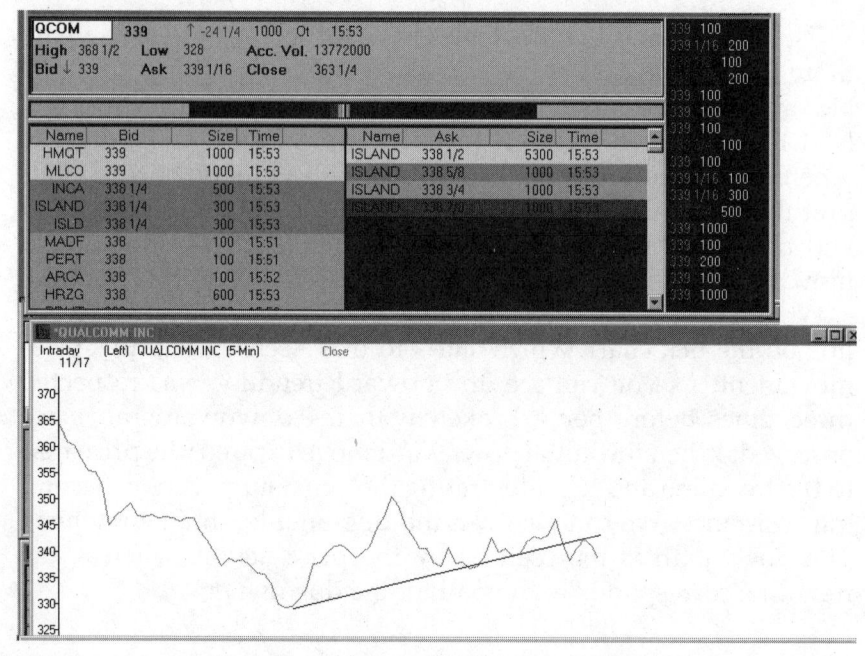

Figure 4-8. Interpreting the Level II screen at the break of an upward trend. (Used with permission of Townsend Analytics, Ltd.)

You can see that the dog's path strays away from the trendline, but never too far. The dog is always pulled back into line with the dog owner's path. Once the dog crosses the owner's path, it finds it difficult to cross back over.

The Level II Screen at the Break of a Downward Trend

This example shows how the Level II screen behaves in the opposite situation. Here we have a security that has been in a confirmed downward trend, and the downward trendline has acted as resistance on three occasions. We are looking to see whether the downward trend is likely to continue or reverse. We will start the display at the point where the downward trend is continuing after a small pullback in the price action. Later on, we will examine this formation a little more closely when we draw in some trendlines, but for the moment, let's focus on the state of the Level II screen as displayed in Figure 4-9.

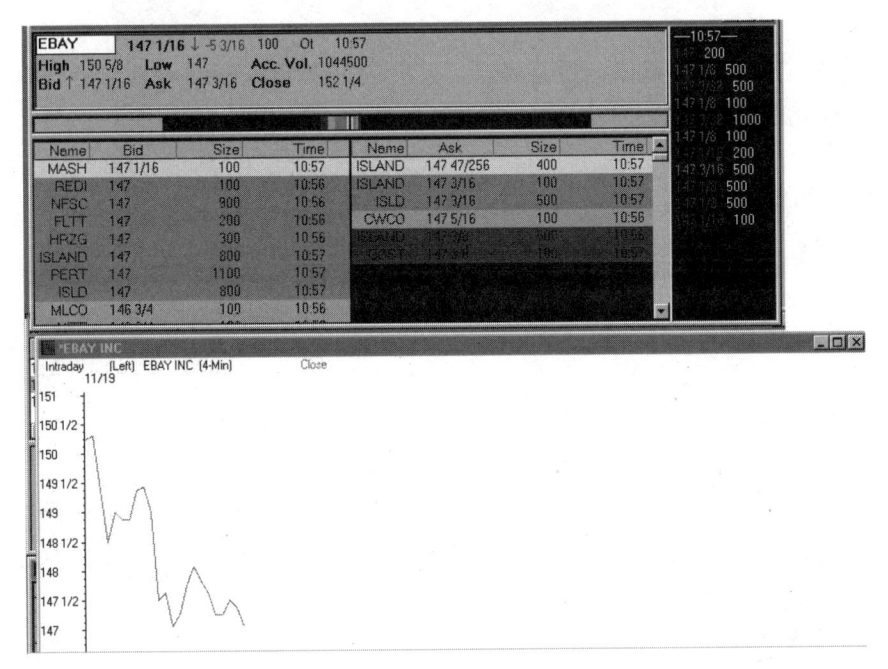

Figure 4-9. Ebay poised at the brink of a break in the downward trend. (Used with permission of Townsend Analytics, Ltd.)

In this display, the best bid is at $147^1/_{16}$, which is where the last trade was executed. Below that, there are lots of supporting bids at 147. The question here is whether the bids at 147 will hold or enough willing sellers to push the price lower. The answer appears in Figure 4-10.

There are straight sells at 147, and the best bid is moving lower. The bid falls straight to 146, where Figure 4-11 shows another set of bids, which this time do not attract sellers and the price holds the 146 level.

146 proves to be the low for the moment. Moving on to Figure 4-12, we see that some lines have now been drawn on the chart. Most important is that the downward trendline that has been in effect from market open can be seen. This downward trendline has presented a couple of opportunities to enter short positions as the price rose to meet the trendline, then continued back down. The upward slanting line in this figure shows the boundaries of a descending triangle in the price action, and as can be seen, when the price action breaches the bottom edge of the triangle, the breakout and subsequent move in price is quite swift.

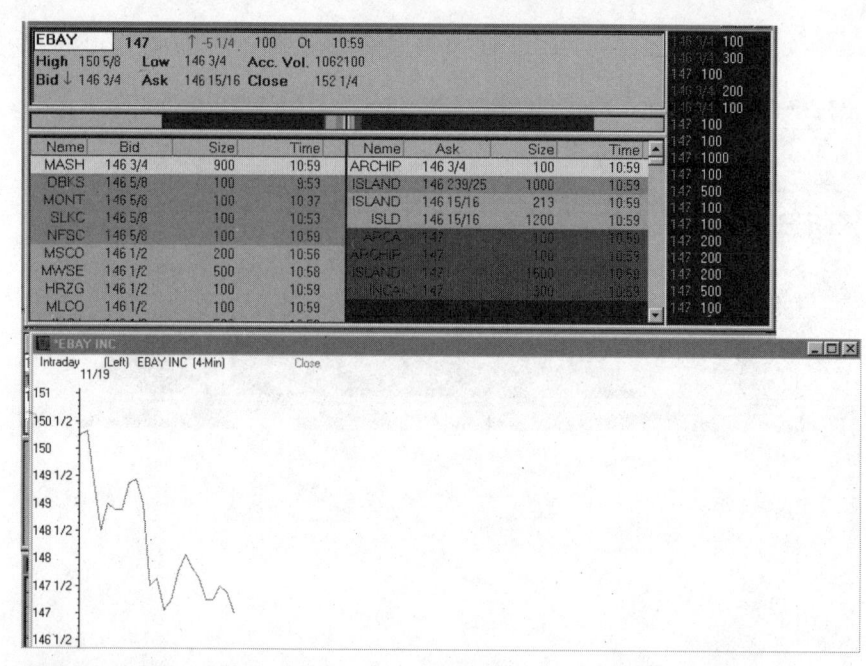

Figure 4-10. The best bid moves lower. (Used with permission of Townsend Analytics, Ltd.)

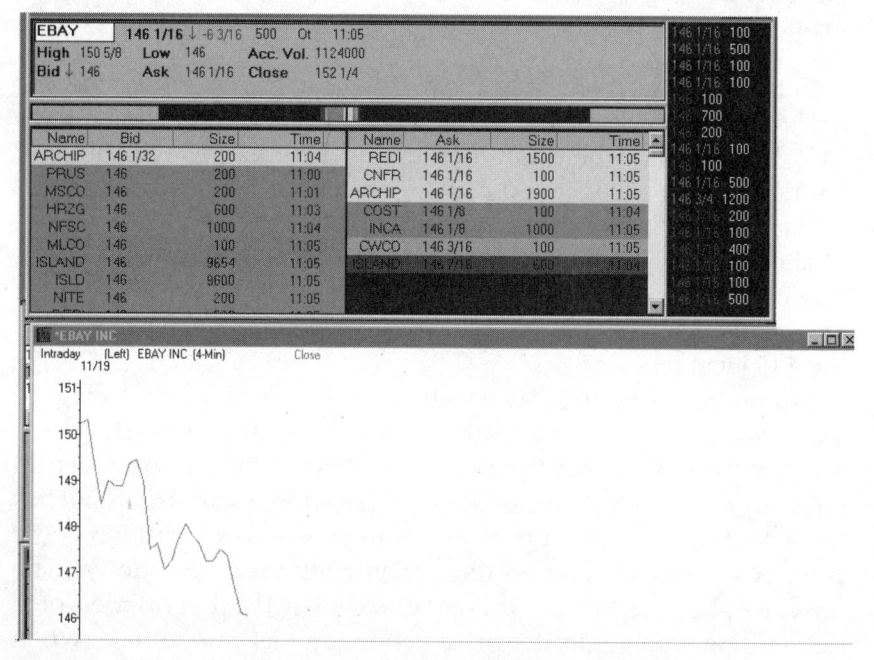

Figure 4-11. The price holds at 146. (Used with permission of Townsend Analytics, Ltd.)

The NASDAQ Level II Screen   **155**

At Figure 4-12, we have a decision to make: Does it look like the trendline will be respected again, or will this be the time that the trendline is broken? The answer is quite clear from the Level II screen. Trades are being executed against the best ask, and there is growing support at the best bid. This is confirmed a few moments later by Figure 4-13. As the bid at $146^{13}/_{16}$ has strong support, with trades taking place at $146^{7}/_{8}$, the best ask.

This proves to be the beginning of an upward trend that takes the price to over 149 with a succession of higher peaks and higher troughs. The most valuable information the Level II screen gave us here was that the apparent support at 147 (it is not a coincidence that lots of bids appear at round numbers; you will see this is commonplace in the market) did not materialize, since traders in the market executed trades against this bid level and exhausted the willingness of market makers to hold it. We also saw that the round number support at 146 held, trades were not executed against this level, and the price rose. Most important of all, we saw that as the price action crossed over and broke the downward

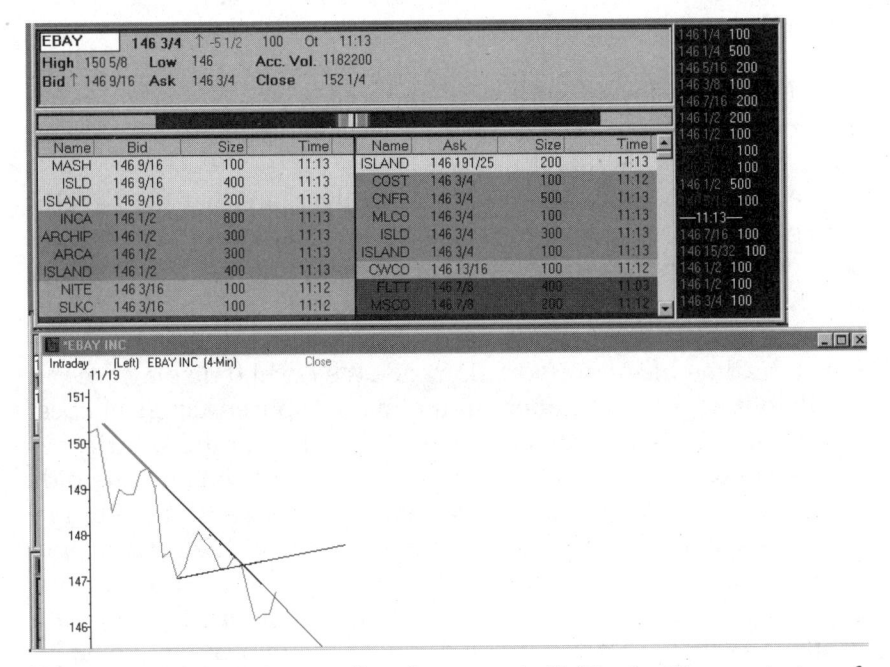

Figure 4-12. Will the trendline be respected? (Used with permission of Townsend Analytics, Ltd.)

156 Chapter 4

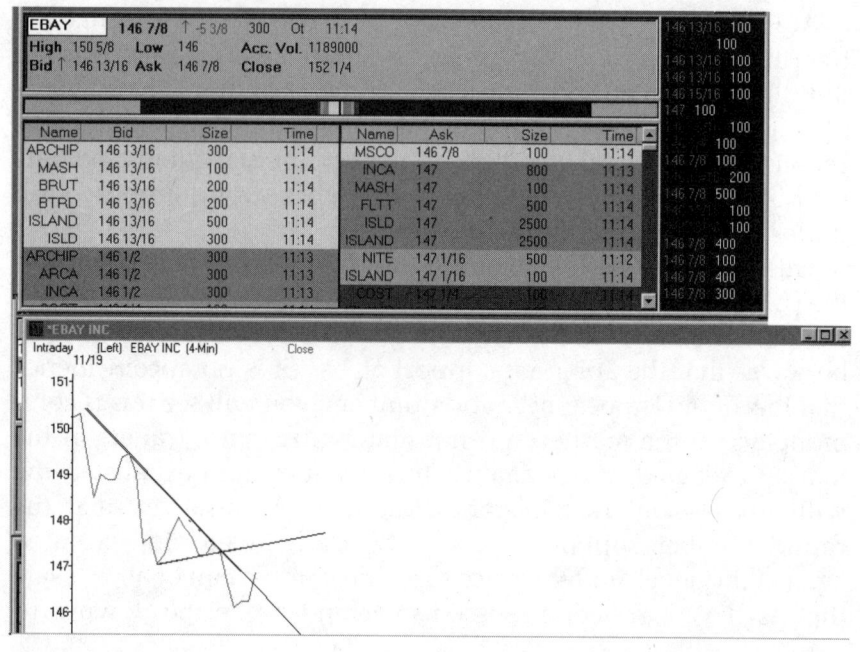

Figure 4-13. The beginning of an upward trend. (Used with permission of Townsend Analytics, Ltd.)

trendline, that support for the bid and trades being executed at the ask persisted, telling us that the price was not going to move down and respect the trendline this time.

The major points to take from this analysis are that the Level II screen taken in snapshot provides no information of any use. By seeing if market makers are adding offers at the best bid or ask or removing their offers, we can determine how eager they are to transact at either the best bid or the best ask. In addition, by looking at the time-of-sales report alongside the Level II display, we can see the willingness of traders in the market to transact at the best bid or ask and thereby determine their appetite for the security.

It is the balance between the trader's appetite to consume bids or asks and the determination of the market maker to hold bid or ask prices that determines the future direction of the price action. As you can see, even when the price is moving steadily in one direction, the Level II screen can frequently look like the direction is about to change. If you trade off of all the indications given by the Level II screen, you will trade yourself out of winning positions. It is only when the chart reaches a critical level that you should be taking your lead from the Level II screen. What Level II can do is let you know if support or resistance is going to hold.

In both of the examples given, we saw a trend in existence, followed by the break of a trendline. In each case, the Level II screen showed the bids, asks, and trades being executed in support of these trends, then a price action reversal seen as sales at the bid drying up followed by purchases at the ask. This was then followed by the trend break, as the price action continued its trend, without pause, through the trendline. Once the trendline had been broken, no more positions should have been taken in harmony with the original trend. Once a new trend becomes established, then it is safe to take positions in the new trend direction. A break of a trendline is enough to stop that trend, but it is not enough to start a new one. A continuation pattern or some other trend indicator, such as successive peaks and troughs (higher for an upward trend, lower for a downward trend), is needed before positions can be entered safely.

PART II
Putting the Plan into Action

5
Executions

So far, we have only covered part of the story regarding how to day trade profitably. It is one thing to identify opportunities in the market. It is another thing entirely to trade only those that fit within a disciplined approach. Without the ability to take a position when you want to, though, at or near the price you want, all the analysis in the world will do you no good.

The thing about electronic day trading (or direct-access trading, to be more precise) is that you have direct access to the trading tools that brokers use, without the broker. This cuts down the time it takes you to make an order and get it to a place where it can be executed. In addition to this direct access, electronic day-trading tools allow you to make offers at the best ask price if you want to sell, or at the best bid price if you want to buy. This allows you to play market maker and capture the spread from transactions. Having said that, I urge you not to base your trading activities on trying to capture the spread. This is a specialized form of day trading that requires its own discipline and tools that are not within the reach of most individual traders.

I first got interested in direct-access trading when I got tired of seeing opportunities in the market disappear because of slow execution by a broker. I was placing orders through a full-service broker to buy and not getting an execution until 10, 15, or more minutes after I had placed the order. This meant that if I placed a limit order (an order to buy at a specific price), I did not get an execution at all. If I placed a market order, I got an execution way off the price at which I originally placed the order. When I questioned this, I was told it was due to the volume of transactions in the market at that time. This is not false, but it is misleading. In general, the problem was that the broker's firm did not have the capacity in either systems or personnel to execute trades that quickly during times of high market volume. I became disillusioned with identifying the opportunity myself, calling a broker to execute it, and being charged hundreds of dollars in commissions for poorly timed executions. My interest then turned to some of the cheaper online brokers, which offered trades at $10 or less, and some promised to execute within a given time frame or complete the trade commission-free. At this stage I figured I would at least save on commissions, and I might even get quicker executions.

What I was not realizing was how these brokers made money at $10 or less per trade. The reason is that $10 per trade is not all they get. Some firms get paid for order flow by other firms that do the actual execution. Other online brokers do execute the trades themselves and profit from the order in the same way as those who pay for order flow. The reason order flow is valuable is that these brokers execute a trade when it is advantageous to them. They match orders, capture the spread, and essentially help themselves to part of the price you pay for the stock. Now, for someone investing for the long term, these small amounts that are shaved off by using a broker should not matter so much, but for a day trader, it is totally unacceptable.

The only way to avoid brokers that are paid for order flow, or who execute the trades themselves and profit from it, is to get your own direct access to the systems those brokers use to enter trades. This will cost more per trade than an online broker, but it gives you the opportunity to take the positions you need when you need them. For trading on NASDAQ, at a minimum, you need direct access to the following trading systems: Island, Archipelago, SOES, and Selectnet. In the sections to come, we'll discuss each one, how it works, when you might want to use it, and when it will not work for you.

Using the SOES Execution Route

Many other books on day trading offer a history of SOES, so I will not present that in detail here. SOES is often seen as synonymous with day trading. It was, in fact, the first tool used by the day-trading community. SOES is a mandatory execution system that allows you to buy at the ask and sell at the bid. The books that originally promoted day trading referred to SOES as a lightning-fast execution system that lets you initiate and close positions almost instantaneously, giving the impression that you could pick off unwary market makers with this execution route. I don't know if that was ever the case, but it is certainly not the case now. There are many aspects of SOES that protect a market maker from having to execute on it until he wants to. Although SOES is a mandatory execution system, using it does not guarantee that you will get an execution at the current market price when you enter an order. You may, and in most instances will, but it is not guaranteed. If a stock is falling sharply and no one wants to buy it, the probability is that you will not get out until buyers return. In the next few pages, we'll review the main features of the SOES system and show how those features have affected actual trades placed via the system.

SOES is a system for transacting against market makers only. You cannot execute against any of the ECNs via this route. It is a way of electronically buying at the best ask or selling at the best bid to the market makers who are offering those prices on the Level II screen. There are a number of features and rules of this system that you should be aware of before using it. The main concept is that there is a queue of orders that traders put into the SOES system, which will be executed against market makers' bids and asks as they become available. A market maker is only hit and transacted against by an SOES order when making the inside market (best bid or ask). You should also know that if an ECN is making the inside market, no market makers can be hit via SOES.

As SOES can only be used to transact at the best bid or ask, it is not possible to enter a limit order that is outside of the best bid or ask. An order entered in this fashion is killed by the exchange. So what happens if you enter an SOES order to buy at the best ask, and an ECN is at the best ask? Your order stays alive for 90 seconds as it waits to see if a market maker will step up to the best ask and accept your order. If that does not happen, your order is killed. Moreover, SOES can only be used during market open hours. ECNs can be used both premarket and postmarket.

SOES will accept odd lot orders from either side, which means you can enter an order size that is not divisible by 100. When it is your turn at the head of the queue, you will get your odd number of shares as long as the market maker at the inside market has a size greater than the size of your order.

SOES is there really as a failsafe, a mandatory means of getting out when you have to. It does not, however, offer a stop order facility. You have to enter either market orders or limit orders at the time you wish to execute on SOES. It will only accept partial orders, which means that you cannot specify the all-or-none type of order. Essentially, this means that you can enter an order for 1000, only get 300 or 400, and have the rest of the order killed. SOES covers the main NASDAQ market but not the small-cap market. In the Real Tick™ Level II display, a security on the regular market will be identified by a **t** in the Level II display, whereas a small-cap stock will have the **s** identifier. There is also the five-minute rule to be aware of when trading on SOES. If you enter an order that is executed on SOES, you cannot enter another similar order on the system for five minutes. As an example, if you enter an order to buy 500 shares of ABC Inc. and that order is executed, you cannot enter an order to buy any more ABC Inc. until five minutes have expired.

It is debatable whether there is any value in entering limit orders with SOES. Let's say you want to sell your position, and you enter a limit order to sell. If the best bid price moves lower than that limit prior to your order getting executed, the order will be canceled by the exchange and you will have to reenter. By entering a market order, you will get executed when you reach the head of the SOES queue at the best bid price at that time. Because SOES should be viewed as a failsafe mandatory execution system, market orders are generally the best route. This advice is given on the assumption that you are using SOES because it is the last option available to you, and that you want to get out at any price.

The two most important features of SOES we will examine in the trade examples are the SOES tier size and the SOES queue. The SOES tier size is the maximum size of trade that can be entered into the system for a given security. SOES tier sizes are quoted as A, which is 1000 shares; B, which is 500 shares; C, which is 200 shares; or D, which is 100 shares. To determine the tier size for a given security, visit the NASDAQ Web site symbol directory at http://www.nasdaqtrader.com/trader/symboldirectory/symbol.stm. Generally speaking, it is a risky thing to trade in excess of the SOES tier size. Let's say you purchase 1000 of a security with a tier size of 500, and despite your best analysis, the stock starts to free-fall and you need to get out. If a stock is in free-fall, ECNs rarely appear at the best bid; therefore, if you want the market price, you have to go to SOES. Your only other option is to offer the stock at the best ask, but if there are no buyers, it is unlikely you will sell the shares. With an SOES tier size of 500, that is all you can sell via that route. The other 500 you are left with can only be offloaded via Selectnet, an ECN, or five minutes later on SOES. Essentially, this leaves you without a guaranteed execution for five minutes. If no one is posting a bid on the ECN you are using, there is no way to guarantee a sale via that ECN.

Just because a security has a tier size of, say, 1000, it does not mean that a market maker must trade in 1000 share lots. It is quite normal to enter a 1000 share trade for a security with a tier size of A and get filled by trades from more than one market maker. What happens in this case is that when your order reaches the head of the SOES queue, it will execute against the market maker on the best bid, up to the size the market maker has advertised he is willing to buy. Once that automatic execution has taken place, the first market maker can choose to refresh his quote and take another lot, or the remaining shares on your order will be presented to the next market maker to appear as the best bid.

The next feature is the SOES queue. Just because you see a market maker on the best bid and you enter a market order to sell does not mean that the market maker will take that trade. When a market maker's bid has reached the best bid level and has been hit by an SOES order, the market maker has 15 seconds to refresh the price and accept more orders. Should the market maker see sell orders building up on the NASDAQ Level III screen (a screen that we traders do not get to see), it is likely that he will not refresh the price, and the next highest bid becomes the best bid. Let's suppose that 30 traders want to sell on SOES at the same time, and you are the thirtieth one to enter your order. If each market maker only takes one trade as their bid hits the best bid level, then removes the quote, the price will fall 30 levels (assuming each market maker is at a different level of bid price) before your turn on SOES. Clearly, this is not what you want, or, in most cases, not what you expected.

So now let's look at what the order entry screen looks like when you come up against some of these SOES features when trading. See Figure 5-1.

166 Chapter 5

Date	Time	Order ID	Action Taken	
11/02/199!	09:35:07	0579-0308-00	Buy 500 GILD at Market on ARCA (500 traded @ 41 7/8)	Executed
11/02/199!	09:37:10		Cancel order 0579-0308-0001-00 sent to exchange	Sent
11/02/199!	09:37:33		Bought 500 GILD at 41 7/8(order 0579-0308-0001-00)	Completed
11/02/199!	09:42:11	0579-0308-00	Sell 500 GILD at 43 Deleted	Killed (User requested cancel)
11/02/199!	09:42:37		Cancel order 0579-0308-0002-00 sent to exchange	Sent
11/02/199!	09:42:38		Order 0579-0308-0002-00 killed by the exchange for reason	Completed
11/02/199!	09:42:52	0579-0308-00	Sell 500 GILD at 42 7/8 Deleted	Killed
11/02/199!	09:43:08		Cancel order 0579-0308-0003-00 sent to exchange	Sent
11/02/199!	09:43:09		Order 0579-0308-0003-00 killed by the exchange for reason	Completed
11/02/199!	09:43:25	0579-0308-00	Sell 500 GILD at Market on SOES (500 traded @ 42.3875)	Executed
11/02/199!	09:44:42		Sold 100 GILD at 42 7/16 with WARR(order 0579-0308-000	Completed
11/02/199!	09:44:50		Sold 400 GILD at 42 3/8 with WARR(order 0579-0308-0004	Completed
11/02/199!	09:57:17	0579-0308-00	Buy 500 GILD at 44 Deleted	Killed
11/02/199!	09:57:30		Cancel order 0579-0308-0005-00 sent to exchange	Sent
11/02/199!	09:57:31		Order 0579-0308-0005-00 killed by the exchange for reason	Completed
11/02/199!	10:17:32	0579-0308-00	Buy 1000 JCDA at 31 1/4 Deleted	Killed (EXCEEDS TIER MAXIMUM 000200)
11/02/199!	10:17:33		Order 0579-0308-0006-00 killed by the exchange for reason	Completed

Figure 5-1. Entering an order on the SOES execution route. (Used with permission of Townsend Analytics, Ltd.)

The first action here is that a market order was entered on Archipelago for 500 shares of GILD (Gilead Sciences). I chose this stock because it had experienced an overnight gap down of about 30 percent, from over $60 to around $40. The stock opened strongly and immediately started to gain ground. I saw lots of activity on Archipelago for this stock, and since it was very actively traded, I wanted to use an ECN instead of SOES, anticipating a long delay in the SOES queue. As you can see, I entered the order to buy at the market on ARCA at 9:35:07. For over two minutes I did not get executed. My interest in the security started to fade, so I tried to cancel the order. Twenty-three seconds after trying to cancel the order, I received a fill at $41^7/_8$. At this point I decided that the weakness I had seen in the security was a continuation pattern in the upward move and stayed with it. At 9:42, I felt that the security had peaked, at least temporarily, and I was up over a dollar, so I wanted to close out. The orders to sell at $43 and 42^7/_8$ were sent to Island. As you can see, the market moved away from my orders and I could see my gains depleting. One of my rules (we will visit the full list of rules in Chapter 7) is to never let a gain turn into a loss, so at 9:43:25 a.m. I entered a market order on SOES to sell the security. I was in the SOES queue until 9:44:42, just over one and a quarter minutes. Fortunately for me, the price had only dropped to 42^7/_{16}$ by this time, when WARR picked up 100 shares. GILD has an SOES tier size of 1000 shares, so I could enter the order to sell 500, but the size at which WARR advertised it was willing to trade on the Level II screen was set to 100. WARR did not refresh its price at 42^7/_{16}$, but moved to $42^3/_8$ and completed the rest of my order at that price. GILD hit a high that day of $51 and closed at $49. I did indeed get out early on this one, but that is what a day trader does who reacts to what happens in the market. If I had held on, I would have been riding out a downturn in the security and hoping that a turnaround would come. Day trading should be about dealing in the reality of price movements and taking small, regular, incremental gains rather than hoping for the big win.

An alternative to entering a market SOES order would have been to enter the order on Selectnet without a preference, at a price lower than the best bid, and hope that a market maker would trade on that. This is not a mandatory execution system, so there is no guarantee that a market maker will pick it up. I do not do this often, but it is an option you should be aware of.

The last part of Figure 5-1 shows that I was attracted to JCDA, which on that day was experiencing a breakout. It opened at $26 and rose to over $37. I saw the strong buying on Level II and the upward trend in the daily tick chart, and wanted to buy 1000 shares at 31^{1}/_{4}$. The only route that appeared to be open at this time was SOES. No ECNs were offering stock at or near the market best ask price. The order could not be completed because JCDA has a tier size of 200 and entering an order for 1000 shares would be violation. When I realized the small size I would be restricted to in this security, I decided to pass on the opportunity.

In the majority of texts on the subject of SOES, the system is described as one that will execute up to 1000 shares. That is true, but not very helpful, given all you've just learned. Before leaving SOES, it is important to know when a market maker has to advertise a size at least matching the tier size and when he may not.

Typically, when a market maker is executed on his advertised price by an SOES order, the size advertised by that market maker is decremented by the amount of the order. So if MASH is bidding for 1000 of ABC Inc. stock and is hit by an SOES order for 500, the size advertised by MASH on the Level II screen decrements to 500 after the execution. Market makers can opt to have their advertised size kept constant automatically, regardless of how many SOES trades are executed against them, the only restriction being that the advertised size must be greater than or equal to the SOES tier size. During normal market conditions, this is a little-used feature, since it leaves the market maker open to virtually unlimited SOES trades at the tier size.

There is some confusion among traders as to whether a market maker has to trade at the SOES tier size. The answer is *no*. There are many instances when a market maker will not trade at the SOES tier size. To simplify the discussion, take the above example of ABC Inc., which has a tier size of 1000. First, MASH is hit with an order for 500, so the advertised size will normally be reduced to 500. Other SOES trades can be executed against this remaining 500 until there is zero left. At that point, MASH will have to refresh at that price for the SOES tier size or move to another price. The only exception is if a market maker is reflecting a customer limit order for less than the SOES tier size. This is important when you are interested in entering an SOES market order to obtain the full SOES tier size.

Let's say you want 1000 of ABC Inc. and your Level II shows that MASH is offering 1000 at an ask of $30, which you like. You enter your market buy order, get 100 shares at $30, and the remainder of the order is canceled. Why does this happen? It takes time for sizes to be updated after a trade has occurred. MASH was probably hit by a total of 900 shares on SOES, leaving the 100 that you got. MASH then did not refresh its price at $30. The next best asking price was advertised by an ECN, and SOES is not able to execute a market buy order with only an ECN at the best ask, so it canceled the order.

In summary, SOES is good as a means of last-resort execution. It is the one way you can be sure of getting out at some point. You can only execute against market makers' bids or asks and only up to the size that they advertise, unless they choose to refresh their quotes. You cannot enter an order in excess of the SOES tier size, and once you execute on SOES, similar orders cannot be processed for another five minutes. The biggest problems with using SOES are that the queue sometimes is long and if ECNs are making the inside market, no SOES orders will be executed.

Why Island (Not Datek) Is the Preferred Route

The main reason Island is the preferred route is that you can execute almost instantaneously against orders that are entered on the Island book. There is no tier size or queue to worry about. If you see an order to buy or sell on Island and you decide to execute against it, as long as you get there first, you will get an instantaneous execution.

Island is also one of the larger ECNs out there in terms of liquidity, ranking second only to Instinet. Still, Island is the ECN of choice for the majority of day traders, whereas Instinet has traditionally been used more by institutions.

The fact that Island is the day trader's route of choice is important not just because of the liquidity it provides. Because so many day traders use Island, many of whom use conflicting strategies, you will often find Island orders on both sides of the market, which means that traders are willing to buy and sell at the same point. This often gives you an opportunity to find a short in a falling stock, but we will cover that in more detail in a later section in this chapter.

Let's start by reviewing the main features of Island. Island only covers NASDAQ securities and only allows you to execute limit order trades against other users of Island. Those other users can be day traders, market makers, or institutions. You don't know who is buying your stock (or selling it to you). All you know is that when you enter a limit order to either buy or sell at a certain price, your trade will be executed if there is a matching order. Let's say you enter an order to buy 500 ADSK at $28 $1/2$. That means you are willing to pay up to, but not more than, $28 $1/2$. Depending on what orders are on the Island book, you will get filled at varying prices up to $28 $1/2$, or not at all if no one on Island is willing to sell at that price. Typically, if there are sell orders for 300 at $28 $7/16$, and 200 at $28 $17/32$, you will pick up these orders and get filled at an average cost lower than $28 $1/2$. It all depends on what is out there.

If there are no matching sell orders and your order to buy at $28 $1/2$ is the best priced order entered into Island at that time, your order will appear on everybody's Level II screen under the ID ISLD. It is then known to all users what your intentions are and someone may choose to execute against them. If this occurs, you are effectively buying at the Island bid price for the security, which may or may not be the best bid price in the market as a whole. Island differs in other ways from SOES. For instance, you can enter limit orders at prices away from the current bid or ask and wait for them to be executed. If you short a stock, for example, you may have determined from the chart that a support level is coming up (assuming that the price continues to fall). Having determined this, you want to make sure that your order to cover your position (in effect, buying the stock back) is the first order on the Island book at that price and therefore the first to be executed when buyers come back in at that level. This is often a good ploy. It is a disciplined approach that will lead to small but regular profits. A riskier proposition is to wait until it looks like the selling pressure is subsiding and then try to cover your position. This can lead to greater profits, but you also run the risk that you cannot cover your position when you want to if no one wants to sell at that time. To clarify these issues, we can look at a real trade executed on Island, as shown in Figure 5-2.

This is the same trade we looked at briefly in Chapter 3, but here we will focus on the execution aspects of the trade. WITC drew my attention as it experienced a strong gap up in the premarket activity. I expected at least a temporary pullback after the market opened. At 9:47:16 I entered the order to sell short 1000 WITC at 23[13]/16, and as you can see, I received fills within one second, at 9:47:17. You will note that I received a better initial selling price for 800 of the 1000 shares. When it came time to buy the shares back at 9:55, I was again given a better purchase price than I expected to cover at and executed within one second. In both of these cases, the sale and then the purchase, I saw the Island orders and picked a level where I expected to be executed quickly. In the case of the short sale, I placed the sell order at the best ask level and had

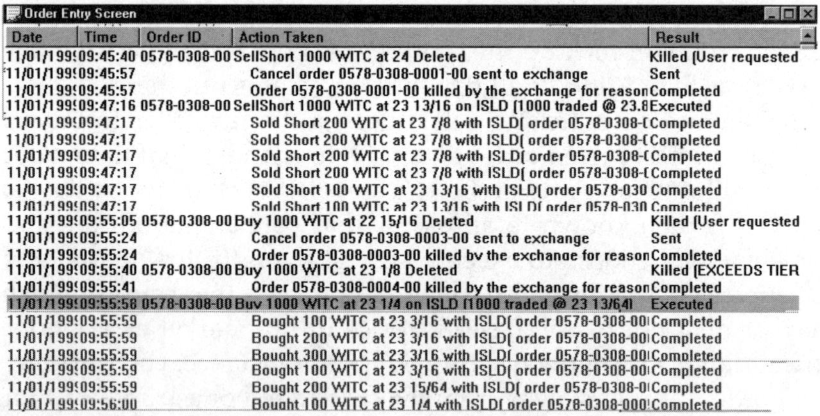
Order Entry Screen

Date	Time	Order ID	Action Taken	Result
11/01/199	09:45:40	0578-0308-00	SellShort 1000 WITC at 24 Deleted	Killed (User requested
11/01/199	09:45:57		Cancel order 0578-0308-0001-00 sent to exchange	Sent
11/01/199	09:45:57		Order 0578-0308-0001-00 killed by the exchange for reason	Completed
11/01/199	09:47:16	0578-0308-00	SellShort 1000 WITC at 23 13/16 on ISLD (1000 traded @ 23.8	Executed
11/01/199	09:47:17		Sold Short 200 WITC at 23 7/8 with ISLD(order 0578-0308-(	Completed
11/01/199	09:47:17		Sold Short 200 WITC at 23 7/8 with ISLD(order 0578-0308-(	Completed
11/01/199	09:47:17		Sold Short 200 WITC at 23 7/8 with ISLD(order 0578-0308-(	Completed
11/01/199	09:47:17		Sold Short 200 WITC at 23 7/8 with ISLD(order 0578-0308-(	Completed
11/01/199	09:47:17		Sold Short 100 WITC at 23 13/16 with ISLD(order 0578-030	Completed
11/01/199	09:47:17		Sold Short 100 WITC at 23 13/16 with ISLD(order 0578-030	Completed
11/01/199	09:55:05	0578-0308-00	Buy 1000 WITC at 22 15/16 Deleted	Killed (User requested
11/01/199	09:55:24		Cancel order 0578-0308-0003-00 sent to exchange	Sent
11/01/199	09:55:24		Order 0578-0308-0003-00 killed by the exchange for reason	Completed
11/01/199	09:55:40	0578-0308-00	Buy 1000 WITC at 23 1/8 Deleted	Killed (EXCEEDS TIER
11/01/199	09:55:41		Order 0578-0308-0004-00 killed by the exchange for reason	Completed
11/01/199	09:55:58	0578-0308-00	Buy 1000 WITC at 23 1/4 on ISLD (1000 traded @ 23 13/64)	Executed
11/01/199	09:55:59		Bought 100 WITC at 23 3/16 with ISLD(order 0578-0308-00	Completed
11/01/199	09:55:59		Bought 200 WITC at 23 3/16 with ISLD(order 0578-0308-00	Completed
11/01/199	09:55:59		Bought 300 WITC at 23 3/16 with ISLD(order 0578-0308-00	Completed
11/01/199	09:55:59		Bought 100 WITC at 23 3/16 with ISLD(order 0578-0308-00	Completed
11/01/199	09:55:59		Bought 200 WITC at 23 15/64 with ISLD(order 0578-0308-0	Completed
11/01/199	09:56:00		Bought 100 WITC at 23 1/4 with ISLD(order 0578-0308-000	Completed

Figure 5-2. A trade executed via Island. (Used with permission of Townsend Analytics, Ltd.)

another trader decide to buy at that time, thus executing my trade. You should see that I tried to exit my position via SOES for this trade, because I forgot the maximum tier size for WITC. That order was rejected and I had to go back to Island to exit my position.

Island is also different from SOES in that you can enter limit orders outside of market hours and trade in the premarket and postmarket. Incidentally, all orders entered during market hours that are still live at market close are deleted at 4:02 p.m., requiring reentry if you still want to trade at that price. As with SOES, it is not possible to preference a market maker, that is, you can't select one out of the list of those with whom to trade. This should make sense since it has already been mentioned how Island orders can only be executed against other orders entered into Island.

Like SOES, Island allows odd lots, which means trading blocks of shares that are not divisible by 100. This is much more common on Island than it is on SOES. On SOES, the other party is always a market maker, and those people tend not to make their lives difficult by trading a strange number of shares. With the large number of day traders active on Island, it does not take much for one trader to enter a lot size of something like three shares to deliver odd lot fills to lots of other traders. What happens, for example, is that a novice trader might be experimenting with Island and enter an order to buy three QCOM, now trading at $371. This is in excess of $1000 total, which is a limit novice traders often work with. If you are long 100 QCOM and enter a matching order to sell at that level, and that three-share trader is the only buyer, you will get three out of the hundred sold. Worse, if the market trades down so that $371 is outside of the bid/ask level (I am assuming you want out of QCOM because this is your expectation), you will be left with 97 QCOM, and your original order will be canceled by Island. This leaves you owning 97 shares and wanting out. Then what you have to do is reenter the trade at a new level for 97 shares. As most order entry systems automatically increment in 100 lots, entering 97 as a size takes valuable time. Something like this will happen to you at some time and leave you with an odd lot. When it does, the best thing to do is enter a market order in SOES for this amount and close the position. If you do enter the order to sell 97 shares at a price that will be matched in Island, the odd lot problem persists and is passed down the line to the next trader.

Due to the speed of Island execution, I have often accepted the Island ask price in a rapidly appreciating stock, even if that ask price is 1/4 or 3/8 above the current best ask price being quoted by a market maker. My experience leads me to do this on rare occasions. When a stock is moving up rapidly, I know that the market makers are unlikely to execute against my order until sellers come back into the market, which could be several dollars above the current asking price. This is a risky ploy, as it does put you immediately in a losing position, but when there has been some event to cause frenzied purchasing of a security, this is often the best way to get in.

One of the features of entering Island orders that can at first appear confusing is when you enter what you think is a reasonable order and you get the return message that the order could not be entered because it would lock or cross the market. There are several situations that can cause this. The first is that you are trying to enter a buy order at above the current asking price on Island, or entering a sell order lower than the existing bid. Clearly, these represent crosses of the market, and it makes sense that they cannot be entered. The most common reason a trader does this is if his market data system is displaying prices that are behind the market and he is unaware that the order being entered would cause a cross. What is not as obvious is that there is a lock zone between the inside market and the best bid/ask on Island, if there is a difference between the two. This is best explained by looking at an example. Suppose that security ABC has an inside market of 20 × $20^1/_8$. These inside prices are quoted by systems other than Island. Let us also suppose that the best bid (purchase order) on Island is $19^1/_2$ and the best ask (sell order) is $20^1/_2$. This creates two lock-out zones, one each for both buy and sell orders. The zone between $20^1/_8$ and $20^1/_2$ covers the region between the inside market ask and the best sell order on Island. You will not be allowed to enter a buy order at the level between $20^1/_8$ and $20^1/_2$. This is restricted to those wishing to enter lower-priced ask (sell) orders. The reason behind this is that there is a two-tiered order-matching process within Island. First, Island tries to match your order with another Island order. For purposes of illustration, let's say you try to enter an Island order to buy at $20^3/_{16}$. The lowest-priced sell order on Island is $20^1/_2$. That order cannot be matched within Island, so Island then looks to offer that out to the market. This is the second tier. At this stage, your buy order coming out to the market will be presented as a bid, which happens to be higher than the inside market ask price and therefore crosses the market, so the order cannot be placed. If you had tried to do the same with a buy order at $20 $1/8$ placed through Island, the order would have failed because it would have been a locked market, which means the bid equals the offer, which is also not allowed.

The zone between $19 $1/2$ and $20 is also restricted. You will not be allowed to enter a sell order on Island at a level between $19 $1/2$ and $20 because that would either lock or cross the market when Island tries to place that unmatched order in the general market. The logic is the same: You cannot offer to sell at a price lower than or equal to the price at which someone else is willing to buy. Of course, it is still possible to enter buy orders at a level between $19 $1/2$ and $20, which will raise the best bid price on Island.

In summary, Island has the best liquidity of the generally available ECNs. It is likely that Instinet will open itself more to individual traders in the future, moving away from its traditional institutional base, and this will then offer even greater liquidity. For now, however, Island is the most liquid ECN for day traders. Island is fast, but it only allows you to enter a limit order. The biggest problem with using Island is getting a partial fill, then having the price move away from your original order and canceling the remainder of your order. This can leave you with the problem of dealing in odd lot sizes.

Some other manuals promote Datek as a means of executing day trades. The logic goes that if you are primarily using Island, which is used by and is partly owned by Datek, why not use Datek? They offer to execute within a short time frame or the trade is commission-free. Datek is a fine vehicle for executing trades when buying and holding securities for the longer term, but it is not appropriate for day-trading activities. During times of heavy market volume, the same order that you can execute very quickly with direct access on either SOES, Archipelago, Island, or Selectnet can take 20 minutes or more via Datek. This is my own costly experience talking. Executing on Datek does not mean that you are executing on Island. Island is just one of the routes available to the Datek traders and trading systems. The simple fact that you can enter market orders for NASDAQ securities on Datek tells you that Island is not being used exclusively.

The Little Helper ARCA and the Other ECNs

Archipelago is represented on the Level II screens as ARCA, and it was one of the original ECNs approved by the exchange. ARCA is radically different in operation from Island, and you need to know how it operates so you know when to use it in preference to Island. It is also important to know how ARCA works so that you do not try to use it in the wrong situation. Whereas Island is geared toward giving you an instantaneous execution should a matching order be available, or canceling your order should the market move away from it before it has been executed, ARCA does some extra work for you.

ARCA was designed as a smart ECN that will look for order execution routes outside of its own internal orders and post to the Level II screen. When I started day trading, I used Archipelago almost exclusively. Once or twice I tried to execute orders at times when Archipelago was not the best route. I received a very poor execution and went away from using it. More recently, Archipelago has become one of my favorite routes again. For those with little day-trading experience, Archipelago is probably the best route to start off with. It works your order through all possible execution routes and can often come up with better execution prices than you will see on your Level II screen.

Let's start with some simple executions. If ARCA is posting the best bid or ask price to the Level II screen, you can trade against those orders in much the same way you do with Island orders. That is, if you see someone posting an order to buy a security at the best bid price, you can sell it to them on ARCA almost instantaneously.

If you wish to make the best bid or offer price, the procedure again is the same as with Island. You merely offer to buy at a level higher than the current best bid posted on the Level II screen as ARCA. Once you do post on the inside market on the Level II screen, you can be hit by other ARCA traders or users of other ECNs that preference you. This means that on their systems' order entry screen, they will preference ARCA to get to your order. We cover preferencing in more detail in the upcoming section on Selectnet.

The situation changes when you go to sell to the best bid or buy from the best ask and there are no ARCA orders there. It is here that ARCA will work for you. Entering an order at the inside market sets off the search capabilities of ARCA. First, ARCA looks to see if any ECNs are posting at the inside market. If there is an ECN on the inside market, ARCA executes against those orders and you get your fill. If there are no ECNs at the inside market, ARCA goes to Selectnet, determines who is the most active market maker in the security you wish to trade, and sends a preferenced order to that market maker. A Selectnet preference order is like an electronic phone call. You are asking the market maker if he would like to trade at the size and price you are offering. There is no guarantee that the market maker will take the trade, so ARCA operates on a timeout basis. If the market maker does not take the offer within 30 seconds, ARCA deletes that Selectnet order and starts again. Essentially, ARCA looks at its own book, then to ECNs, and finally seeks to preference active market makers via Selectnet. It does not access the SOES execution route for you.

Here's an example of how ARCA works in practice. Assume the inside market for security ABC is as shown below:

GSCO 21   10   MASH 21$^{1}/_{8}$ 10

This shows that the best bid is $21 from Goldman Sachs, who is offering to buy 1000 shares. Mayer and Schweitzer is offering to sell up to 1000 at 21^{1}/_{8}$. You decide to sell on ARCA at $21. Clearly, there are no ECNs at the best bid at this time, so ARCA will try to preference GSCO. Let's suppose you have decided to get out because you see the market weakening. As a result of this weakening, the inside market slips to the following:

MLCO 20$^{15}/_{16}$ 5   MASH 21$^{1}/_{8}$ 10

ARCA will realize this and offer your order out at the inside ask as follows:

MLCO 20$^{15}/_{16}$ 5   ARCA 21   10

You can see that ARCA has automatically selected the probable best route for you to get the price that you are looking for in the market (or better). ARCA will accept orders for up to 10,000 shares and will work the order for you, placing orders at the routes most advantageous as the price offered in the market changes. ARCA will only work with round lots, however. If you have received an execution from Island that has left you with an odd lot, ARCA cannot offload all your stock for you.

All this effort on your behalf comes at a price, and that price is speed of execution during fast-moving markets. ARCA can perform badly during a fast market due to the 30-second timeout when preferencing market makers. Should you choose a market ARCA sell order as your exit route in a rapidly falling security, and if no ARCA buy orders are available, the price could fall rapidly while ARCA is waiting for the 30-second timeout to expire. ARCA then has to start all over again looking for orders on its own book, ECNs, preferencing market makers, offering the stock out, etc. ARCA gives the best results in quiet markets, when there is time to obtain the best possible price. One exception to ARCA's weakness in fast markets is when you want to buy a rapidly appreciating security. You know that the SOES queue will probably stop you from getting your fill at the price you want. If no matching sell orders are available on Island, but matching sell orders on other ECNs, like REDI or BRUT, look attractive to you, you can enter a matching limit order on ARCA for these prices, and ARCA will execute against these ECNs for you.

SelectNet Can Be a Good Friend

We have already discussed Selectnet to some degree. Here we will cover the material previously discussed in more detail.

Selectnet really exists as NASDAQ's ECN, that is, it reflects orders placed on it by participants, and it is not a mandatory execution route. A market maker does not have to trade with you via Selectnet if he does not want to. If you see a market maker on the best bid and want to sell to him, SOES is the only mandatory route, but as we know, if the market maker has fulfilled his obligation on SOES and does not want to trade any more at that price level, your order will not be filled. Placing your order on Selectnet is really just a way of advertising it and hoping that someone will take you up on it. There are two modes for Selectnet, a broadcast to all market makers and a more directed preference to a specific market maker. We will see the pros and cons of each.

Selectnet can execute trades to all market makers and all ECNs. When you enter an order on Selectnet, it is not seen on everybody's Level II screen. It is generally only seen by the market makers. On the Townsend Analytics Real Tick™ screen, it will show other users' preferred Selectnet orders, when appropriately configured. This is not all the Selectnet orders of course, only the subset of those entered using that firm's software.

Selectnet requires limit orders to be entered. There is no option for market orders. As it is a nonmandatory execution route, you can offer to buy stock at the best bid or sell at the best ask, and place quotes outside of the best bid/ask spread. An interesting feature is that Selectnet will allow you to select an all-or-none trade, meaning that you will not get a partial fill of the order. The party on the other end of the trade either accepts all of the stock or none of it. If you do ever take a large position in a security, well above the SOES tier size, Selectnet is one of the routes that will allow you to enter trade sizes above the SOES tier.

Offering to buy or sell stock on Selectnet can be broadcast (this is selected by posting *no preference* in the order entry screen), which means that all market makers will see your order. Alternatively, you can elect to preference your order to only one market maker by entering that market maker's four-letter ID in the preference box on your order entry screen. You may choose to do this if you notice a particular market maker has been very active in the stock and you do not want to reveal your order to the whole market. Preferenced orders generally get better attention from market makers than broadcast orders. There is one instance when you can force a market maker to do something via Selectnet, and that is if the market maker is at the inside market and you preference him to trade at that price. In that instance that market maker must trade or move price. It is questionable whether you would want to do this, since if the market maker is at the inside market and willing to trade at that price, SOES is the faster and simpler option.

You can do all of these things both in the premarket and postmarket on Selectnet. At this time, there are three sessions for Selectnet trading, which are currently from 9:00 to 9:30 a.m. ET, from 9:30 a.m. to 4:00 p.m. ET, and the final session from 4:00 to 5:25 p.m. ET. At the end of each session, orders are canceled.

The times when I have had the most success with Selectnet were when I had the misfortune to be long in a rapidly falling stock, could not get any ECN participants to buy, and the SOES queue kept my order from being filled for too long. In those instances, I preferenced a market maker at one or two levels below the best bid and occasionally got a fill. This is risky. By doing this, you are getting less than the inside market at the time of the trade. If, however, that price is better than the price you would have gotten waiting for your turn in the SOES queue, you have done well. Of course, there is no way to tell from the trader's position whether it was the best thing or not, but at least it reduces the stress of waiting to see if you get a fill.

Getting Shorts in the Market

Let's look at a day in the market when I felt shorts were the best option for plays early in the day. My attention was drawn to BLDP and ELCO, for the following reasons. Both had experienced a gap up of over $2, and their daily charts looked like they had limited upside potential. ELCO had experienced a breakout, and the gap this day looked like it might be an exhaustion gap. The daily chart is shown in Figure 5-3.

BLDP had been in a long-term downward trend and looked as if it had gapped up to a resistance level as shown in Figure 5-4.

I was also interested in both these securities because my broker had a borrow available on both, allowing me to short them. Both had a tier size of 1000, allowing me to trade 1000 shares with some confidence, and there was premarket volume in both securities, indicating real interest in the securities that day. At market open, I could see prices start to tail off in the market in general. This was most easily seen by looking at the value of the net ticks symbol, which keeps track of the net number of securities showing an uptick in the bid price. This value started at around 160 and proceeded to fall rapidly. My ideal pattern for an early short is to see the security continue up after market open, then reverse down within the first 10 minutes (we will go through market-open patterns in different market scenarios in more depth in Chapter 6). BLDP was the first to do this after only a couple of minutes. When a security reverses this quickly, I am cautious and only look for quick profits. After a security has started to fall, the tick direction

Elcom Int'l

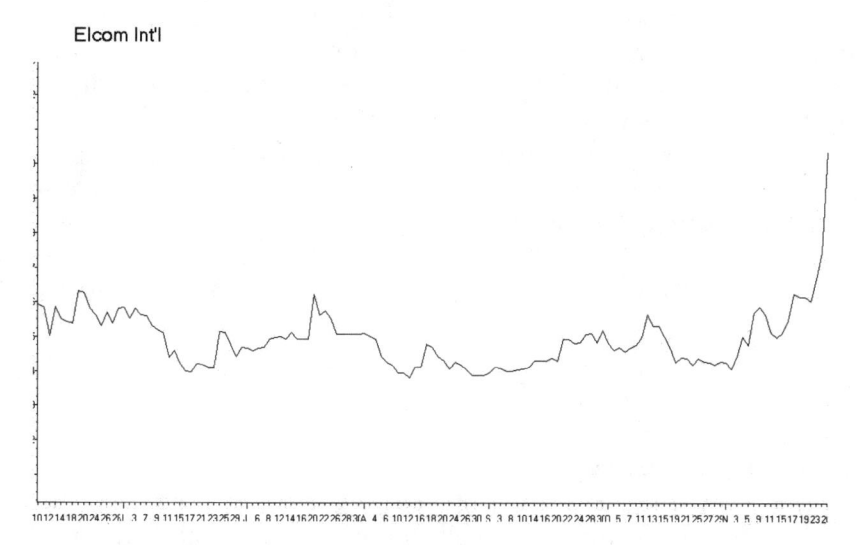

Figure 5-3. Getting a short; ELCO daily chart. (Used with permission of Townsend Analytics, Ltd.)

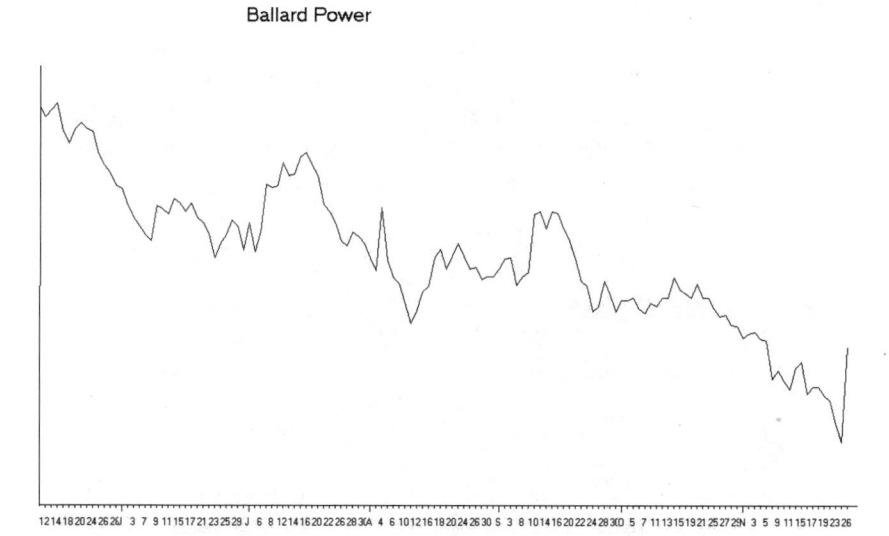

Ballard Power

Figure 5-4. Another shorting opportunity; BLDP gapping up. (Used with permission of Townsend Analytics, Ltd.)

for the bid value is obviously down. There is a NASDAQ rule that disallows selling short to the best bid price during those conditions, so you have to offer stock you want to short at a level above the best bid. Essentially you are creating a new best ask price and hoping that someone chooses to hit that ask price and trade against it to give you a fill. Clearly, in this situation, you have to offer the stock out on an ECN, since you are trying to sell at the new ask price. You can only sell to the bid on SOES, so to short on SOES, the bid must be on an uptick. The arrow in the Level II screen tells you if the security is in a bid uptick or downtick situation. At market open I do not try to anticipate a top. I need to see the security start to come back first, so I always end up using an ECN to offer stock at the ask, and due to its liquidity, Island is almost always that ECN.

My actual trading actions are shown in Figure 5-5. My first action was to try to advertise a short for BLDP on Island and hope somebody would take it. I could not sell at the bid as the stock was already on the downtick. Two seconds after I offered the stock for sale, it was bought, and I was short 1000 BLDP. Soon after I sold the stock (about three minutes), I was not happy with the way it was moving. There was no decisive position being taken by the market makers. The amount of stock offered at the bid and ask became quite close, indicating a balance in supply and demand. The excess supply previously seen by more market makers on the ask side (as confirmation of the tick chart price action) had disappeared. I then started to look at closing my position. Trying to get out at $26^{13}/_{16}$ did not work, since the price moved above that, but I was able to execute a trade of some shares at $27⅞. Here I took my eye off the ball and started to see how ELCO was doing, with-

```
11/26/199:09:31:50 0591-0308-00 SellShort 1000 BLDP at 27 1/8 on ISLD (1000 traded @ 27 1/8 Executed
11/26/199:09:32:00                  Sold Short 200 BLDP at 27 1/8 with ISLD[ order 0591-0308-(Completed
11/26/199:09:32:02                  Sold Short 800 BLDP at 27 1/8 with ISLD[ order 0591-0308-(Completed
11/26/199:09:35:35 0591-0308-00 Buy 1000 BLDP at 26 13/16 Deleted                Killed (User requested cancel)
11/26/199:09:36:06                  Cancel order 0591-0308-0002-00 sent to exchange    Sent
11/26/199:09:36:06                  Order 0591-0308-0002-00 killed by the exchange for reason Completed
11/26/199:09:36:14 0591-0308-00 Buy 1000 BLDP at 26 7/8 on SOES (300 traded @ 26 7/8)   Executed
11/26/199:09:36:22                  Bought 300 BLDP at 26 7/8 with HRZG[ order 0591-0308-00 Completed
11/26/199:09:36:25                  Order 0591-0308-0003-00 killed by the exchange for reason Completed
11/26/199:09:37:22 0591-0308-00 Buy 700 BLDP at Market on SOES (700 traded @ 27 1/8]    Executed
11/26/199:09:37:26                  Bought 700 BLDP at 27 1/8 with PRUS[ order 0591-0308-00 Completed
11/26/199:09:40:23 0591-0308-00 SellShort 1000 ELCO at 12 1/8 on ISLD (1000 traded @ 12 1/8 Executed
11/26/199:09:40:32                  Sold Short 1000 ELCO at 12 1/8 with ISLD[ order 0591-0308 Completed

11/26/199:09:44:40                  Bought 100 ELCO at 11 9/16 with NITE[ order 0591-0308-00 Completed
11/26/199:09:44:41                  Bought 900 ELCO at 11 7/16 with SHWD[ order 0591-0308-( Completed
```

Figure 5-5. Trading action with BLDP. (Used with permission of Townsend Analytics, Ltd.)

out realizing I had only bought 300 shares and not 1000. I had made the mistake of entering a limit SOES order and not a market SOES order. I chose SOES because there were no ECNs available on the ask side. The reason it ended up being a limit SOES order is that the previous trade was done on Island, which only allows limit orders, and I had not changed my order entry screen parameter to market. After looking briefly at ELCO, I saw in my market minder screen that I still had a position. Cursing the previous day's Thanksgiving celebration, I entered a market order to exit BLDP. Instead of making 3/8 on 1000 shares, I only made that on 300 shares, since my purchase price for the remaining 700 matched the price of the short. My problem with entering a limit order in this case was that after I got my first fill at $26⁷/₈, the market moved away from this price and the order was canceled. Had it been a market order, I would probably have received a fill at the next best ask price (which was actually $26¹⁵/₁₆). The only time you do not get an SOES fill at the next price level is if the only offer at the next price level is from an ECN and no market makers come to the inside market within 30 seconds. If this is the case, your remaining order will be canceled with the message that there were no market makers available. This error in order entry cost me $250 in execution price and commission costs. As it turned out, it was a wise choice to exit. BLDP continued up to over $29.

I quickly turned my attention to ELCO, since it was behaving more like the typical candidate for a reversal down. The price action had moved up strongly in the first 10 minutes of trading after a strong premarket gap up with volume. At the magical 9:40 a.m. time (we will cover this magical time in more detail in the next chapter), I attempted to enter a short. Eleven seconds after entering the short at the best ask price, I was filled by someone else on Island purchasing those shares. ELCO moved down nicely from this level, with trades being executed at the bid and market makers chasing down the ask price. Some support was shown for ELCO at $11³/₈, the price started to move up, and as I had already shown myself not to be 100 percent on top of the game, I decided to exit and take my profit early, this time with a market SOES order. As it turned out, this rise was a continuation move down and I would have made more money holding my position. You never go broke by taking your profits in day trading, however. The intraday chart for ELCO is shown in Figure 5-6, which also shows the actual peak at 9:36 a.m.

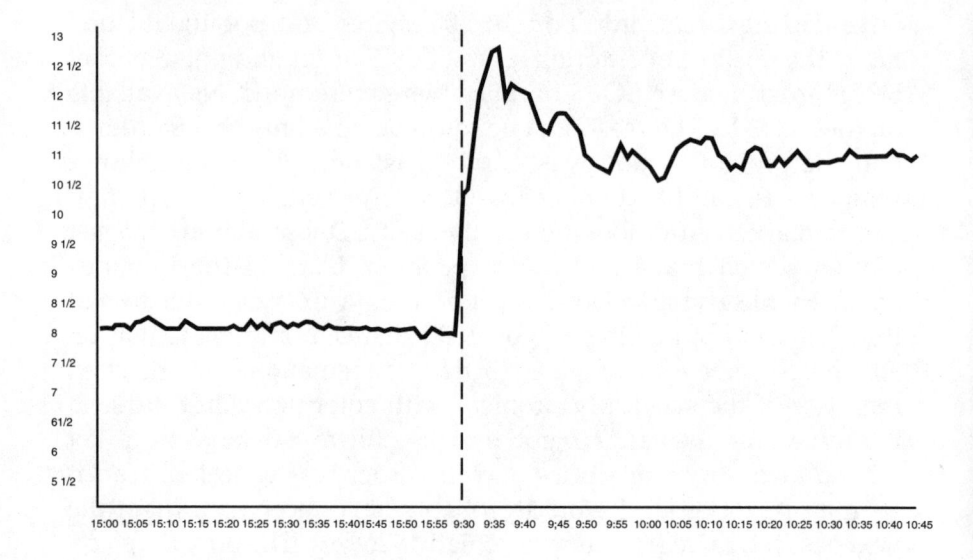

Figure 5-6. ELCO's intraday chart. (Used with permission of Townsend Analytics, Ltd.)

Some of the other premarket movers gave greater opportunities for profit, but at significantly greater risk. ADSP closed the previous day at $10 and moved straight up to $57 by 10:10 a.m. I tend to stay away from securities that move so wildly. You never know when the bottom will fall out of them, and when it does, you often have no way out. Had my broker had a borrow available on ADSP, I might have looked for the reversal, but that was not available, so I couldn't short it. Although the gains I made look insignificant when compared to moves like that in a security, you have to realize that going for those types of gains will expose your capital to tremendous risk. If you chase stocks that move like ADSP, you often get whipsawed trying to cap your losses. This means that you get in and out of the security as it gyrates and, on average, end up losing money, even if the stock moves up strongly. Yes, it is possible to catch them occasionally. I have done so a few times, but more often, I have seen stocks moving like that have thin levels (few market makers at each price on both the bid and ask side) and got caught with my pants down, so to speak. With a stock like that, it is easy for it to move $2 or $3 against you before you can react. ADSP was actually back to $18 during the day on Monday,

November 29, so practically all of those tremendous gains disappeared.

So, there you have two examples of getting shorts in the market. Both were obtained on Island. I waited for the security to start falling before I entered the short. Due to the uptick rule, I could not short by selling to the best bid when the bid has just ticked down, so in effect, I had to offer the stock at the best ask and hope somebody would take it. Due to the liquidity of Island, I was hit by other traders wanting to buy when I wanted to sell, so I got my fills. Net of commissions, I made over $500 in 15 minutes of trading, even though I did not make the most of the opportunities open to me. If I was offered that prior to the market opening, I would have taken it, so I counted myself lucky and spent the rest of that day researching, writing, and being with my family.

6
A Trading Week

In this chapter, we bring together many of the ideas presented earlier in the book and add the final pieces to the puzzle of assessing overall market direction. I cannot stress too strongly that the behavior of the individual security on the day you are trading is the most important thing. Assessment and tracking of the overall market can only help to place a bias on your search for opportunities. In the strongest market, some securities will go down, and in the weakest market, some will go up. Particularly in short-term day trading, paying attention to the individual security's behavior is by far the most important activity. The principle I follow is to look first for opportunities that lead me to take a position in harmony with the overall market direction. If none present themselves, however, I will take positions contrary to the overall market direction at that time if the opportunity is compelling enough.

Looking at the daily chart of market indexes can set your bias when looking for opportunities, but, as we shall see, if you can determine the direction of the market each day by reference to a one-minute tick chart of the Composite and net ticks figures, your best opportunities are realized by trading in harmony with the direction of those indicators.

Typically, the majority of my trading activity occurs in the 45 minutes before market open and the first hour of market trading. This is the time when the patterns discussed here repeat themselves most frequently and when the pace of trades is at its greatest, thus providing the most liquidity for our trades. It also helps by keeping the market makers honest with their quotes.

The most difficult thing about day trading is getting yourself in the position to trade when a security has just started to make its move. I find the most success when I concentrate my efforts on a few securities that are likely to behave according to one of the patterns I have presented and trade a security when it does. I do not anticipate a security behaving as I expect. That is a sure way to lose money when day trading. I only trade when I see evidence of pattern compliance.

For the rest of this chapter, we will progress through the various means for examining overall market strength and direction, then look at a typical trading week, including how to approach the market and which trades to make. I understand the criticism that even the worst trader can be profitable for a week, and that providing one week's worth of data is not a true test of any method. But I would challenge those same critics to try these methods themselves before applying their criticisms. In fact, the week presented in this book is not the best of weeks, nor is it the worst. I just happened to choose it when I was at the point of writing this chapter.

Assessing the Market Direction: Charting Methods

This section looks at chart patterns used in point-and-figure and candlestick charting. When assessing the overall strength of the market, I like to take input from several sources. The most important is reading the daily chart and analyzing trends, areas of support and resistance, and possibly moving averages. Supplementing these studies with point-and-figure and candlesticks is useful in confirming your opinions.

Candlesticks

The basics of real body and shadow description were covered in Chapter 1. It is the analysis of multicandlestick formations that yields the predictive qualities of this particular type of chart-reading. Over three centuries ago, rice-futures traders noticed the repetitive patterns in candlestick charts, which predicted future price movements in the commodity contracts traded. It should be noted that candlestick analysis is somewhat more sensitive than regular daily chart analysis in that it generates more signals. Given this profusion of signals, it is important to be aware of when those patterns appear in the trend so that more or less weight can be assigned to them in your analysis. The example from Chapter 1 holds true. If a candlestick reversal pattern appears at the end of an extended trend, you tend to believe it more than a reversal pattern that appears at the beginning of a new trend.

Patterns formed using multiple candlesticks tend to carry more weight than single candlestick patterns. We will begin with analysis of specific, well-known single-candlestick formations, which will become part of multicandlestick formations as we progress.

The "doji," as illustrated in Figure 6-1, is a warning signal. It signifies equal strength between those who are bullish and those who are bearish on a security (or whatever is the subject of the candlestick study). As such, the doji by itself can indicate an uncertain future, since neither the bulls nor the bears have the upper hand. When the doji appears in multicandlestick formations, it makes those formations more accurate in their prediction of future price action.

The single-candlestick patterns are typically indicators of reversals. There are two other single-candlestick formations of note, the "hanging man," and the "hammer." As with all single-event patterns, they are difficult to use and are only of real value when they appear in multicandlestick formations. The hanging man reverses

Figure 6-1. The classic doji, showing opening and closing price equal to each other.

Figure 6-2. (a) The hanging man; (b) the hammer.

an upward trend, whereas the hammer reverses a downward trend, as shown in Figure 6-2.

These are essentially the inverse of each other. The hanging man has more predictive quality when it is black, indicating a lower close, and the hammer has more predictive quality when it is white, indicating a higher close.

Two-candlestick patterns all consist of one candlestick of each color in the pattern and are most commonly reversal patterns. The second candlestick will be black if the pattern is predicting the end of an upward trend, and white if predicting the end of a downward trend. The first two that we will look at are variations on a theme and are illustrated as topping formations. The first pattern is known as "dark cloud cover," the concepts of which are extended to form a bearish engulfing line. Both are depicted in Figure 6-3.

In this figure, the candle on the left is the final white candle in the upward trend. The next candle initiates the first downward move, with the price closing lower than it opened. When the real body of the second candle extends down into the body of the first candle, the formation is considered dark cloud cover. When the second real body extends down lower than the close in the previous candle, it is known as a "bearish engulfment."

Figure 6-3. On the left, dark cloud cover. On the right, the second candlestick extends to form a bearish engulfment.

Figure 6-4. On the left, a bullish Hirami; on the right, a bearish one.

These two candle reversal patterns are complemented with continuation patterns, which are called *Hirami* patterns, and are shown in Figure 6-4.

These are considered weaker reversal patterns and therefore are taken to be a sign of a continuation. As you can see in this figure, the second candle has its real body within the range of the previous candle's real body. These patterns have more potency if the second candle is a doji rather than a candle with a real body.

The most common three-candle patterns to look for are the "morning star" and "evening star." The morning star occurs after a downward trend. The first element is a strong black candle, which indicates that most of the pessimism in the market is being expended, followed by two white candles, the second of which needs to make significant inroads into the real body of the first candle. The evening star is essentially the inverse. It starts with a strong white candle that indicates the bulls have bought all they can. The pattern is followed by two black candles, the second of which must extend well into the body of the first candle. Both of these patterns are shown in Figure 6-5.

Figure 6-5. On the left, the morning star; on the right, the evening star.

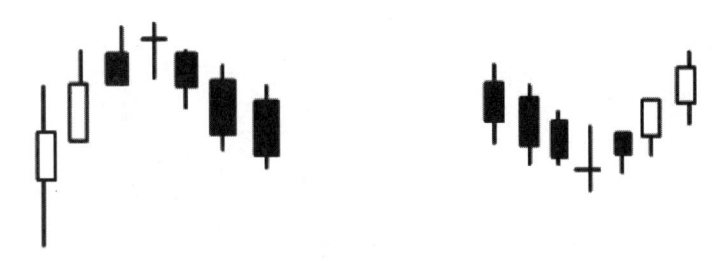

Figure 6-6. On the left, the tower top; on the right, the tower bottom.

There is one seven-candle pattern that is worth noting, the "tower" pattern. This pattern is shown in Figure 6-6, for the tower top and tower bottom. The elements of bulls and bears exchanging leadership are essentially the same as for the star patterns noted previously.

This can only be taken as an introduction to the subject of candlestick charting analysis. There are many good texts available should you wish to go further with your study of this subject. The important point to keep in mind when looking at candlestick charts is that the white candles show bulls having the upper hand, and black candles show bears having the last word. Should strength be shifting from one group to the other, it will show up first in a candlestick chart, which could change the bias for the type of positions you look for in your day-trading opportunities.

Point-and-Figure

The other charting method I use to assess the overall strength of the market is point-and-figure charting. The basics of point-and-figure were also covered in Chapter 1, but here we will look at reading these charts to get a feel for the overall market direction.

The first point-and-figure analysis you should be aware of is the use of trendlines, both the bullish support line and the bearish resistance line. These trendlines are not drawn the same way as they are on bar or line charts. The bullish support line is essentially a 45-degree line sloping upward from left to right, starting at the bottom of a recent low. This is illustrated by the line of plus signs in Figure 6-7.

The bearish resistance line is the inverse. It is a line sloping down from left to right, drawn from the top of a recent high on the

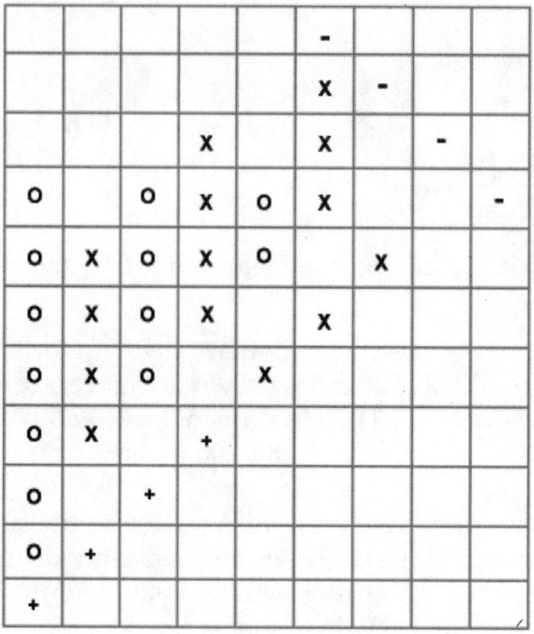

Figure 6-7. Bearish resistance and bullish support line on a point-and-figure chart.

point-and-figure chart. This line also slopes at a 45-degree angle. This is shown in Figure 6-7 as a line of minus signs. These lines make it simple to come to a general conclusion regarding the object of the study. If the price action is above the bullish support line, one looks to go long. If, however, that line is broken with a downward move in the price action, one looks for shorting opportunities while the price action is below the bearish resistance line.

Beyond these simple trendlines, there are patterns within the point-and-figure chart that are worth looking for. The most common are of two types, either breakouts of multiple tops or bottoms, or breakouts from triangle patterns.

The breakouts from a triple-top and a triple-bottom are shown in Figure 6-8.

These charts make it easier to spot breakouts from areas of price congestion, since they take out the time element inherent in a normal bar or line chart and focus purely on the price movement. Again, these patterns are easily interpreted: A market that has completed a bullish breakout of a triple-top suggests that longs

				X
X		X	O	X
X	O	X	O	X
X	O	X	O	X
X	O		O	X
X			O	

O	X			
O	X	O		
O	X	O	X	
O	X	O	X	O
O	X	O		O
				O

Figure 6-8. (a) Bullish breakout from a triple-top; (b) bearish breakout from a triple-bottom.

provide the best opportunity, whereas one that has just broken out from a triple-bottom suggests that shorts are the way to go. Triangles on point-and-figure charts are interpreted similarly to the way they are on line or bar charts. A triangle breakout is shown in Figure 6-9. The direction of the breakout will indicate whether longs or shorts are preferred. Obviously, a breakout to the upside suggests longs and a breakout to the downside suggests shorts.

I tend to look at candlestick and point-and-figure charts of the NASDAQ Composite and NASDAQ 100 indexes not more than twice per week to set my bias for whether I prefer longs or shorts as day trades.

X				
X	O			X
X	O	X		X
X	O	X	O	X
X	O	X	O	
X	O	X		
X	O			
X				

Figure 6-9. Bullish breakout from a triangle formation.

The VIX Index

Before continuing our discussion of overall market direction with noncharting methods, it is worth discussing the only piece of contrarian thinking I find valuable, the VIX index. Contrarian thinking can be a very dangerous thing when day trading. It is very unwise to try to be contrary to the majority when going long or short an individual security for an intraday move in that security. If you see a stock falling and all the market makers are lining up on the ask and leaving the bid, it is dangerous to buy the security. It is safer in this instance to wait for a change in market conditions and see some buying come into the market before taking a position.

VIX is the CBOE (Chicago Board Options Exchange) Volatility Index, which is a good indicator of the levels of fear and overconfidence in the market. The CBOE started VIX in 1993. It is calculated by taking a weighted average of the implied volatilities of eight OEX calls and puts with an average time to maturity of 30 days. Before going into how this index is used, it is worth a short explanation of the terms used.

Volatility is a percentage measure of price change, without regard to its direction. As volatility is a percentage measure, the absolute size of price movement has no effect on the value of volatility. For example, a move from 50 to 52 is a 4 percent change and is equivalent in volatility terms to a move from 100 to 104, or for that matter, from 100 to 96. Volatility can be calculated on a historical basis, on some expected value, or on the aforementioned implied volatility, which is a value based on the current price of an option. If you are unfamiliar with derivatives, think of implied volatility as a ratio that is equivalent to price-earnings ratios in the equity markets. It is a way of comparing different options at different price levels on the same basis.

It is not important to understand in detail what implied volatility is, or how to choose the eight contracts used to calculate the VIX index. What is important when interpreting the VIX chart is relating what the VIX tells you to the trend and pattern formations in the market indexes. It is also important to know how other market participants use this chart.

Think of the VIX as indicating the level of fear in the market. One of the few rules that always holds true is that the greatest level of fear in the market occurs within a few days of a market bottom.

Conversely, when the level of confidence in the market is at its peak, so, invariably, is the market. If you print out a chart of the VIX, it looks like an oscillator that varies between the value of 20 and 30. This is the normal range. At times of overconfidence, the value dips below 20, and at times of greatest fear it spikes above 30. I would not suggest that just because the VIX jumps over 30 that you call a market bottom and start to look exclusively for opportunities to buy securities. What I do suggest is that if you see the VIX rise above 30, look to see if there are any confirmations of a bottom in the market action of the NASDAQ Composite. If you see a high VIX level at the same time that the daily chart of the Composite has made a higher low (has failed to make a new low in its current downtrend), you should start thinking that the bottom in the current market action has occurred. If the Composite is still making new lows, it does not matter how high the VIX goes. It means the bottom has not been reached.

While we are looking at the operation of VIX at a market bottom, it is worth considering the effect of margin clerks at this time as well. As we know, most trading accounts are margined, particularly those that are actively traded. Margin allows the account holder to buy $100,000 worth of securities with $50,000, or $50,000 of securities with $25,000 by using a margin level of 50 percent, the most that is normally available. If someone were to do that, they would have used all the margin available to them. If the securities bought on margin decline in value, the overall account becomes more than 50 percent margined, meaning that the account holder still owes $50,000 to the broker, but that $50,000 is now more than 50 percent of the value of the account. If the decline is sharp and the $50,000 borrowed from the broker comes to make up 60 percent of the account value, the broker will typically start to monitor the account very closely. Should the level of that borrowed money come to represent 70 percent of the account value, the broker might force the account holder to sell some securities and pay back some of the $50,000 to bring the level of debt in the account back to 50 percent. The exact level of equity in the account at which the broker forces the hand of the account holder varies from firm to firm and is set by the broker's house rules.

It is the job of margin clerks to monitor the level of margin in accounts. When the margin clerk decides action is necessary, he or she will typically call the account holder and give that person until 2 p.m. that day, or thereabouts, to rectify the situation. The account holder can either deposit more cash to pay off the debt, or can sell securities. When there is no new cash placed in the account and the account holder has not sold any securities, the margin clerk can issue what is termed a *maintenance call* and sell whatever he likes in the client's account to reduce the debt to an acceptable level.

I explain this in such detail at this point because watching market action, including maintenance calls, in the afternoon during a market decline gives good information about how ready the market is to hit its low point and start heading up again. While the decline is still in effect, market selloffs can be seen in the afternoon as margin clerks execute maintenance calls. When afternoon selloffs no longer appear in the market action, it is a sign that all of the forced selling has taken place and the fear in the market has been realized by margin clerks forcing customers to take losses.

Analyzing this type of market behavior complements analysis of the VIX index. When a decline in the NASDAQ Composite occurs, you can call a turn to the upside with a high degree of confidence if the VIX is well above 30, afternoon selloffs are no longer occurring, and the market fails to make a new low. This combination of events tends to indicate the start of a new upward trend. The final piece of evidence to convince you of a market turning to the upside would be to see volume confirm the upward price action by increasing when the market moves higher and decreasing when the market pulls back.

When looking at a market top, the converse is true regarding failure of the NASDAQ to make a new high and the VIX being below 20. However, margin clerks do not have the same sort of impact on market action at tops as they do at bottoms.

Assessing the Market Direction: Noncharting Methods

The nonchart indicators I look at on a weekly basis are as follows:

- The NASDAQ bullish percentage
- Percentage of NASDAQ stocks trading above their 10-week moving averages
- The hi-lo index

The NASDAQ Bullish Percentage

Let us first look at the NASDAQ bullish percentage. This is an indicator that crosses the boundary between charting and non-charting indicators. The bullish percentage figure is simply the percentage of NASDAQ stocks that are on a point-and-figure buy signal. In this case, the buy signal is defined as a security whose point-and-figure chart is in a column of Xs that has exceeded the level of the previous column of Xs. Once you have found the value for the bullish percentage, you turn to a point-and-figure chart of the bullish percentage figure itself to determine what your market posture will be. This indicator was originally designed for the NYSE by A. W. Cohen of Chartcraft, and was later refined by a Mr. Earl Blumenthal by breaking things down into six categories:

- Bull alert
- Bull confirmed
- Bull correction
- Bear alert
- Bear confirmed
- Bear correction

The *bull alert* state occurs when the point-and-figure for the bullish percentage chart has reversed from a column of 0s to a column of Xs, with its value below 30 percent. This is an alert to start looking for long opportunities, primarily securities that have reached an area of significant support on the bar or line chart, or those resting on the bullish support line on the point-and-figure.

The *bull confirmed* state is an extension of the bull alert state, as its name would suggest. This is when the point-and-figure chart for the bullish percentage is in a column of Xs and has exceeded the high set by the previous column of Xs. This condition gives a strong signal to look for longs, provided it occurs below the 70 percent value in the bullish percentage figure.

The *bull correction* state has the bullish percentage point-and-figure chart in a column of 0s and reversing down at a level that is below the 70 percent value. This is a warning to be cautious when taking long positions and to get out earlier, rather than later. This does not signal the end of the bull market, but it signals that until the bull run resumes, more caution is called for when entering long positions.

The *bear alert* state looks similar to the bull correction state. With the point-and-figure chart in a column of 0s, a bear alert is defined as the column of 0s taking the chart from above to below the 70 percent line. When this occurs, you need to be cautious when assessing both long and short opportunities. It signals a potential change in the direction of the market.

The *bear confirmed* state occurs when the point-and-figure chart for bullish percentage is in a column of 0s and drops below the low of the previous column of 0s. Anytime this occurs, you should be cautious about longs. If this happens when the value of the bullish percentage is at or near 70 percent, you should just be thinking shorts.

The *bear correction* state is typically a temporary pullback in the downward trend. This is similar to the bull alert in that the point-and-figure chart is reversing from a column of 0s into a column of Xs, but it occurs when the value of the bullish percentage index is above the 30 percent line.

The Percentage of NASDAQ Stocks Trading Above Their 10-Week Moving Averages

This is also a good indicator of the general health of the market. It is usually a better short-term indicator than the bullish percentage state, which changes relatively infrequently. As its name suggests, this indicator just calculates the percentage of stocks on the NASDAQ that are trading above their 10-week moving average figures. If this indicator reverses down to a level below the 70 percent figure from a level that was above 70 percent, the outlook is negative and shorts are preferred. If, however, the value starts off below 30 percent and moves above 30 percent, the outlook is favorable for longs. Most commonly, you look for agreement between the bullish percentage reading and the percentage of NASDAQ stocks above their 10-week moving averages to provide the strongest signal.

The Hi-Lo Index

The hi-lo index is calculated by taking the number of NASDAQ securities reaching new highs and dividing it by the number of securities reaching new lows for each day. The resulting figure is interpreted the same way as the previous indicator. A reversal from above to below the 70 percent mark is negative, and a reversal from below to above the 30 percent level is positive.

When using these indicators, remember to not get too caught up in analyzing them on a daily basis. As a day trader, you need to be most concerned with what is happening that day. You increase your chances, however, when you are trading in harmony with the overall market direction. As stated previously, these indicators are only worth tracking once or so a week, to keep the appropriate bias in your search for opportunities. The result this analysis should have is that if you see equally attractive opportunities to go short or long, you choose the one that is in harmony with the market's direction at that point.

Some Other Nonchart Indicators

If I am considering trading a set of stocks in the post-open Phase 2 market, I will also consider the relative strength of the sector of the stocks I am tracking, as well as the relative strength of the stocks themselves.

An example of how to use relative strength is as follows. Suppose your overall market analysis tells you we are in a bull market. You would first look for sectors that are gaining in relative strength compared to the overall market. Then you look for securities within that sector that are gaining in relative strength compared to the sector itself. The aim is to generate a list of the strongest stocks from the strongest sector. Once you have this list, you look for one of the selected securities to exhibit a sustainable upward trend on the one-minute tick chart, buy it, and hold it until the upward trend gives a signal (break of trendline, failure to make new high, etc.). Of course, the reverse is true if the market is head-

Chapter 6

ing down. You then look for the weakest stocks in the weakest sectors for shorting opportunities.

If you are interested in this indicator, the calculations are performed by computer and are available from many sources. As an example of how it works, consider a theoretical sector and look at its relative strength compared to its index. Suppose the security is trading at $50 and the index of the sector of which it is a part is trading at 500. Dividing the stock price by the index value gives us a value of 0.1. If, the next day, the security declines to $49 and the index declines to 450, the new relative strength figure is 0.109, rounded to 0.11. Even though both instruments have declined, the relative strength of the security has increased. When you get a series of these values, you can plot them on a regular chart or a point-and-figure chart, depending on your preference, and look for breakouts—a high that is higher than a previous high or a low that is lower than a previous low. Although initially attracted to this indicator, I seldom use it these days. It tends to perform better as a long-term indicator.

Finally, there are two indicators that I look at as the day progresses to get a feel for how the market is trading that day. First is a one-minute tick chart of the NASDAQ Composite. Second is a one-minute tick chart of the net ticks figure. The NASDAQ Composite should be familiar to you. It is the index of all securities on the NASDAQ exchange. When I can, I trade opportunities that are in harmony with the direction of the Composite that day. The same is true of the net ticks value. This indicator shows the net number of securities that are on an uptick, i.e., the number of securities that have a bid price higher than the previous bid price. This is a broad market indicator. When positive, it can indicate widespread buying in the market.

In all of this, assessment of the overall market must only be viewed as secondary to what is happening on that day in the actual securities you are considering trading. Do not get too caught up in doing excessive analysis of the overall market. It will only confuse your trading decisions. If you do wish to track the market by using the indicators discussed above, visit either www.dorseywright.com or www.chartcraft.com, both of which offer tracking of these and other indicators.

Daily Premarket Preparation

My day starts at around 8:45 a.m., when I establish a connection to the Internet and run a sort program to determine which stocks are moving that day. This is an analysis of the premarket bids and asks posted by market makers and ECNs prior to trading. It is worth examining what I am actually looking for in this, first of all for securities with rising bids in the premarket.

In this instance, in the premarket, I am looking for securities whose bid prices are at least $1 above the closing bid of yesterday's trading. In the premarket, market makers are not obliged to trade, so the only way they can entice potential sellers to sell to them is to offer them a bid price that is attractive enough. In the premarket, you will typically see ask prices untouched by the market makers until close to market open. The reason for this is that for a rising security, the market makers are not interested in selling and would not transact at the advertised ask if they were preferenced by an ECN. For a falling security, the market makers will lower the ask price and leave the bid alone until close to market open. The reason is that the market makers want to offload the depreciating security, and the only way to do that outside mandatory trading hours is to offer a price low enough to attract value buyers. When stocks move like this in the premarket, you see lots of backwardation, in which the bid price is higher than the ask. On the face of it, this presents an arbitrage opportunity, with the market willing to pay a higher price than it is asking. This is, not the case, of course, because no market makers have to execute at the posted prices before the market opens.

On the sorting software I use,* I enter the following criteria to identify gap-up candidates:

Symbol=<ALL>,Last Price Between (5,100),Vol>10,000, Bid>0, Exchange=NAS, Pre-Mkt Gap Up>1

This tells the software to look for all securities listed on the NASDAQ exchange with prices between $5 and $100, bid prices $1

---

*If you are looking for sorting software, you can visit the www.mbtrading.com Web site to see available examples.

or more higher than yesterday's closing price, and volume in excess of 10,000 shares. The bid-greater-than-zero entry is there to eliminate bad data. The search criteria for securities gapping down is the same except for the last entry, which is changed to Pre-Mkt Gap Dn<-1. This looks for securities whose ask prices are more than $1 lower than yesterday's closing price.

Having the capability to search for securities in premarket conditions is absolutely essential to trading the opening period. There are some systems that only allow searching for most up and most down once the market has opened. This is of no value to a day trader wanting to trade the opening period. There is simply too much that needs to be done before you are able to safely trade a security during the open period. Before you trade the open, you need to determine for each security whether a short is available and what the tier size is. You then assess the daily chart and make a trading decision to catch the first move, all of which is too much to accomplish in a couple of minutes.

Once I have determined what is up and what is down (normally by 9:00-9:15 a.m.), I look to see which securities are trading with sufficient volume. Sufficient means different things for different securities. I want to see trading activity that is above the average for that security. This is difficult to assess in the premarket, so I look for something that is trading over 50,000 shares premarket. Once the market opens, I want any candidates I am looking to trade to have at least one trade per second executed. Much slower than that is indicative of a security for which you may not be able to close a position very easily. The easiest way to assess this on the Real Tick™ system is to view the dynamic time-of-sales screen that is attached to the Level II window after market open. Let's go back to the premarket preparation, though. Once I have found the upward and downward movers, I visit the NASDAQ trader Web site and determine the tier size for all the securities. The securities whose tier sizes are 500 or 1000 and whose price allows my margin to buy that many, receive the most attention from me.

The next thing I do is go to my broker's Web site and determine which of the securities are borrowable, which allows me to short them should I desire to.

Finally, I look at a daily chart of all the candidates and see which premarket movers have reached a level of support if gapping down, or resistance if gapping up. Having assessed the daily chart of my candidates, I write down the play I expect to make should the security's price action behave as I expect. If the security does not behave as expected, I strike it from my list and move on, or at least leave it alone to see if it will behave according to one of the patterns later in the day (by later, I mean within about 30 minutes).

The next thing is to make sure that all candidate securities are entered in the market-minder window, so that when I do decide to trade, I can do so purely by mouse clicks. I also want to make sure I have a window set up to display the one-minute tick chart of each security I am interested in. I use this to determine whether trends are in effect, or are broken. Once I have taken a position, I only look at the Level II screen (with attached dynamic time-of-sales window) and one-minute tick chart of that security—plus some broad market indicators, like the net ticks figure and NASDAQ Composite index—to get a feel for the overall market direction. If, for example, I am long in a security and I start to see some weakness, as indicated by slowing trades and less market maker support at the bid, there may be times when I will hold the position, whereas my most normal action would be to sell. For me to hold, I have to have seen over a 3/4 point appreciation, which gives me room to get out should the weakness turn into a reversal. Also, the Composite and net ticks need to continue to move up strongly. If these conditions exist, holding a position through some weakness can be profitable. Of course, it all depends on your risk tolerance. If you consistently see that you are picking stocks that go through some weakness only to continue upward one play is to sell half your position to protect profits and still have some exposure to further potential gain.

The last—and a very important—thing to do is after you have done your preparation, to read your own set of trading rules prior to any trading. This is a daily activity and is meant to improve your chances of trading in a disciplined manner. In Chapter 7, I will share my personal set of daily trading rules. However, each trader's rules should be drawn from his or her own experience, from analyzing winning and losing trades and seeing the mistakes he or she is prone to. Another goal of reading your rules is to ensure that you have the mindset for seeking opportunities when stocks move the way you expect them to, rather than rushing to get in on a stock without having done the preparation to trade it properly. In addition, the rules are intended to keep emotions like greed and fear out of your trading decisions as much as possible. When we look at a week's worth of trading data later in this chapter, we will see that the premarket analysis provides several candidates for trading. Not all of them follow the patterns that I trade. Some will, however, and it is those that I trade. The most important, and most difficult, rule to live by is to only trade opportunities that the market presents to you, rather than trying to seek out ones that do not exist. This may sound trivial to those with little or no day-trading experience, but those who have traded for a year or more will know this tendency.

Before we move on to look at the range of market open patterns I look to trade, we should cement these concepts with a look at one day's premarket activity and the resulting trade. The day in question is December 1, 1999, and my trade report from that day is given below.

```
Terra Nova Trading, LLC DAILY TRADE LIST Page 1
STCS 4.4.65 (SWST) 12/1/99 19:16:22

Account: XXXXXXXX-YYYY
                                    Unit       Total
Tick   Typ  Symbol  B/S    Shares   Price      Price      System  Time   By
3286   2    TECD    Buy    1000     21 1/4     -21,250    SOES    09:37: MONT
3999   2    TECD    Sell   1000     21 15/16   21,937.5   ISLD    09:40: ISLD
5393   3    ARDT    Shor   100      31 7/8     3,187.50   SOES    09:46: NITE
5612   3    ARDT    Buy    100      31 1/2     -3,150.0   ISLD    09:47: ISLD

Total Gain         725
Commission         91.80
Total Net Gain     633.20
```

My search for premarket movers with volume yielded the following candidates.

NETR

Was up in the premarket; SOES tier size C; in a downward trend and was not shortable via my broker. The play I would choose for this security would be a short once the early buying subsided. Since it was not shortable, however, and I could only trade 200 shares of it with confidence (due to the tier size), I passed on this one. As it turned out, this security followed the pattern of rising in the first 10 minutes of market activity and then falling off sharply. Its price action during the day made it a good shorting candidate, but the tier size and lack of short facility discounted it.

ASFD

I discounted this one since, again, it was a premarket gainer I could not short because my broker did not have a borrow available on it. Also, the tier size was C.

ARDT

This security had been progressing in an upward trend within a well-defined channel, and the premarket upward move had brought it to the resistance line at the upper part of the channel. With upward trend, the upper line of the channel is the most likely to be broken, so I monitored this security closely and decided that if I did take a position, it would be with plenty of caution.

My search found two more gap-up securities, ESAT and WBVN, which I discounted because both looked too strong to short on their daily charts.

As this was generally a positive, upbeat premarket, there were few securities declining in value enough to get my interest. I did find two, however.

VONE

One look at this daily chart told me all I needed to know about VONE. It had experienced a wild spike up in the previous two days' trading; therefore, I did not want to touch it. Securities that experience these wild spikes are too unpredictable for day trading.

TECD

This looked like a gem. The daily chart showed a downward trend that appeared to have reversed with an inverse head and shoulders, and the premarket gap down, taking the stock to strong levels of support. TECD also had a tier size of A and was within my price range to buy 1000 shares. I would look to go long this security when the Level II screen indicated excess demand.

As it turned out, the system I use had difficulty getting all order routes available prior to market open. Since I had opened my trading system prior to market open, access to SOES was not there at 9:30 a.m. When I saw the market open, TECD started to move up almost instantly, so I tried to purchase on the order routes available to me, ARCA and ISLD. I could not get a fill on either, so I had to restart my system in order to get SOES access.

Once I had gotten SOES access back, I went long at $21 1/4$ at 9:37 a.m. TECD had already moved up over \$1, so I was looking to get out at the first sign of weakness, which came at \$22, and I closed my position at $21 15/16$ at 9:40 a.m. As it turned out, this was a continuation pullback, and TECD carried on to over \$23. If I had taken a long position earlier in the day, I may have held on to see if it was a continuation, but as it was, the right thing to do was to take the available profit.

The Long and Short of It

ARDT also looked to be moving down nicely, but as you can see from the trade report, I only got a short of 100 shares at my target price, even though I tried to execute for 1000. ARDT did move down nearly \$2 in the next half hour, but I missed the opportunity to get in at a price level I was comfortable with. Missing this trade motivated me to get out early and close my trading system, happy with the profits I made that day. In addition, my overall market assessment told me the market was in a strong move upward and that I should be careful of shorts. Having made profits on a long position and seeing the market move from heavy Phase 1 trading to slower Phase 2 trading meant it was time to leave with my profits, rather than trade them away.

Market Open Patterns to Look For

This is the crux of what trading the open is all about. We are looking for securities that are up in the premarket and are likely to fall, or securities that are down in the premarket and likely to rise. As discussed in the previous section, I use a sort program that lists all these premarket movers in order of percentage change. Here, we will look both at securities that have gained in the premarket and those that have lost value in the premarket. First, those that have lost.

What we are looking for is a security that, prior to today, was in a sustainable upward trend, and for which today's premarket price action brought the price down to the trendline support. This was exactly the case with the TECD that we examined in the previous section. For securities that have gained in the premarket, the following chart patterns are the most likely. Now those that gain.

In Figure 6-10, a security has moved up in the premarket and has continued up after market open. If the security is to reverse

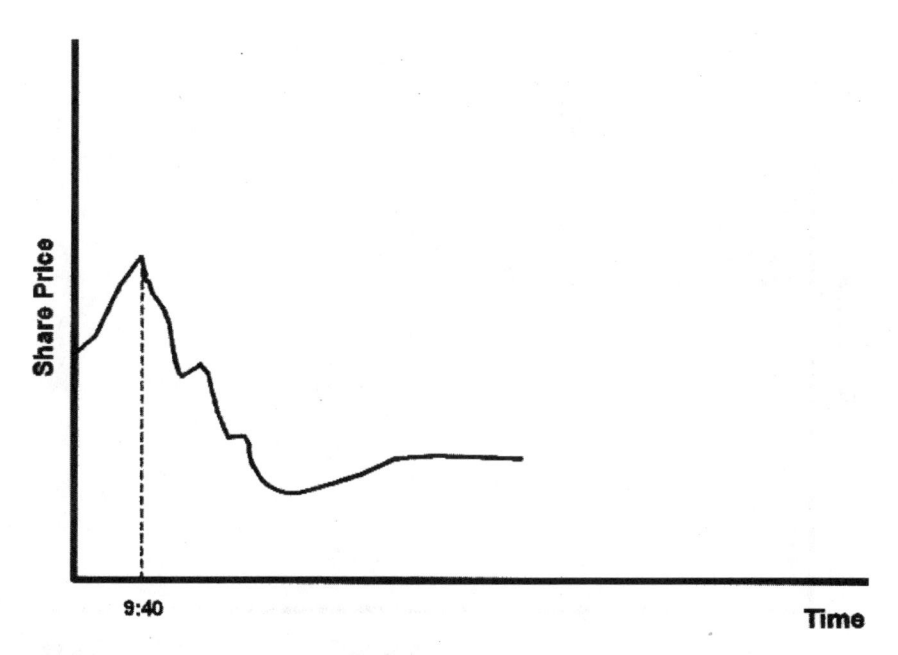

Figure 6-10. A security that has moved up in the premarket and continued up after market open.

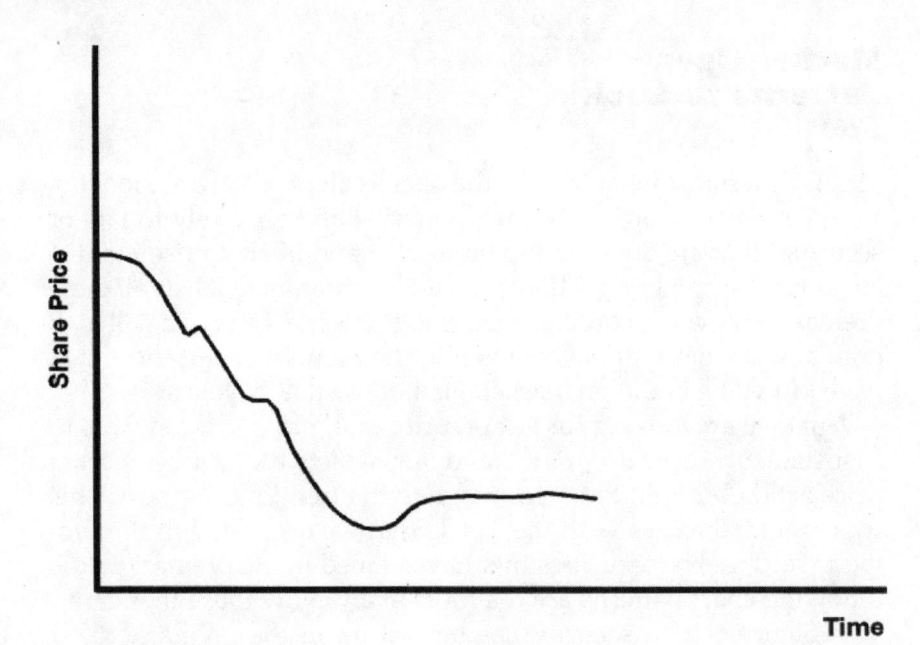

Figure 6-11. Up in the premarket, with a reversal down soon after open.

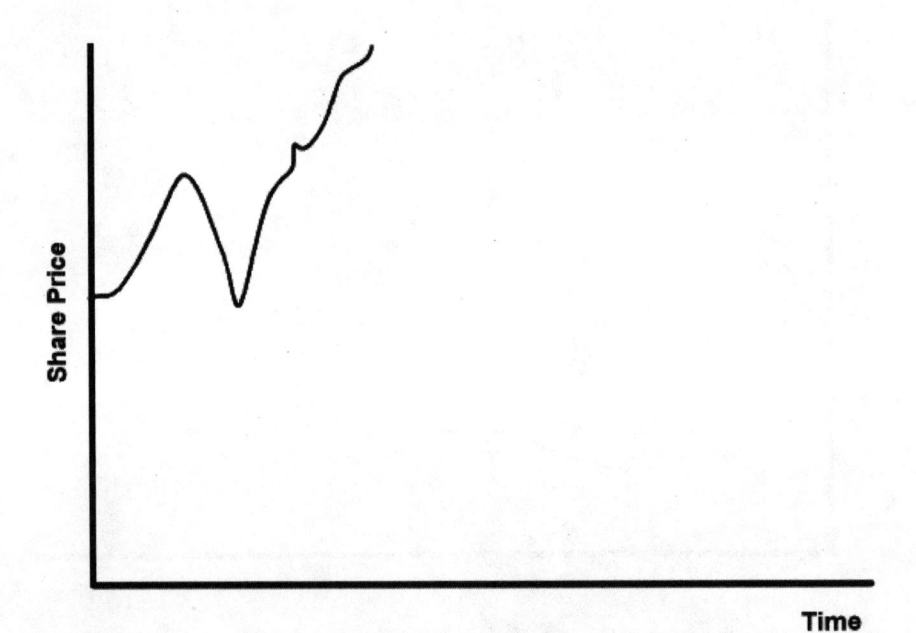

Figure 6-12. Up premarket, reversal down, and a second reversal up.

Figure 6-13. Up premarket, a continuation pattern, then up again—a nightmare to trade.

down, the most common time is at or around 9:40 a.m., although this is by no means fixed. Currently, reversals are tending to happen earlier in the trading day. The second option is Figure 6-11.

Here the security reverses down quite soon after market open. For a security to behave this way, it is most usual for the overall market to be heading downward from the market open.

Figure 6-12 is a pattern that became more common during the bull run in NASDAQ securities that gained momentum during 1999. The key movement is that after the security has reversed down, it regains positive momentum when the price has declined to the opening value.

Figure 6-13 shows the worst of all situations for a security that has gained significantly in the premarket. Initially, the price action moves up, looking like it is peaking, but it is actually generating a continuation pattern and moves up again. This tends to occur on days when the market as a whole is moving up strongly, the security in question is in a strong upward trend, and the premarket gap up has taken the security through an area of resistance. This illustrates the importance of understanding the implications of the price action in the daily chart.

There are other methodologies for trading the market open period that assess the value of the news stories coming out and drive the movement of the price action. This has not led me to consistently correct assessments. Virtually the same news story that comes out one day on a security can have a completely different effect on another security a few days later. I typically do not bother with reading the news stories that come out on these securities. The premarket movement and postmarket price action tell me all I need to know.

For securities that have fallen during premarket trading, the patterns are the reverse of those I have given for securities moving up in price. The most common patterns are for the security either to continue to fall in price for a short time after market open, then climb, or to climb from the open immediately.

The goal is to trade the first move down for a gap-up security and the first move up for the gap-down security. I will only trade a security when I see evidence of the following two situations occur: (1) demand for a gap-down security, as displayed by market makers lining up at the best bid and increasing the best bid at every opportunity, accompanied by trades going off at the best ask price or better; (2) excess supply of a gap-up security, as displayed by market makers lining up on the best ask, trades going off at the best bid, and market makers moving away from the best bid price. Once I have taken a position, the tick chart and Level II screen get all my attention.

Some traders like to use oscillators as a confirmational tool during this period of trading. This is okay if you wish, but the oscillator will not tell you anything more than the premarket move and postmarket open price action tell you. Taking the example of a gap-down security, the fact that the security has gapped down will cause the oscillator to move into oversold territory (assuming you have an oscillator that spans yesterday's and today's price action). In the case that the security moves up in price immediately after market open, the oscillator cannot provide any advance notice. Using an oscillator can provide comfort for those who like oscillators, but it gives no real added value for this case. An oscillator might be of use when you are looking to liquidate a position taken on the early reversal of a security. If the price action is showing some weakness and you want to assess whether this is a pullback, or indeed the end of this move, an oscillator can sometimes give an indication, although it is by no means infallible. If the oscillator has not yet reached the overbought or oversold level (depending on whether you are holding a long or short), you may continue to hold in the belief that the oscillator will reach one of those levels before the existing move expires. This is not a guaranteed thing by any means. Reading the Level II screen and watching the overall market indicators is just as likely to tell you whether or not the initial move is over.

Let's now focus on the classic daily chart pattern to look for when trading gap-up and gap-down securities.

The ideal market situation for trading a security that has gapped up is for lots of other leading securities on the NASDAQ to be gapping up slightly, which gives the Composite index room to start falling soon after market open. The net tick figure will start to decline and you will be trading a gap-up security whose daily chart is similar to that shown in Figure 6-14. The security is in a confirmed downward trend and has gapped up to resistance.

The converse is true for the gap-down security. For gap-downers, it is preferable to see a slightly negative opening, with the overall market in an upward trend and the net tick figure rising. With daily chart evidence like that shown in Figure 6-15, where

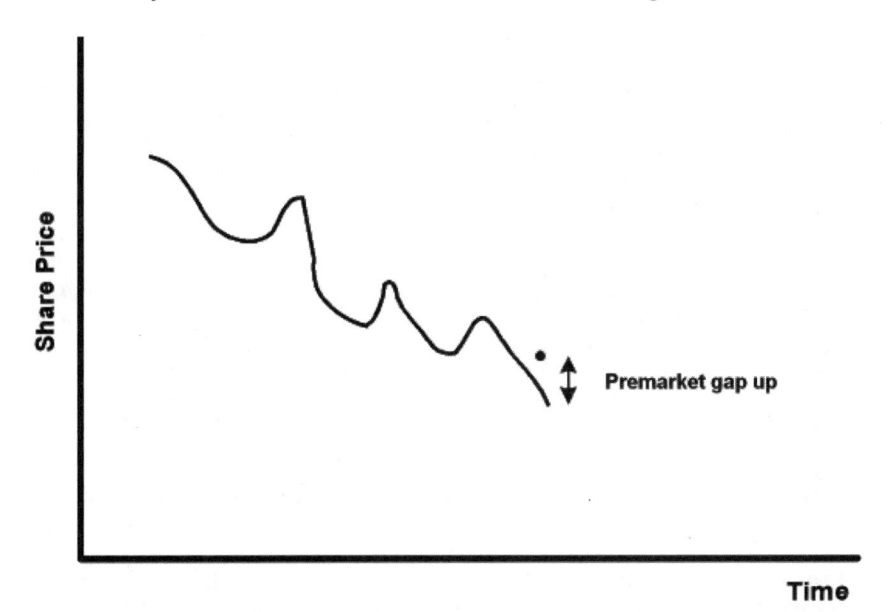

Figure 6-14. Ideal daily chart for a gap-up security.

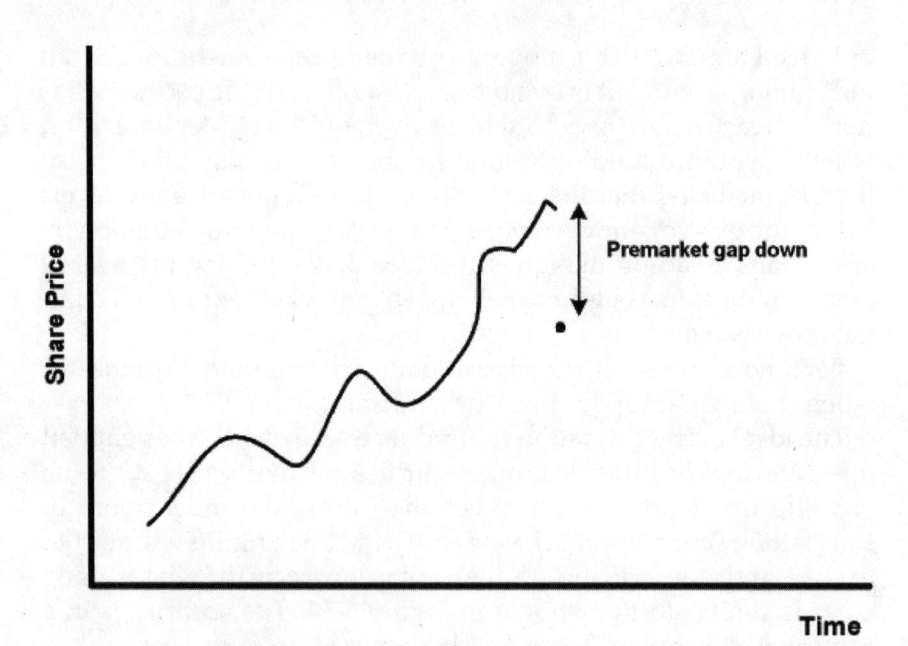

Figure 6-15. An ideal chart for long position opportunities.

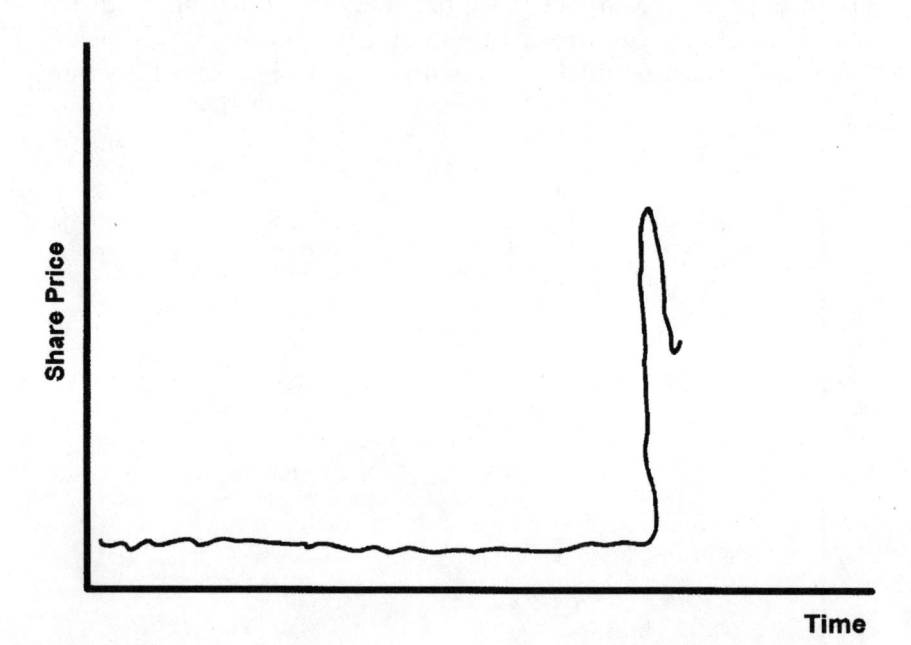

Figure 6-16. A daily chart pattern to avoid when trading gapping securities.

the security is in a confirmed upward trend and has gapped down to support levels, you should be comfortable seeking long position opportunities.

These patterns will hold true for most, and probably the majority of days. If you experience a day in which none of these patterns hold and the market is not trending, the best thing to do is take the day off and wait for the opportunities to return.

There are also some daily chart patterns to be aware of that should direct you *away from* trading the security, no matter how appealing the premarket percentage moves in price and volume. If you see a daily chart for a security of interest that looks anything like Figure 6-16, do not trade it, no matter what the direction of the premarket gap.

The large spike we see in this daily chart comes out of a trendless security and indicates wild speculation. With securities like this, there are generally wide spreads, thin levels, and rapid movement, often blocking the day trader from exiting positions at a favorable price when required. It is possible to make spectacular gains trading these types of securities, but the risk of loss is just as great. My whole approach is to take regular, small, and low-risk gains, rather than looking for the wild-swing home-run trades.

The final pattern I look for, which really is as a backup if no opportunities arise that match my preferred patterns, is to glance at the previous day's gappers and see if there are any tradable moves in those securities. The goal of trading the previous day's gappers is to look for moves in the same direction you would have traded the first day. For example, if a security loses 20 percent in the premarket one day and made nice tradable gains from the open on the day of that loss, you look to go long to profit from the gap. The same is true of the second-day trade. If the gapper from yesterday is experiencing heavy premarket volume today, it indicates that yesterday's price action has attracted renewed interest in the security, so it may be worth trading again. Whatever the direction of the premarket move, you look to trade only in the direction you would have traded on the gapper's first day. In the example given above, if the security lost 20 percent or so yesterday, you look for a move upward today, regardless of the direction of the premarket action, or even the price action immediately after the open. In this case, if the price action moves upward immediately after market open, you would look to go long. If, however, the price action moves down, you would look for a reversal upward before taking a position. If these moves are not supported by market maker positioning on the Level II screen (market makers repeatedly lining up on the best bid available and not refreshing ask prices) and trades going off at the best ask price, do not trade the move upward.

Generically, the methods described here can be called *trading against the gap*. This has been the subject of some study by MBA students at Harvard Business School and has resulted in articles presented in *Technical Analysis of Stocks and Commodities* magazine (which can be viewed online at www.traders.com). One student looked at the constituents of the Dow and researched how effective trading against gaps was when holding the position for different numbers of days. Statistically, it was found that trading against the gap for Dow securities yielded positive gains.

I advise against the individual day trader trading any method blindly. You need to be more selective. Trading is an art, more than a science, and I do not support the concept of black box trading systems that tell you when to take positions and when to exit. The reason I mention this is that if trading against the gap in this blind fashion with Dow securities (predominantly NYSE) is profitable, think how much safer it is to trade this way when analyzing the extra information available on NASDAQ securities and choosing which ones you will look to trade based on their existing trends.

I would not have expected the trading that the MBA student's article studied to have been successful, but it was, which just adds to the validity of looking for opportunities to trade against the gap.

Trading the Post-Open Periods

I tend to trade the post-open periods far less frequently than when I first started day trading. Now, my goals are to start premarket preparation at about 8:45 a.m. and be finished trading by 10:00 a.m. EST. With $20,000 capital, I would look to get between $500 and $1000 per day when I win, and to keep losses minimal, less than $200, when I don't. Trading the market open period gives plenty of opportunity to make between $50,000 and $100,000 per year. The reason I trade less frequently during the post-open periods is that I am not as motivated to do so any more. The gains are harder to come by and slower to materialize. Certainly it is possible to add to your daily profits by trading post-open periods. You need a very high tolerance for stress. If you are driven and highly motivated to make the most of every opportunity, you may be able to keep the discipline necessary for trading throughout the day. It is no longer a desire of mine but we will discuss it anyway.

Trading the post-open periods requires as much discipline as trading the market open, but it is discipline of a different kind. Here, you are looking for sustainable trends. The discipline you need is to not enter a trend when it is reaching a peak in the zigzag upward motion but to wait until the price has pulled back to the trendline. Should the stock take off and not return to the trendline for the rest of the day, you have missed that opportunity, so just move on. It is rarely wise to chase a security once it has lifted away from its trendline. Trading securities in the post-open requires you to analyze the overall market, choose a sector to operate in, and then find an individual security to trade. The concept is that you look for a sector that is heading in the same direction as the overall market, preferably the sector that is driving the market at that time. Then, within that sector, you look for the securities that are driving the sector. For upward-moving sectors, that will be the strongest stocks making the greatest percentage gains. For declining sectors, the weakest are driving the decline. Clearly, this is a different type of analysis than that used for the market open, and it will yield a different set of securities to trade. For each of these cases, your goal is to enter on a pullback within the trend and exit when the trend is still moving in your favor.

For the post-open period, you can either choose to move sectors as the market shifts, or you can stick with one sector and follow its oscillations and changing leadership. In either case, what you are doing is putting together a plan for how you expect a small basket of securities to behave. This is the only similarity between trading the open and the post-open periods. For both periods, you must have your basket of securities and an expectation for how you anticipate them to behave. Of course, not all the securities will behave as you expect, but you only have to trade the ones that do, and it requires discipline to stick to that.

A Sample Trading Week

Monday

Our sample trading week begins on Monday, December 6, 1999. This week was chosen simply because this was the week I was trading when I reached this part of writing the book. You can see that all the examples of trades in previous chapters have led in a roughly chronological order up to this point. It is rare these days that I trade every day of a week. What I choose to do with my time does not accommodate that. However, I cleared the mornings for this particular week so I could trade during the period that is most comfortable for me. I am showing five consecutive days because usually, during any five trading days, you will see a mixture of market environments for day trades, some in which shorting is more appropriate, and others where you look to go long. In addition, it is very unlikely that I will trade perfectly for five days in a row. Something will go wrong, either in my analysis, my concentration, or my technology. This is a function of day trading over the Internet. Day trading requires quick decision making, and the Internet can be an unreliable medium.

Choosing a week to record and display for all to see is a somewhat daunting task. Recording decisions and market conditions for inclusion in this text added an extra dimension of complexity to the trading process. Incidentally, independent verification of the fact that these trades took place is available at www.mbtrading.com/r/lewis.asp. This shows my trading account activity for the week, verifying that the gains I claim are real and that I only executed the trades I claim to have and am not hiding any losses.

The first task is to assess the overall market condition. The NASDAQ market is in a strong bull phase, with no clear sign from any form of analysis that the end is near just yet. Of course, it only takes one key reversal day to indicate weakness in the trend, but that has not happened yet. My preference, then, will be to take longs where possible and only take shorts should there be no long candidates moving the way I expect—with the market as a whole giving back preopen gains. My sort program turns up the following candidates for premarket open gaps. First, those gapping upward:

INFM is up $3 at $8½, essentially as a result of a *Barron's* story. *Barron's* can turn a lot of investors on to a stock. Often, they will buy at the open and expect to hold the security for an extended period of time (in the eyes of a day trader). Two things drive up the bid on a security like this, first, the market makers knowing that there will be demand for it, second, traders with the ability to trade in the premarket getting the security before others can trade at the open. This often produces a shorting opportunity. As INFM has an SOES tier size of 1000, I will monitor this security for a possible short, should no long candidates behave well.

MSPG has shown a downward trend on the daily chart, but the premarket gap (up over $8 to $40½) has taken the chart up and through resistance, from which there is typically a temporary pullback in the new upward trend. MSPG is shortable through my broker and has a tier size of 1000. I will monitor this also.

ELNK is also up over $8 to $62 and looks similar on the daily chart to MSPG. With a smaller-percentage premarket gap, I prefer to look more closely at MSPG, but will keep an eye on ELNK, since it is shortable and has a tier size of 1000.

BGST is up only $1, to $7½, has a tier size of 200, and is not shortable. I pass on BGST.

NMGC has gapped up $1⅜ to $10¹¹/₁₆ and appears to have gapped to an area where there may be resistance, which I will watch closely for the first signs of weakness.

The securities gapping down are as follows:

CHRX is down over 50 percent at $14⅝. Prior to this move, CHRX did not have a strong trend. This drop, however, breaks the price action down through any support. Despite the massive move, CHRX does not appear to have stopped its fall at any support level, and I am therefore cautious about its chances of recovery today. This may be a candidate to track tomorrow for signs of recovery.

CTIX has been in a confirmed downward trend, and this gap-down does not bring the price action to a level of support, so I do not look to trade this security today.

FREE shows a spike formation, which means I will not trade it. Additionally, it does not have enough volume for my liking.

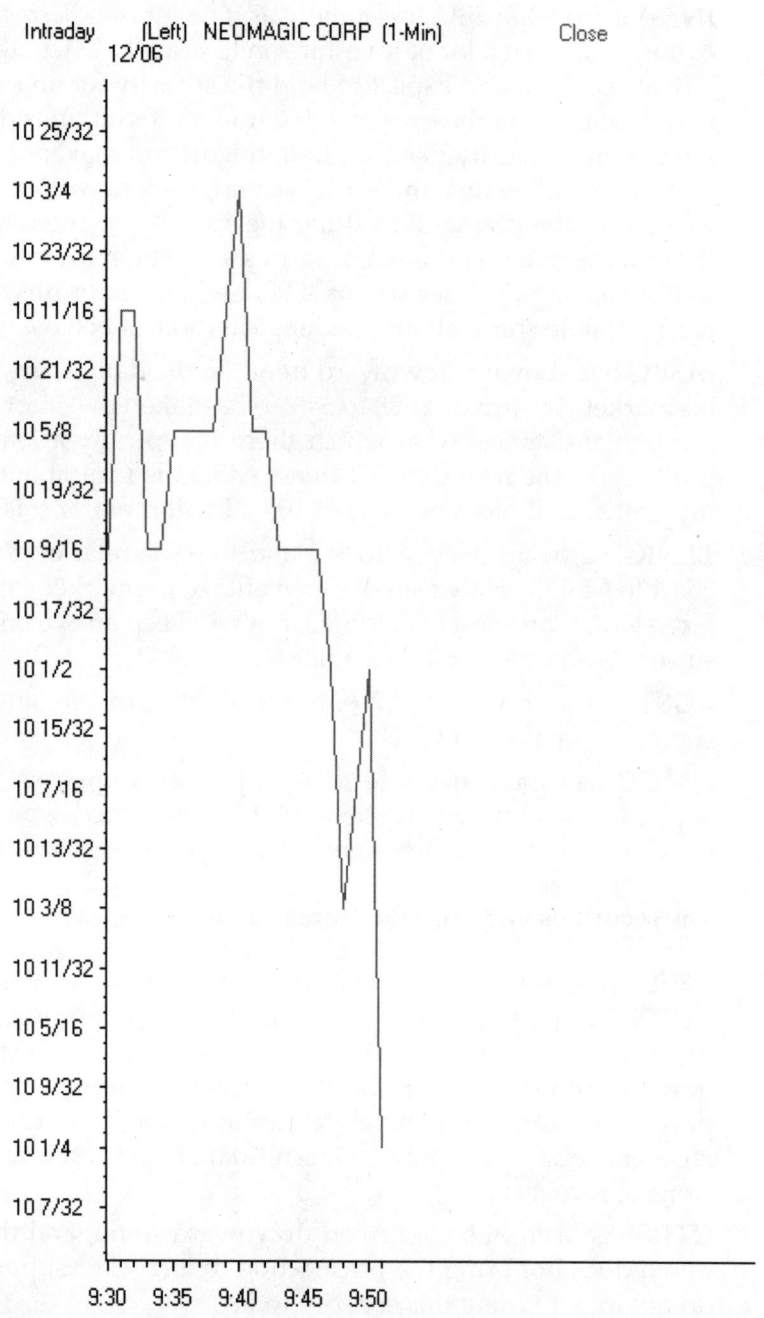

Figure 6-17. NMGC's one-minute tick chart: a chance to short. (Used with permission of Townsend Analytics, Ltd.)

XEIK, like CTIX, does not have support at the level at which it is trading in the premarket. I doubt this will recover and decide to give it a miss.

Since today does not appear to be very exciting for the longs, shorting opportunities will be my focus, even though the market as a whole is in a bull phase.

As the market opens, I am looking for securities in the premarket gap-up group that show signs of weakness on the Level II screen. NMGC is the first candidate, and its one-minute tick chart is shown in Figure 6-17.

For the first couple of minutes, NMGC continues up, then comes down off the $10^{11}/_{16}$ level. The Level II screen shows excess supply so I enter a short at $10^9/_{16}$ just before 9:32 a.m. and get executed just after. From there, the price action does not behave as I expect. If NMGC really were ready to fall, it would continue to do so. I see demand start to build on the bid of the Level II screen, so I get out at $10^9/_{16}$, losing the cost of commission. This was the right thing to do. As you can see from Figure 6-17, however, NMGC did actually fall quite nicely a few minutes later, from above $10^3/_4$ to below $10^1/_4$.

I turn my attention to other securities and see that I have already missed a good part of the move down on MSPG. I short MSPG at 9:42:43 a.m. at $38^5/_{16}$ and see it continue to fall briefly before rallying to $38^1/_2$. I decide that $38^9/_{16}$ is my stop loss and hold on. The rally to this level is nowhere near a higher high, or even the level of the previous low, so the downward trend is intact. And the Level II screen is not showing strong demand. I continue to hold the short until 9:48:39 a.m., when I decide to close my position at $37^5/_8$. At this point, the existing trend has experienced three attempts by the bulls to rally the price, and the Level II screen is showing stronger demand, with ECNs and market makers populating the inside bid quite heavily. Fortunately, I get out at just the right time and make a profit. The one-minute tick chart for MSPG is shown in Figure 6-18.

I have not started well. The first trade that lost me money on NMGC was a good stop. I showed discipline in exiting my position when the price was not behaving as I expected and thereby cut my losses. If I had held, I might have been tempted to cut my losses with a quarter-point move against me and ended up losing more. On the second trade, MSPG, I chose a poor entry point. The

218 Chapter 6

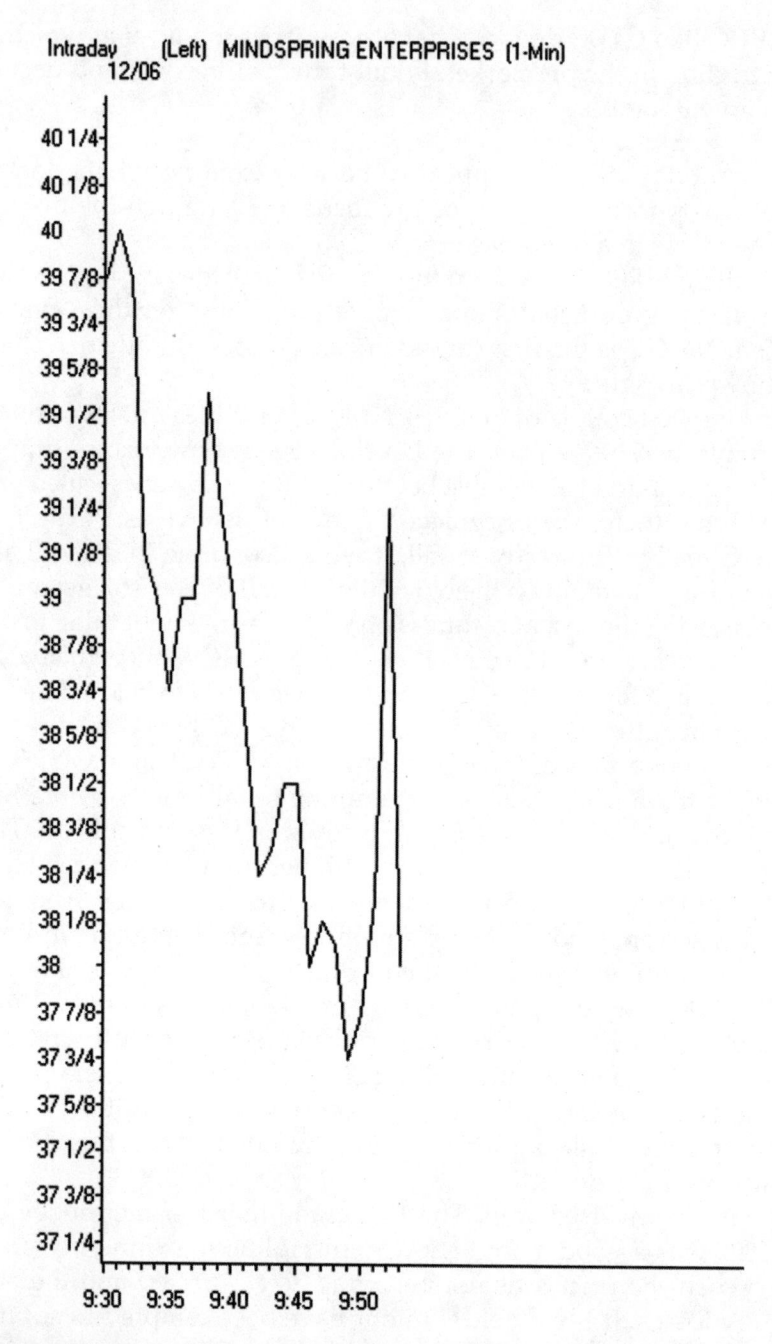

Figure 6-18. Another short; the one-minute tick chart for MSPG. (Used with permission of Townsend Analytics, Ltd.)

Date	Time	Order ID	Action Taken	
12/06/1999	09:31:48	059b-0308-00	SellShort 1000 NMGC at 10 9/16 on ISLD (1000 traded @ 10 9/16)	Executed
12/06/1999	09:32:04		Sold Short 1000 NMGC at 10 9/16 with ISLD(order 059b-0308-0001-00)	Completed
12/06/1999	09:32:42	059b-0308-00	Buy 1000 NMGC at 10 9/16 on SOES (1000 traded @ 10 9/16)	Executed
12/06/1999	09:32:49		Bought 1000 NMGC at 10 9/16 with MSCO(order 059b-0308-0002-00)	Completed
12/06/1999	09:42:43	059b-0308-00	SellShort 700 MSPG at 38 5/16 on ISLD (700 traded @ 38 3/8)	Executed
12/06/1999	09:42:44		Sold Short 700 MSPG at 38 3/8 with ISLD(order 059b-0308-0003-00)	Completed
12/06/1999	09:48:39	059b-0308-00	Buy 700 MSPG at 37 5/8 on ISLD (700 traded @ 37 5/8)	Executed
12/06/1999	09:49:05		Bought 700 MSPG at 37 5/8 with ISLD(order 059b-0308-0004-00)	Completed

Figure 6-19. Summary of a trading day, Monday, December 6, 1999. (Used with permission of Townsend Analytics, Ltd.)

rule here is that if the security is in a downtrend, I look to enter the short on a brief rally. I did not do so. I salvaged the situation by picking my exit well, but I am not pleased with the way I have traded today. I choose to quit while I am ahead and try again tomorrow. My trading activity for the day is shown in Figure 6-19.

Tuesday

The premarket trading is showing a marginally positive opening, but some well-known tech securities, like Yahoo and Redhat, are showing big gains. As usual, my first activity is to run my premarket sorting program and look at the daily trends for the premarket gainers and losers.

>CYGN has almost doubled in price in the premarket to 17^{7}/_{16}$, is shortable, and has a tier size of 1000. CYGN has been mainly trendless. If anything, the price action has shown a bias toward a downward trend. In this situation, I will look to short the security should the Level II action after the open show excess supply.

>GERN is up nearly $6 to 17^{1}/_{4}$ in the premarket. It is shortable, has a tier size of 1000, and is exhibiting a downward trend prior to this gap, making this a perfect candidate to short when weakness in the form of excess supply appears on the Level II screen.

>AMEN has been in a sustainable downtrend prior to the gap up, and with a tier size of 1000 looks to be a perfect candidate for shorting. The problem is that on this security there is no borrow available from my broker, so I decide not to monitor this one.

>LASE is up 2^{1}/_{4}$ to 13^{9}/_{16}$. LASE has been oscillating in a trading range on the daily chart and this gap up seems to have brought the security to an area of congestion. Again, with a tier size of

1000, I will look to short this security on signs on the Level II display of oversupply, but it is not shortable from my broker.

ANCR, with today's gap up, looks, on the daily chart, like a breakout from an ascending triangle. I will not look to short this security near the open. With strength in the overall market and in this security, the odds of getting a profitable short are less than with some of the other securities.

Now for the gap-down securities. In the current positive market environment, my bias is to go long, rather than short, and securities gapping down to areas of support on the daily chart are most likely to deliver those opportunities.

VISX is down nearly $38 to close to $50, at which level there is evidence of support on the daily chart. With a tier size of 1000, I am attracted to this security, but at $50, I can only buy 700 shares with my margin in this account. My decision is to buy this security if demand on the bid appears close to market open.

BEAM was down nearly $6 to just over $15 in the premarket trading to areas of support seen on the daily chart. With a tier size of 1000 and a low price, I will look to buy this security if I see demand on the Level II screen.

TWMC shows a slight downtrend, and the premarket gap takes the price action to below support levels. Given the small level of the gap (just over $1), I will pass on this security.

TURF is a low-level gap-down security with a tier size of 500. I pass on this.

So, my short list for securities to monitor are VISX and BEAM for longs, and CYGN and GERN for shorts, depending on how the overall market trades when it opens. ANCR is not on the list of shorts, but from its opening at $80, it traded up to $94 and came down to $74. It would have been a good security to monitor, but I was not observing this stock when the opportunities in it arose.

Within the first minute of trading, VISX behaves closest to my expectations, and since my preference is for longs, I decide to buy this security. At 9:32 a.m. I see share availability on Island at 50^{1}/_{8}$ and look to purchase it. The problem is that the order entry system has lost its connection to Island and I cannot execute on that route.

ARCA has no shares available, so I have to take my chances in the SOES queue to buy VISX. I enter a market order (limit orders on SOES at this time of day are useless for a rapidly moving highly traded stock), and I get my 700 shares about one and a half minutes later at $50^3/8$. This technical hitch has cost me $1/4 in the purchase price, but I am still long an appreciating security, so I cannot complain too much. At 9:40:50 a.m. I see demand start to moderate, evident in the pace of trades slowing, and fewer market makers willing to jump onto the inside bid. I have enjoyed a nice ride up to $53 and decide to take my profit, so I enter a market order to sell on SOES, since there are no buyers on the available ECNs. For a minute and 42 seconds, I sit in the SOES queue watching the price fall. During this time I see numerous market makers on the inside bid, but each one is taking its time about refreshing its price or stepping off the inside market as traders ahead of me get their trades executed. Finally, at 9:42:32 a.m., my order is canceled because an ECN has come back onto the inside market. I have to start all over to enter a sell order. I have seen a broadcast message from my broker that Island is now available and I see buyers, so I put in an order to sell at $52^3/{16}$. This is not actually smart trading at this stage. I have become frustrated by waiting in the SOES queue so long and then getting my order canceled by the exchange, and I overlook the fact that if ECNs are appearing on the best bid, buyers must be coming back into the market. This is the case, because my order is executed at a better price than I entered, at $52^1/2$ and $52^7/{16}$ immediately after it has been entered.

The order record is shown in Figure 6-20.

Figure 6-21 shows the one-minute tick chart of VISX for this morning's trading. You can see that by getting out at $52^1/2$, I did not maximize my gains but I did choose the best time to exit, because a steep selloff to the $50 level followed.

Date	Time	Order ID	Action Taken	
12/07/1999	09:32:44	059c-0308-00	Buy 700 VISX at 50 1/8 Deleted	Clerk Rejected (No connection to
12/07/1999	09:32:57	059c-0308-00	Buy 700 VISX at Market on SOES (700 traded @ 50 3/8)	Executed
12/07/1999	09:34:25		Bought 700 VISX at 50 3/8 with MLCO(order 059c-0308-0002-00)	Completed
12/07/1999	09:40:50	059c-0308-00	Sell 700 VISX at Market Deleted	Killed (NO SOES MM AVAILABLE
12/07/1999	09:42:22		Order 059c-0308-0003-00 killed by the exchange for reason: NO SOES MM AVAILABLE	Completed
12/07/1999	09:42:32	059c-0308-00	Sell 700 VISX at Market Deleted	Killed
12/07/1999	09:43:01		Cancel order 059c-0308-0004-00 sent to exchange	Sent
12/07/1999	09:43:03		Order 059c-0308-0004-00 killed by the exchange for reason:	Completed
12/07/1999	09:43:06	059c-0308-00	Sell 700 VISX at 52 3/16 on ISLD (700 traded @ 52.4732)	Executed
12/07/1999	09:43:06		Sold 400 VISX at 52 1/2 with ISLD(order 059c-0308-0005-00)	Completed
12/07/1999	09:43:06		Sold 100 VISX at 52 7/16 with ISLD(order 059c-0308-0005-00)	Completed
12/07/1999	09:43:06		Sold 200 VISX at 52 7/16 with ISLD(order 059c-0308-0005-00)	Completed

Figure 6-20. My order record for VISX. (Used with permission of Townsend Analytics, Ltd.)

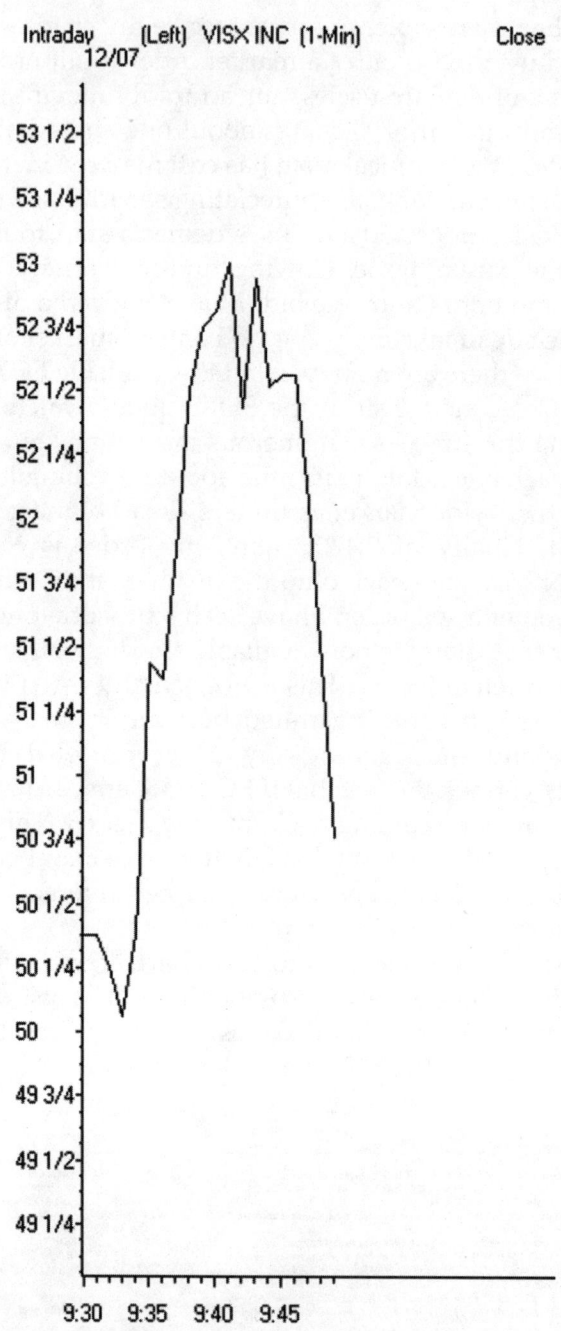

Figure 6-21. One-minute tick chart for VISX—a disciplined exit. (Used with permission of Townsend Analytics, Ltd.)

Several of the other securities identified by the premarket gap report behaved as expected. CYGN, and especially GERN, showed nice tradable moves down. But due to margin restrictions, I can only trade one security at a time in this account and chose the security that allowed me to go long, which was in harmony with the overall market direction. With a gain of over $1400 on the day, given the technical and execution problems I faced, I am happy with the result and look forward to tomorrow's opening.

Wednesday

So far this week, I have had two positive days, and generally speaking, I have traded with discipline. The days have not been stellar in their returns, but the trades I made were of the type that can be repeated week-in and week-out to produce a regular income. This morning, however, I feel caution. The main reason is that I feel fatigue. During my morning run, which is normally a relaxed jog, I had difficulty maintaining my normal speed. My 13-month-old son has a cold and kept his mother and me awake most of the night. This may seem like spurious information in a book on technical analysis, but it is highly important. You must know yourself and know if you are 100 percent, meaning you are able to concentrate and focus at the level needed to day-trade profitably. If you are not fully prepared and focused, the best thing, normally, is to not trade. This is one of my rules, more fully discussed in the next chapter.

Given my goal to show a whole week's worth of trading in this chapter, I decide to continue, with extreme caution, and here is what happened.

My premarket search for gapping securities yields the following results for gainers:

TRAC, which has been in a sustainable downtrend on the daily chart and has just gone through what looked like a continuation pattern of the downward trend, is now experiencing a gap up that there is promise of it falling back from. I choose to monitor this security at the open to see if I can see signs of weakness on its Level II display. As it turns out, the pace of trades in this security is not fast enough for my liking. I like to see a constant stream of trades going through the dynamic time-of-sales screen, which indicates enough participants involved to ensure ease in exiting a position when I wish. I eliminate this security from my watch list soon after the open.

ISLD is a big gainer in the premarket. However, the premarket gap looks like a breakaway gap in an extremely strong and wild upward move. I decide to pass on this one also.

VRSA is in a sustainable upward trend, and does not fit the high probability trade profile of a security in a downward trend, so I pass on it.

As it turns out, this was the best candidate to have traded on the day. After the initial move upward after open, this security reversed almost all of its gap up by 2:00 p.m. (a tradable move down from $45 to $35). If I had been feeling more confident in my abilities this day, I would probably have tracked this more closely. As it was, with decreased confidence in my powers of concentration and focus, I needed to restrict myself to the highest probability trades.

TSCN's daily chart action is not inspiring. It looks like TSCN has experienced a breakout to the upside and has just completed a continuation pattern, with the premarket gap-up forming the breakout from that continuation pattern. Therefore, I do not feel that TSCN holds the highest probability of giving back its premarket gain, particularly as the whole market is still strong.

XICO has been in a sustainable uptrend on the daily chart, but it looks as if the premarket gap is overextending the upward trend, so I decided to monitor this security at the open. Once trading started, there was not enough pace in this security's trading, nor were there tight enough levels on the Level II screen, so I pass on this one also.

For securities showing premarket gaps down, I have only two candidates:

CATT has been largely trendless on its daily chart, but it has shown strong support at around the $13 level. The premarket action has taken it to $10, so I expect a move back upward toward $13.

CTXS, on the daily chart, shows a strong and sustainable upward trend, so I look for an upward move in this security. I decide not to trade CTXS in this account because the margin available and the stock price of over $115 mean I cannot purchase many stocks. This would require me to capture a far bigger move than normal to make sufficient money on the trade to justify the risk. I pass. (Ultimately, CTXS did behave as expected. After a continuation of the move down after market open, a nice tradable reversal occurred at 10 a.m., and the stock appreciated $5 in one move.)

I do not trade CATT because I have taken my eye off the ball. It behaves exactly as I expected, gaining almost a $1 to $10^3/$_4$ immediately after market open, and to over $12 by early afternoon. Missing this opportunity is probably the result of not being able to concentrate 100 percent. I then go to my backup plan, which is to look at yesterday's gappers. This shows that VISX is attracting lots of volume. VISX gapped up in the premarket, but gives up some of those gains immediately after market open. My pattern for trading gappers on the second day is to look for a move in the direction of the first day's tradable move, and since VISX was a significant gap-downer yesterday, I look for a tradable move up today.

The one-minute tick chart of VISX for that day, as shown in Figure 6-22, VISX traded down from $57^1/$_8$ to around $55^3/$_4$. Then a reversal upward occurred.

I see the reversal upward, and that it is confirmed by a good pace of trades going off at the ask and market makers building up on the best bid available, indicating strong demand for the security at this price. So I take a long position, as shown in Figure 6-23.

VISX continues to appreciate, but I am stuck in the SOES queue for about a minute before getting my fill at $56^1/$_4$ and $56^3/$_8$. I watch VISX continue to appreciate for the next one and a quarter minutes, mindful of the fact that I am trading a second-day gapper, which requires even more caution than when trading a first-day gapper. I see some potential weakness in the demand, a slowing of the pace of trades, followed by roughly half the trades going off at the bid and half at the ask. This is also close to 9:40 a.m, when I had seen VISX reverse down yesterday, so I look to get out. I close at $56^{11}/$_{16}$ with a profit of close to $300 before commission.

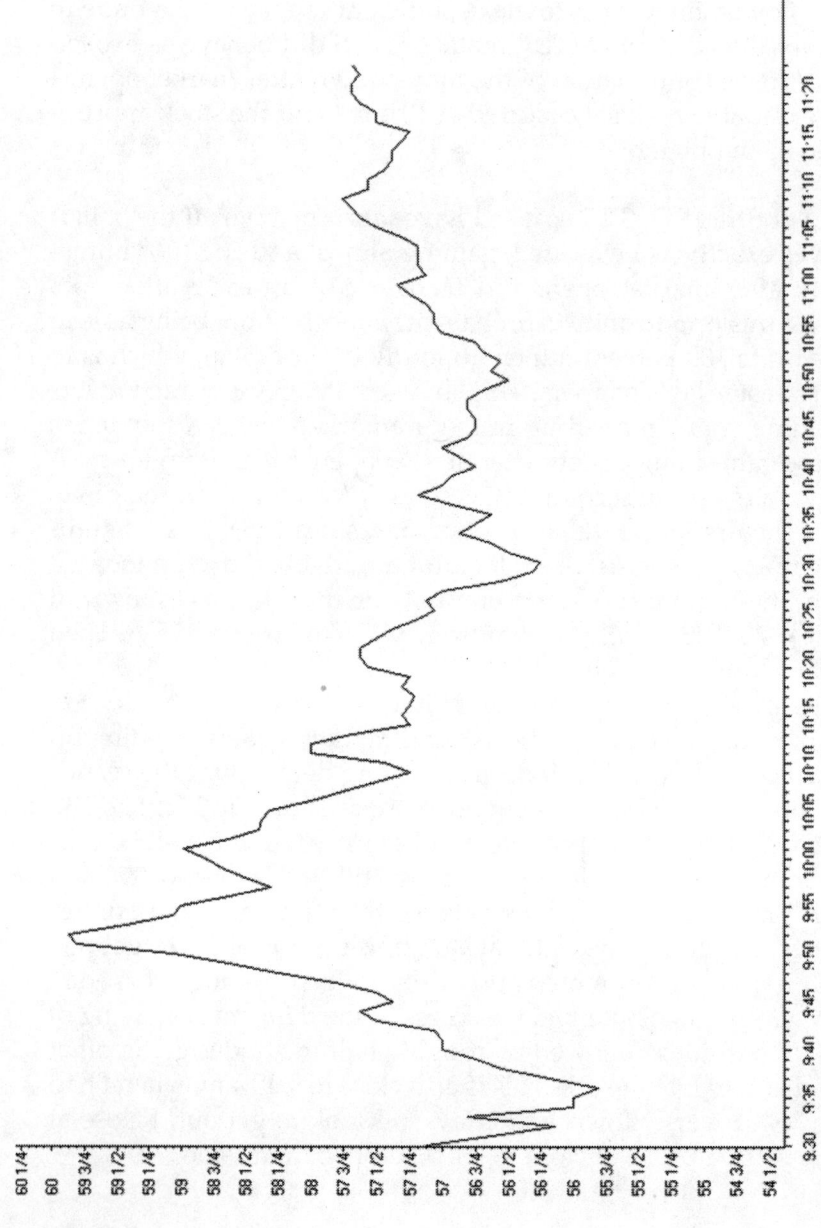

Figure 6-22. VISX one-minute chart—looking for a tradable move up. (Used with permission of Townsend Analytics, Ltd.)

Date	Time	Order ID	Action Taken	
12/08/199	09:36:57	059d-0308-00	Buy 700 VISX at Market on SOES (700 traded @ 56.2679)	Executed
12/08/199	09:37:53		Bought 100 VISX at 56 1/4 with AGIS(order 059d-0308-0001-00)	Completed
12/08/199	09:38:00		Bought 500 VISX at 56 1/4 with GSCO(order 059d-0308-0001-00)	Completed
12/08/199	09:38:15		Bought 100 VISX at 56 3/8 with COWN(order 059d-0308-0001-00)	Completed
12/08/199	09:39:27	059d-0308-00	Sell 700 VISX at 56 11/16 Deleted	Killed (Would loc
12/08/199	09:39:28		Order 059d-0308-0002-00 killed by the exchange for reason: Would lock or cross market	Completed
12/08/199	09:39:40	059d-0308-00	Sell 700 VISX at 56 11/16 on SOES (700 traded @ 56 11/16)	Executed
12/08/199	09:39:49		Sold 100 VISX at 56 11/16 with WARR(order 059d-0308-0003-00)	Completed
12/08/199	09:39:52		Sold 100 VISX at 56 11/16 with NITE(order 059d-0308-0003-00)	Completed
12/08/199	09:39:53		Sold 100 VISX at 56 11/16 with HRZG(order 059d-0308-0003-00)	Completed
12/08/199	09:39:55		Sold 100 VISX at 56 11/16 with AGIS(order 059d-0308-0003-00)	Completed
12/08/199	09:40:01		Sold 300 VISX at 56 11/16 with AGIS(order 059d-0308-0003-00)	Completed

Figure 6-23. Taking a long position in VISX. (Used with permission of Townsend Analytics, Ltd.)

VISX then moved up to $60. Deciding to exit VISX based on yesterday's reversal time was foolish, since the security had already undergone its reversal at 9:37, and that was a reversal upward. I was acting out of fear. Due to fatigue, I did not have confidence in myself. Noticing this, and with the market emphasizing the point by letting me see what should have been $2000 in profit come in at only $300, I decide to rest and try again tomorrow.

Thursday

Although we had another disruptive night, my effort during the morning run tells me I am in better shape than yesterday. I am still not feeling up to par, but better, so I decide to continue. Energy levels and the ability to focus are more important to an individual online trader than to a trader working for a large organization. The effects of a losing run when you trade your own account are far more significant to the individual than to a corporation. When you trade, and especially day-trade for yourself, the first goal is to not lose money, which is all too easy to do at times, especially if you cannot concentrate fully.

So I will approach the market with caution and only trade patterns that I know, discarding all other apparent opportunities. When you trade outside of your known patterns, it is easy to take a position and have the trend reverse against you. This is something I am purposely bringing to the forefront of my consciousness today. Not functioning at 100 percent again means that I must redouble my efforts to keep my trading to known patterns and stack the odds as much as possible in my favor.

As usual, the first thing I do is to use my sort program and find those securities gapping up and gapping down today. As the whole market is up strongly, there are more securities gapping up than gapping down, so my options for looking for stocks to rebound upward today are limited, making shorts after the initial runup after market open the best bet. Faced with this situation, I will keep in mind the tendency in the current market for reversals to happen at around 9:40 a.m. I will also bear in mind, though, that the market is still in a strong bull phase, that caution is therefore necessary, and that I must cut losses quickly should what looks like a reversal turn into a continuation pattern for a security that has moved up after the open. Here, then, is the list of gapping securities I found attractive in terms of gap size, security price, and sufficient premarket volume. As usual, I give the gappers-up first:

> **CORL** has experienced a dramatic runup in the past few days, and this looks like it might be an exhaustion gap. It is priced within my margin range and trades at an SOES tier size of 1000. This looks like a good candidate for shorting, should the overall market start to give back its premarket gains, and should it show signs of weakness on the Level II screen. The problem here is that my broker does not have a borrow on it, so my planned play is not possible, because I cannot short this security.
>
> As it turned out, a short on this security would have been very lucrative. CORL fell from $43 to near $35 in a single move after market open.
>
> **ETEL** has been within a range of between $2 1/2$ and $7 for some time, and this looks like a breakout from that range. If the market shows early weakness, ETEL should be a good shorting candidate, if supported by Level II screen action. Again, though, a borrow is not available on ETEL, so I cannot short it.
>
> ETEL moved up from $7 3/4$ to over $9, where it started to fall. It would have been a good short candidate, but the play was not open to me, so I passed on it.
>
> **ANDN** is an initial offering, so I will stay away from it. Anything can happen at any time with these. It is not borrowable anyway. ANDN dropped $10 after market open and then gained it all back again. I do not trade these securities. It cannot be done in a disciplined manner.

MESG, at last, is a premarket gainer that I can short. Overall, the daily chart shows that MESG has been in a range, but is in a secondary upward trend. This gap up does not provide a breakout to new highs. In fact, it only brings it into an area of congestion. This is almost always a sign that the gap up will reverse downward after market open. MESG has a tier size of 1000 and is well within my margin reach, so I treat it as one of my prime candidates to watch for a reversal down.

ACSC has been in a sustainable upward trend for several months on the daily chart, has just completed a flag continuation pattern, and has broken out to the upside with this gap. The size of the gap suggests that if the market shows weakness after the open, some of this gap could be given back, so I mark it as a potential short candidate. A borrow is available, I have the margin to trade this security, and it has a tier size of 1000.

INIT looks very much like ACSC on the daily chart, so I treat it the same way. It will need the market overall to start to give up its premarket gains before I consider this a shorting candidate. It is shortable through my broker, but there is a problem with the tier size of 200, which limits the confidence level I have when day trading a security.

The only gap-down security I found of interest was PERL.

PERL has been trendless and is now experiencing a wild spike up, which fits the profile of a security to avoid. It gains significantly after market open, but experiences wild swings, thin levels, and no definite Level II screen indications. I am happy to pass this one up, since it is not possible to trade in a disciplined manner.

So we get to the action part of the day. The market has opened and I am screening my list of potential shorts. The market opens weakly and continues down, giving up its premarket gains and heading toward negative territory (I am referring to the NASDAQ Composite here). This gives me confidence to look for shorting opportunities. ACSC is not generating enough volume for my liking, so I pass on it. This leaves me with INIT and MESG. While I

Date/Time	Order ID	Action	Status
12/09/1999 09:40:44	059e-0308-00	SellShort 1000 MESG at 18 7/8 Deleted	Killed (User requested cancel)
12/09/1999 09:40:53		Cancel order 059e-0308-0001-00 sent to exchange	Sent
12/09/1999 09:40:54		Order 059e-0308-0001-00 killed by the exchange for reason: User requested cancel	Completed
12/09/1999 09:45:26	059e-0308-00	SellShort 1000 MESG at 19 7/16 Deleted	Killed (Would lock or cross mar
12/09/1999 09:45:26		Order 059e-0308-0002-00 killed by the exchange for reason: Would lock or cross market	Completed
12/09/1999 09:46:01	059e-0308-00	SellShort 1000 MESG at 19 1/4 Deleted	Killed (User requested cancel)
12/09/1999 09:46:20		Cancel order 059e-0308-0003-00 sent to exchange	Sent
12/09/1999 09:46:21		Order 059e-0308-0003-00 killed by the exchange for reason: User requested cancel	Completed
12/09/1999 09:47:57	059e-0308-00	SellShort 1000 MESG at 18 7/8 on ISLD (800 traded @ 18.9321)	Executed
12/09/1999 09:47:58		Sold Short 500 MESG at 18 241/256 with ISLD(order 059e-0308-0004-00)	Completed
12/09/1999 09:47:58		Sold Short 200 MESG at 18 15/16 with ISLD(order 059e-0308-0004-00)	Completed
12/09/1999 09:47:58		Sold Short 100 MESG at 18 7/8 with ISLD(order 059e-0308-0004-00)	Completed
12/09/1999 09:47:58		Order 059e-0308-0004-00 killed by the exchange for reason: Would lock or cross market	Completed
12/09/1999 09:49:57		Bought 800 MESG at 18 1/2 with ISLD(order 059e-0308-0005-00)	Completed

Figure 6-24. Trading summary for Thursday, December 9, 1999. (Used with permission of Townsend Analytics, Ltd.)

am examining the overall market and looking at the Level II and tick chart movements for my securities, I miss the first move down of INIT. This is annoying, but I decide that if I have missed the first move, I should leave the security alone. This turns out to be a mistake, and by hindsight I can see that with the market falling quite dramatically and as long as the Level II screen and trade action confirmed further moves down for INIT, it would have been worth shorting.

However, I did not have the benefit of hindsight at the time, so I focused my attention on MESG. In Figure 6-24, you can see the trades I entered for Thursday.

At 9:40, I saw some weakness, so I entered a short at $18 7/8. Almost immediately, the Level II screen showed more market makers coming on to the inside bid and some leaving the inside ask, indications of strength (remember, at this time of day, I tend to believe the Level II screen action), so I canceled. MESG rallied further to over $19, then started to weaken again. I tried shorts at $19 7/16 and $19 1/4, but there were no takers with MESG starting to fall fast. I entered my last attempt at $18 7/8 and got 800 out of the 1000 requested at 9:47. MESG then started to fall nicely, and I entered an order to buy back at $18 1/2. At the time of order entry, this was well below the best bid price. I just wanted to mark my place for a price at which I was willing to cover to ensure that I got covered when the price fell to that level. As you can see, it did not take long—only six seconds—after entering this order to get a fill, meaning I held the short for about two minutes.

Looking at Figure 6-25, you can see that MESG started to climb again after reaching $18 3/8. It went over $18 3/4, but later in the day fell below $17. I was happy that I had traded with discipline, even though I was tired, and made profits again from the consistent patterns that form out of premarket gaps.

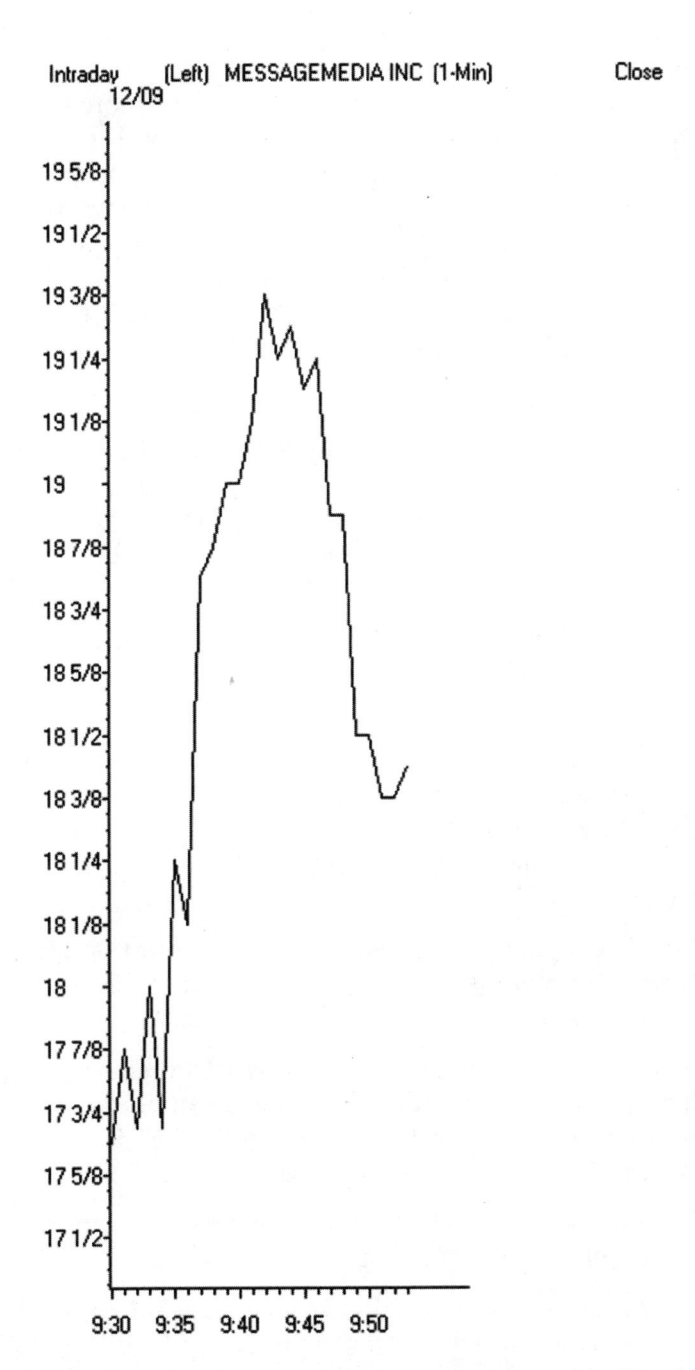

Figure 6-25. Covering a short for MESG—the aftermath. (Used with permission of Townsend Analytics, Ltd.)

Friday

A better night for the Lewis household, and I feel more energized and better able to concentrate and focus. The overall market conditions for the NASDAQ remain exceptionally strong, so my preference is to look for longs rather than shorts. As always, however, the individual behavior of the securities I choose to follow this morning will have the most influence on my decisions. The premarket gap report from my sorting software yields the following candidates. First, the up securities:

BTWS is up strongly in the premarket, and in an existing upward trend, the current action looks like it might be an exhaustion gap. The only high-percentage play here will be if a strong move downward is seen at or near the opening, and because my broker does not have a borrow available on BTWS, I have to pass on this security.

MTMC is the same story as BTWS. It's a similar trend, but not borrowable, so I have to pass.

ODIS also looks as if it is in a strong upward trend, and the current gap looks like an exhaustion gap. It has a tier size of 1000 and my broker has a borrow available on it. This is one of the securities I will watch closely at the open, and I will attempt to short it should the market makers start building the ask and dropping the bid.

CSPI has a tier size of 1000 and is shortable, but I decide not to watch this security, since in recent days' trading, it has experienced the spike formation that I always avoid.

SMSI shows a nice downward trend, with a premarket gap up and tier size of 1000, making this an ideal candidate to monitor at the open. It is not shortable with my broker, however, so I have to pass.

PERL has an SOES tier size of 500 and a spike formation, meaning that I will not play this stock.

CORL is a similar story to PERL. No matter what happens with this security, the presence of a substantial spike in the last few days' price action means that it is too unpredictable to make it worth the risk.

GBIX's recent market action shows this security reversing up out of a downward trend. This reversal up could be a continuation pattern, or it could really be the start of a new trend. I have no real bias on this security. However, with a tier size of 1000 and a borrow available, I will monitor GBIX for a possible short.

TMCS had been in a sustainable downward trend until recent days, and it looks to me as if the premarket gap up may, at least temporarily, have exhausted the current upswing. Because it is shortable and has a tier size of 1000, this is my best candidate for a short should market conditions make shorting appropriate.

Now to those securities gapping down. The market has been very strong in the premarket, and there are few securities gapping down. My list is short:

VIRS has been in an upward trend, and the premarket gap down brings the security to levels of support. With a tier size of 1000, I am looking to VIRS as my prime candidate for a long position.

JAZZ is an IPO, so I will not trade it. There is no history, and technical analysis requires history, so today, JAZZ is not for me.

RAMP has a tier size of 200, which means I have no interest in RAMP, so I pass on it.

That makes my short list for stocks to watch at the open ODIS, GBIX, and TMCS for shorts, and VIRS for a long. Since this is a low number of securities to watch, I add MESG as a second-day gapper to see if an opportunity arises there.

Although, in general, I want to trade in harmony with the overall trend of the market, which is decidedly up, every trend takes a breather from time to time. The market makers are the ones who know this best, since they have the orders coming into them. This helps them take advantage of some investors by raising the prices in the premarket for hot stocks that day, knowing that many individuals do not have the ability to trade in the premarket and will put in orders to buy at the open. This provides a perfect opportunity for market makers to sell short at high prices and cover later on at a lower price. With this in mind, I will give as much attention to my short candidates as my long candidate.

With better concentration and more focus, I see the market sell off almost immediately from the open. Scanning my short candidates, I see TMCS has market makers building the ask and shying away from the bid. I also see Island orders for the security have not settled down, so I attempt a short at 9:31, as can be seen in Figure 6-26.

Date	Time	Order ID	Action Taken	
12/10/1999	09:31:05	059f-0308-00(	SellShort 800 TMCS at 45 9/16 on ISLD [800 traded @ 45 9/16]	Executed
12/10/1999	09:31:06		Sold Short 100 TMCS at 45 9/16 with ISLD[order 059f-0308-0001-00]	Completed
12/10/1999	09:31:17		Sold Short 700 TMCS at 45 9/16 with ISLD[order 059f-0308-0001-00]	Completed
12/10/1999	09:35:47	059f-0308-00(	Buy 800 TMCS at 44 Deleted	Killed (User requested cancel
12/10/1999	09:36:06		Cancel order 059f-0308-0002-00 sent to exchange	Sent
12/10/1999	09:36:07		Order 059f-0308-0002-00 killed by the exchange for reason: User requested cancel	Completed
12/10/1999	09:36:18	059f-0308-00(	Buy 800 TMCS at Market on SOES [800 traded @ 44 1/4]	Executed
12/10/1999	09:36:35		Bought 100 TMCS at 44 1/4 with HRZG[order 059f-0308-0003-00]	Completed
12/10/1999	09:36:36		Bought 100 TMCS at 44 1/4 with MONT[order 059f-0308-0003-00]	Completed
12/10/1999	09:36:38		Bought 100 TMCS at 44 1/4 with TWPT[order 059f-0308-0003-00]	Completed
12/10/1999	09:36:54		Bought 100 TMCS at 44 1/4 with MONT[order 059f-0308-0003-00]	Completed
12/10/1999	09:36:54		Bought 400 TMCS at 44 1/4 with HRZG[order 059f-0308-0003-00]	Completed

Figure 6-26. Shorting TMCS. (Used with permission of Townsend Analytics, Ltd.)

My advertised short for 800 at $45^9/_{16}$ is taken almost immediately by 100 shares. The remainder go 12 seconds after order entry. After I get the short, I see TMCS start to sell off nicely. Four and a half minutes later, I try to cover by placing the best bid on Island, which is still below the inside market by 1/8, but in a quickly falling security, Island orders near the inside bid will often be taken by those desperate to offload their long positions in the security, since the Island order is instantaneously executable with no SOES queue. I see the pace of trades slow, however, and nobody takes my bid. Twenty seconds after entering the bid, I cancel it and enter a market order to buy 800 and cover my position. I see plenty of market makers at the best ask and supporting the best ask, so SOES should get me out. Forty seconds later I am out, having made over $1000 profit before 9:40 a.m. For anyone trading a $20,000 account, that should be enough in one day, so I quit while I'm ahead and stop trading for the day.

The one-minute tick chart for TMCS is shown in Figure 6-27, and the daily chart is shown in Figure 6-28.

Today, I am pleased with the trading action, and not just because of the profit. I have traded with discipline. I had a number of qualified candidates and picked the one that followed the expected price action. Other securities did follow the pattern, but they were not shortable, and some candidates did not behave as expected. With more energy and better focus, I was able to monitor all the securities at the open and pick the best one, which led me to meet-

A Trading Week **235**

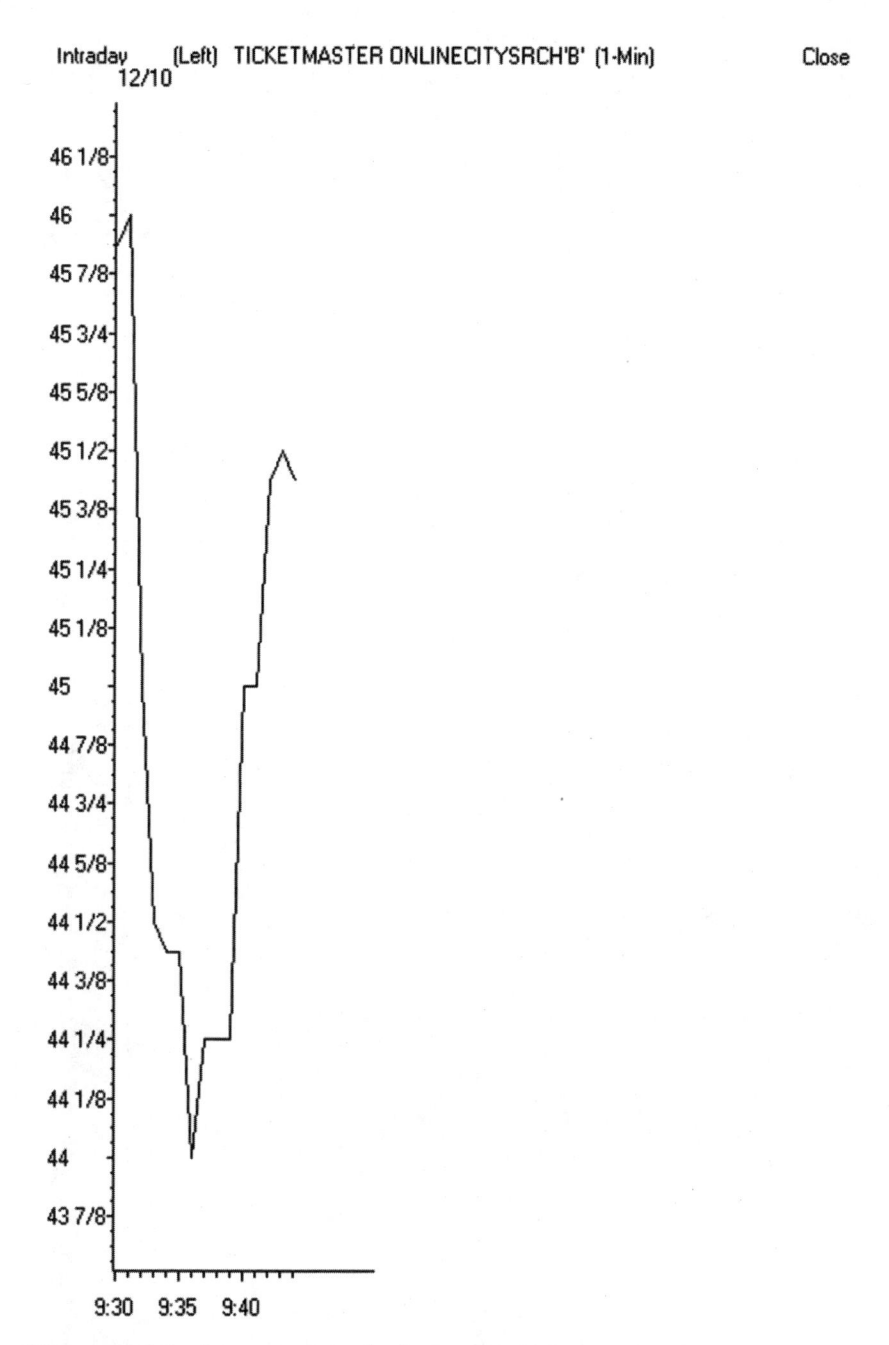

Intraday (Left) TICKETMASTER ONLINECITYSRCH'B' (1-Min) Close
12/10

Figure 6-27. One-minute tick chart to TMCS. (Used with permission of Townsend Analytics, Ltd.)

Figure 6-28. Daily chart to TMCS. (Used with permission of Townsend Analytics, Ltd.)

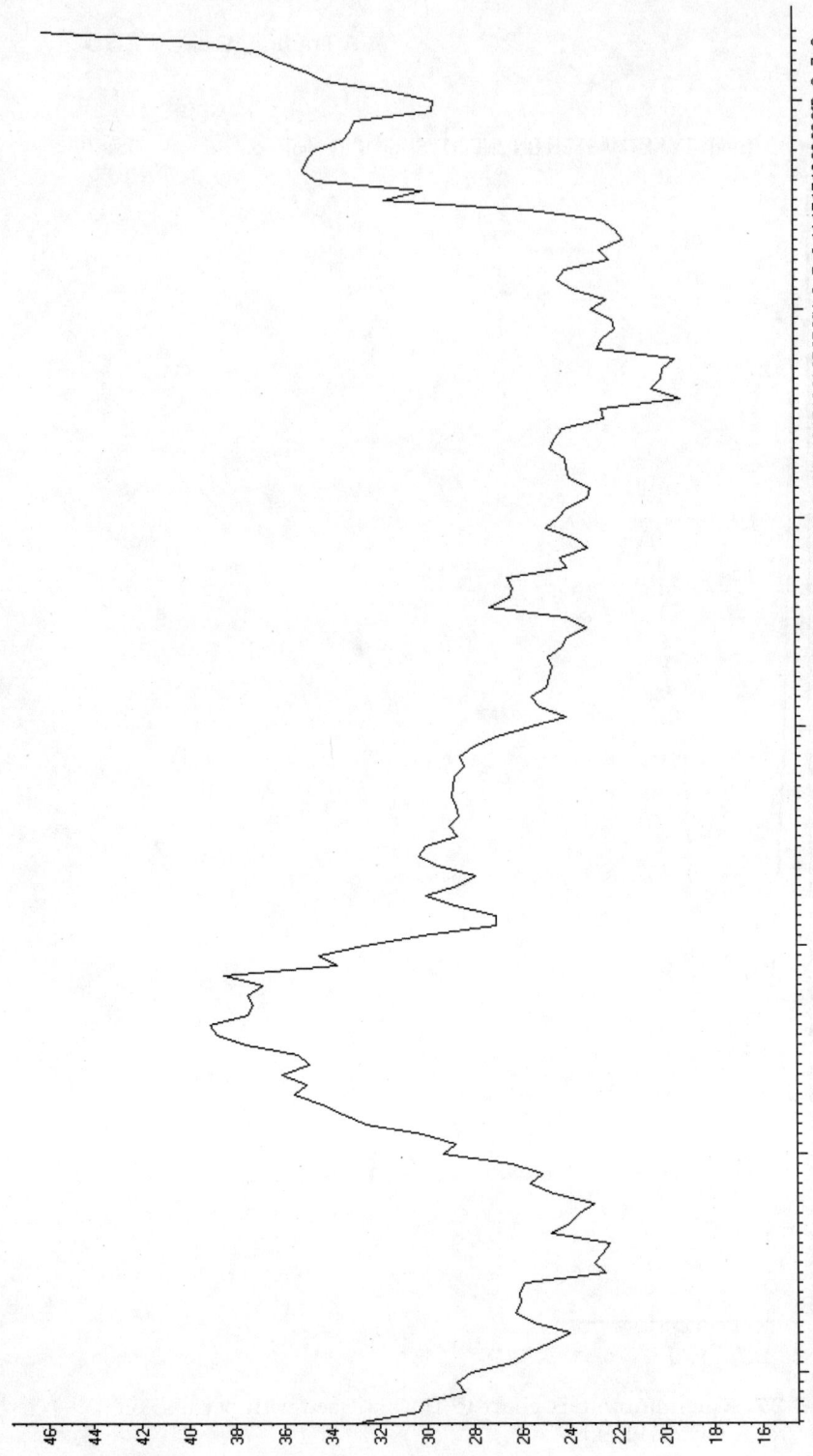

ing my daily goal within seven minutes of the market being open. I do not think I would have been able to evaluate all those opportunities and make trading decisions as quickly as that on either of the past two trading days.

Evaluation of the Week's Trading

This was an average week of trading. I made a little over $3400 with an account size of $20,000. My trading did not rely on catching any of the wild gyrations of stocks like Yahoo!, which moved $67 in one day, or the latest hot Internet IPO. My trading was based on a sound analysis of market gaps, and with respect to the existing trend of the security. I followed this with careful reading of the Level II display to assess supply and demand in order to take positions.

By no means was it a perfect week. There were problems with execution routes on Tuesday, with no connection from my order entry system to Island. I had domestic demands that led to me being too tired to focus fully on a couple of days. Furthermore, you can see from the tick charts included in the narrative above that I did not always make the most of my opportunities, or even pick the best opportunity each day.

With all of this going on, I was still able to make a profit by making trades out of the opportunities that present themselves each and every day in the market.

I have seen estimates of income in some other books on day trading suggesting that your goal should be to make four trades that will each yield $1/4 profit. The idea is that it is easier to make $1/4 on a trade than $1. This is not likely to happen. I prefer to look for good opportunities and stay with them for as long as there appears to be a good reason. If you trade with discipline, there is no reason why you, too, cannot repeat this performance each and every week. These returns can be made by going both long and short, enabling you to make profits no matter what direction the market takes. In fact, some simple analysis shows that I made these profits using twice as many shorts as longs in a market that was making new highs throughout the week. Clearly, this was not a case of buying blindly into a raging bull market.

Again, some simple math shows you that if you trade like this for a year, the income can be in excess of $150,000 from an original

$20,000 investment. Do I expect a novice to reap these returns? Probably not. That is not because using the gap, and, trend analyses is too difficult, but because the likelihood of overtrading and losing the profits made is too great. At the beginning of the book, I stated that $20,000 should yield an income of between $50,000 and $100,000. This week's trading shows that those figures can be beaten quite handily—if you can trade with discipline. The methods I use do not require either a bull or bear market, just volatility, which is probably the only thing we are guaranteed in the market for the foreseeable future.

Incidentally, the profit figure of $3400 for the week is a little low, since trading this amount will get you a rebate on the cost of trades. Because no positions are held overnight, my broker, MB Trading, sweeps the money into an interest-bearing account, so I get interest too. If you are new to trading, MB Trading does offer $5 trades for a limited period so that you can gain experience at a lower cost. I mention MB Trading purely because I use them and have received good service. I am in no way associated with them except that I am a customer.

7
Trading Psychology

This chapter gives a brief overview of the kind of thinking that has helped me in my trading career. In day trading, your profitability is not driven by the amount you know about all the different market indicators, nor all the news stories, nor even knowledge of all the charts there are. What makes the difference between a profitable and an unprofitable day trader is the ability to work with discipline and self-control. Fear and greed are what drive intraday swings in the value of securities, and the patterns caused by both will become recognizable to you if you day trade for any length of time and are aware of your own emotions. In Chapter 6, I gave enough information for a day trader to become profitable and proved the worth of that information with an example in which I put my own money on the line. I would like to see other proponents of day-trading methodologies put themselves to the same test and illustrate daily profits through both long and short positions. What stops some traders from being profitable every week (and on occasion stops me also) is lapse in discipline. Instead of suffering from greed for more money or fear of losing it, your focus needs to be greed for trading in accordance with your rules and fear of making a trade that does not fit with your planned activity. For a day trader who is active on a weekly basis, the first and most important activity is to avoid losses.

It took me close to a year of barely keeping my trading capital intact before I developed my own set of rules, which, if followed, lead me to regular and healthy profits. At times, especially after long winning streaks, when I become lax about regularly reading my rules, I am still hit with a loss that was completely avoidable if only I had not broken one of my own rules. Some losses are unavoidable. You do the right thing and the security's price still moves against you. For the market-open trading I illustrated in the last chapter, this is rare, but it does happen. It happened on the first day of trading with NMGC. The right thing to do in such instances is to cut your loss as soon as the security is not behaving the way you expect. With NMGC all I lost was the commission of $46, which is a small loss indeed. For most traders, this is one of the most difficult things to do. Most humans tend to hold out and hope things will turn in their favor. In day trading that is almost always a mistake.

When I break one of my rules, I am now actually thankful for the loss that ensues, because reinforcing the discipline, and not my ego, is what leads to regular profits. Thankfully, my lapses are getting less and less frequent, and I look forward to the day when my only losses come as a result of stopping out of a well-thought-out trade that fit my model. So, let's look at stops.

Learning to Love Stops

This is one of the simplest tactics for keeping your capital intact, but one of the most difficult rules to keep for a trader hooked on the excitement generated by the experience of a winning trade. There are no hard-and-fast rules for stops. You will have different limits for stops, depending on what stage of the day you are trading. For the market-open trading I have illustrated, stops have to be very tight. Essentially, I exit my position at the first sign of trouble for my position. The process is the same whether I enter either a long or short. When the security stops moving in the direction I expect, I liquidate immediately. This may mean taking a small loss. Similarly, if I have made a small appreciation of something like $1/4 or $3/8, I often exit to preserve that profit at the first sign of trouble. The only time I do not exit at the first sign of a slowdown in the direction of price movement favoring my position is when I have made over $1 and the market conditions suggest that the pullback is a continuation rather than reversal. During the week's worth of trading shown in Chapter 6, you saw me exit with a loss when the price movement was not as expected for NMGC. Other than that, I exited at the first sign of trouble for all the other positions I took and thereby preserved my profits. This should tell you how often I try to ride out continuation patterns during market-open trading: not often.

If you find that Phase 2 market trading fits your personality better, you need to set stops that are not as tight. Stops in Phase 1 trading kick in as a result of a slowdown in price movement and a shift in the side of the market favored by the market makers. The same in Phase 2 trading would be harmful to your capital. When trading Phase 2 continuation patterns, or if you must, reversal patterns, you have to set a reasonable loss limit to allow the pattern some room. Typically, anything more than $3/8 is a bad idea, but much less will lead you to cut losses too early.

If you are active in the Phase 3 market and trade breakouts, you need to revert back to the tighter stops of Phase 1 trading. The reason Phase 1 and Phase 3 trading require tighter stops is that the price movement tends to be more violent, and reversals equally so, which can leave you in a losing position that is difficult to close out of.

By keeping these types of stops, you preserve your capital. However, if you start to enter ill-advised trades, trades that violate your own personal set of rules, no type of stop will save you. There are many reasons traders enter ill-advised trades, from trading on emotion and looking for thrills to feelings of omnipotence because of a modest winning streak. Generally, these and other reasons for failure happen because traders focus on the wrong thing. The only worthwhile thing to focus on is the process of performing disciplined trading. The next section deals with some concepts that may help you understand what it takes to keep an appropriate focus.

Focus on the Process

The first example here borrows from the thinking of a professional basketball coach. Coaches' lives are all about winning, but that is not what they focus on when making their plans. Sure, they make plans to win, but thinking about winning the championship and the glory it will bring them gets them nowhere in and of itself.

What coaches focus on is getting their team to do the things that they believe will ultimately lead to the best chance of winning on the most occasions. The media typically focuses on one shot missed or made at the end of the game and points to that as the reason a team lost or won. In just about all cases, the game was lost by what happened leading up to that moment. If the team had performed better during the whole game, it would not have had to rely on that one last shot. If all the players do their part, the odds are stacked in favor of the team winning. It is when players do not play their part of the plan that coaches get upset. They know that winning is about doing the right things consistently, not the occasional flashy (albeit personally satisfying) play. Perhaps an illustration will help.

I live in New York and am a New York Knicks fan, which has led to as many heartaches as trading Internet securities. What has struck me in watching the Knicks play is how similar the coach's job is to that of a trader. We both pick our starting lineup (the coach picks players; I pick the securities I am interested in). We both make substitutions to try to enhance our results. We both want to win. The coach wins by having his team end up with more points than the opposition, and I win by growing my capital. What we have in common is that we must both focus on the *process* of doing the right thing, not looking for (often irrelevant) things to blame. Here's a concrete example from each world.

The Knicks were in a close playoff series and the coach decided to make a change in the starting lineup. The Knicks lost. When questioned, the coach said that considering how poorly his team rebounded and defended, it would not have mattered what the starting lineup was. The next game, the coach used the same starting lineup and the team won. The point is that the focus for improving from a losing to a winning position is not the seemingly obvious one of player selection, it is in the discipline of the team. It has to do with the team getting back on defense, making rebounds, and doing all the things necessary to get the team in a position to win.

This is closely connected to experiences I have had in trading. What pays off there is a focus on being disciplined and paying attention to the process, not getting overly concerned about the results of one trade. If I do all the little things, such as proper premarket preparation, keeping good records, analyzing my trades, and avoiding entering risky positions, in other words keeping to my rules, I will win. If I seek out thrills and don't analyze my actions as much as I analyze the market, I will lose. In the world of trading, you can give a successful trader and an unsuccessful trader the same securities to trade and the same information upon which to trade. The successful trader will make money by keeping discipline and trading only when real opportunities present themselves, whereas the unsuccessful trader may make one or two gains, but is just as likely to trade away the profits and end up losing.

There are many ways that a trader can be distracted and neglect discipline, and it takes continual monitoring of your actions to identify what leads to your lapses. The first time I noticed this effect in my own trading was early in my trading career. I noticed that if my first trade was a losing trade, I tended to compound my losses by taking more ill-advised positions. Now I recognize that the first trade being a loser is not necessarily a bad thing. If I have traded a high-percentage situation and limited my losses by exiting when the security did not behave as expected, I have done a good job. Back at the beginning, however, that first loss would adversely affect my judgment in subsequent trades. At times, I would get into a profitable position only to see it turn to a loss. This happened because I sometimes was guilty of holding onto a position in the hope of getting an extra quarter, trying to cover an earlier loss. Inevitably, the opportunity to exit with a profit disappeared, and I had to exit with a second loss. At times like these, it is easy to look back and by hindsight see a big move in a security that I missed and blame my stock selection for the loss. I thought that if I could only have come up with some form of analysis that would have led me to look at the other security, I would have been okay. This, of course, is ridiculous. The fault was not with my stock selection; it was with my discipline. No form of analysis will put you in position to execute on the best opportunity all the time. Your goal has to be to execute the opportunities you do discover in a disciplined fashion, not to worry about the ones you missed. There are always more opportunities than you can possibly execute on.

The difference between these two stories is that the coach focused on the discipline needed by his players to win rather than on the issue of the starting lineup. I should have focused on making the best exit point for the trade rather than getting drawn into making decisions based on where I started my trading day. The message really is that consistent application of disciplined trading will lead to profits, and you must not allow your end goal of profits obscure your better judgment on individual trades.

If you have read up to this point, you have enough information to day trade profitably. What will determine your financial success is your ability to keep to your rules and trade with discipline. If you find yourself thinking that maybe just learning one or two more "market secrets" will open the door to better profits, you are kidding yourself and need to evaluate why you are trading and what you really want to get out of it. The notion of market secrets is perpetuated by the host of market gurus and Internet chat rooms that aim to get your subscription dollars for as long as possible. Successful traders do not believe in market secrets. They know that the market behaves now as it did in the days of Charles Dow. There is no secret to that.

Obstacles to Trading Success

There is plenty of information in this book and others that tells actual and aspiring traders how to make a profit. Lack of information is not an obstacle. What is an obstacle is people's behavior. Too many people don't know how to accept success when it comes along. They need adversity to strive against, rather than being able to maintain focus on winning consistently. This is not a conscious decision by any individual trader. It is the tendency to change trading behavior when success comes along and not stick with the hard work of analysis, both of the market and of one's own actions, that is necessary for on-going success. In the rest of this section, we'll look at some of the things that prevent traders from winning consistently, all of which come from within the trader.

Among the things that attracts many people to day trading is the freedom it offers. There is no boss, no one to tell you when to come to work, or that your work is not good enough. In fact, there is complete freedom to do as you please. What can often happen, however, is that instead of this freedom being the deliverance that people expect, they are sidelined by the lack of control and feedback. In all of society there are controls to keep us on track and to give us warning signs, like a bad review at work warning us of dire consequences unless improvement is made, or a traffic cop handing out tickets for bad driving. Feedback is constant, and whether we realize it or not, we expect it to be there. One of the dangers in trading your own account is that there is no feedback, only the level of capital in your account. For many people, that lack of feedback can allow destructive behavior to become entrenched in their trading actions. When trading your own account, you have to let the level of capital in your account be your boss. If it is declining, or not advancing as quickly as you expect, do not trick yourself into believing that next month will be any different without a change in your trading behavior.

In other walks of life, when people enter into destructive behavior, there are generally self-help organizations to assist them in their recovery. To my knowledge, there is no such help group for traders. If you find some Internet chat room or other support group that you like, that is fine. Just don't use that to make your trading decisions.

Just because there is no well-established trader's self-help group does not mean that there are no lessons to learn from existing self-help groups in other areas. In his book, *Trading for a Living*, Dr. Alexander Elder points to Alcoholics Anonymous as an organization that can help traders. The discipline an alcoholic must live with to avoid alcohol is similar to the discipline a trader must live with to avoid losses. Dr. Elder's profession as a psychiatrist took him to many AA meetings, where he heard how just one drink led the alcoholic down a slippery slope to drunkenness, and he noticed a similarity with his trading activities. Just one lapse of discipline could lead him to lose control and compound losses. In other words, Dr. Elder equates the losses of a trader to alcohol for an alcoholic. So the same way an alcoholic avoids getting drunk one day at a time, which adds up a week, then a month, a year, and a decade, a trader avoids losses one day at a time. Anyone who trades knows that a winning streak inevitably ends when you start to become too sure of yourself and lose discipline.

There are many people who are not alcoholics, but who have had a little too much to drink at one time or another. Few people set out to get drunk, but how many people have gotten up in the morning with a hangover, swearing that they will never do that again? Plenty. No one thinks about tomorrow's hangover at the time he takes that one-drink-too-many. It is the same in trading. It can be difficult to avoid the lure of an ill-advised trade that holds some promise of getting back your day's losses, and then only deepens them.

I like the analogy up to this point, but Dr. Elder takes it a little further by saying that if someone who has to avoid alcohol is called an alcoholic, a person who has to avoid losses is a loser. He advocates telling yourself each day before trading starts that you are a loser. The idea is that this will remind you that without utmost care, you will generate losses rather than gains during the trading day. Here is where Dr. Elder and I part company, because this is a little too negative for my taste. I do applaud the goal of reminding oneself daily that any cavalier trading actions will likely result in generating and compounding losses. But I stop at recommending that you read your rules every day before starting to trade and stating that your goal that day is to trade in a disciplined fashion consistent with your premarket plan. This should be adequate to keep your focus on avoiding losses.

The other self-help organizations that are interesting from the viewpoint of trading psychology are the weight-loss folks. For most people, a simple plan that includes a healthy, low-fat diet and regular exercise is enough to lose weight and keep it off. But if it is that simple, how can a huge weight-loss industry derive millions of dollars from helping people lose weight?

It seems many people are looking for that magical something: a new food additive, prescription drug, or fat-burning exercise machine that makes losing weight easier. Many people seem to take a similar view when it comes to trading. The majority will look for some market secret that successful traders know and they don't. Again, though, there are no market secrets. What leads to long-term trading success is simple to say, but difficult to adhere to. You have to become your own self-help organization and remind yourself constantly of the rules and disciplinary measures needed to reach and maintain trading success. Those who promote market secrets that you can follow blindly and promise to deliver easy returns are about as believable as those who promote the latest exercise machine or miracle weight-loss drug that will give you a model body effortlessly.

Just because you know what to do does not mean you will be able to do it. Doing what leads to success on a long-term basis is a challenging proposition.

There are many warning signs that you should heed when trading. One of the most common is the reluctance to take a break when you lose. If you enter a losing streak and find it impossible, or even difficult, to stop trading for two weeks or so for self-evaluation, you may be in trouble and in need of help. You should consider Gamblers Anonymous or serious psychotherapy. Equally common is the desire of traders to hide losses, or to claim that money obtained from other sources has actually come from trading. Both of these problems are indicative of an emotional rather than intellectual involvement in trading, which will only lead to depleted capital.

Your best defense in dealing with these obstacles is a set of rules that is customized to your strengths and weaknesses, which can only be generated from analysis of your own trading actions. In the next section, I share with you my own set of personal rules that guide my trading actions on a daily basis. Whenever I break one of these rules, I end up losing money.

Forming Your Own Set of Rules

Getting your own set of rules to trade by is a very personal thing. You need to critically assess your motivations and trading actions in order to develop your rules. Once you have determined that a rule should exist for you, your goal must be to never break it again. In my early career, this was one of the most difficult things to do. Adhering to a rule that prevents you from making a trade will always mean missing out on an opportunity here and there that would have made money. The temptation then, of course, becomes to break that rule at some point in the future so as not to miss out on the next opportunity. The first rule I had to force myself to live with came about by analyzing my Phase 1 trading. I would watch the price action of a security that I had a position in move against me and try to convince myself that it was a continuation of the price action direction that I had bought into. This was, of course, a fallacy. During Phase 1, there tend to be wild swings, and no trends have established themselves on the intraday chart, so there are no trends present for a continuation pattern to act upon. This rule now leads me to take profits very early in Phase 1 trading and to exit a position at the first sign of a reversal in price action direction. This was evident in the week's trading illustrated in the previous chapter. What made it difficult for me to live with this rule at first was that even though I held positions through what I thought was a continuation, only to see profits turn to losses, on occasion I also saw the price action move in my favor and give me big returns. The reason I now make a rule of early exits in Phase 1 trading is because keeping good trading records showed me that over time, I have done better by exiting early and avoiding the losses that come from looking for the price action to turn back in my favor. This is the key to making day trading a profitable long-term source of income. You must do what works for the majority of the time all the time and not be tempted to act on impulse to take advantage of a perceived opportunity that is not in your normal trading routine.

One of the concepts I take from long-term investing, which actually helps my discipline, is the idea of limiting the number of trades I execute in a week. The concept for long-term investing is that you can allow yourself to make 20 stock picks in your investing life. The rationale is that with such a small number of decisions available to you, you have to research each one extremely carefully before making the commitment for that investment to be one of your 20. This concept helps me particularly well when I have taken a break from trading for a while. What I do is start by allowing myself only two trades per week. This forces me to trade only the very best of opportunities. Usually this means waiting for an opportunity in which the market heading up can be combined with a security experiencing a premarket gap down to areas of support, but trending strongly upward on the daily chart. This sort of thing does not happen every day, but the discipline needed to wait for it is a valuable thing. Once I have kept to that level of trading and profited, I can increase the number of trades I allow myself as long as I maintain discipline and trade within my rules. If ever my discipline fails, I cut back on the number of trades. Ultimately, I want to get to the point where I allow myself two trades per day.

Here, then, is my list of trading rules, followed by an explanation of each one, where necessary.

1. For Phase 1 trading, only execute trades that agree with your premarket plan.
2. If you are sick, unable to concentrate 100 percent, or have not done adequate premarket preparation, do not trade that day.

3. If you only get a partial fill on a limit order and the stock runs away from you, do not chase the stock; trade only the amount of shares you have from the partial fill.
4. Do not chase stocks past a half point.
5. Never let profits turn to losses. Particularly in Phase 1, exit winning positions early so that you get out when you can, not when you have to.
6. If trading the first move after the open, initiate positions by 9:33 a.m., and always respect the 9:40 a.m. reversal time.
7. When looking for reversals after market open, only trade those securities that reverse into the direction of the market. The best opportunities come when a security reverses into the direction of the market either right at the open or close to 9:40 a.m.
8. If you find yourself rushing to get a position in a stock that you have not analyzed before the market opens, don't.
9. Keep stop losses to 1/4 and always execute them when they are hit.
10. Always remember that you will never know it all or get it all right. Lose respect for the market and it will take your capital.
11. Never allow yourself to trade anything other than one of the well-known patterns (especially no spiking securities).
12. Never trade above the SOES tier size.
13. Having closed the trading system down, do not open it again to take advantage of a perceived opportunity.
14. If a trade goes immediately against you, get out immediately.
15. Do not hold a position in a stock that has stopped moving. In that situation there is equal probability that the stock will continue to go nowhere, will go up, or go down.
16. Do not trade stocks that have either wide spreads (anything greater than 1/8 for any period of time) or thin levels. This is indicative of a security with a small float that can swing wildly. You don't need these types of securities to make money.

This is not a comprehensive list of things to avoid, or of things to do to ensure profitability. What it is meant to be is a list of things that I know are my weak points, things that I need a daily reminder to be cautious of.

Let's discuss each of these rules in a little more detail. Rule 1 I cannot stress enough. As you have seen, my preference is to trade during the first half hour of the market. This fits with my personal style and preferences and provides plenty of opportunity for profit, without tying me to the screen all day. If you look at a one-minute or five-minute tick chart, you will see that the sharpest moves tend to occur during the opening period. Each day, I do my premarket analysis, come up with no more than five potential plays, and look to see which security behaves as I expect. If I restrict myself to only executing on one of those preidentified plays, I will do well. If I get tempted by a strongly moving security that pops into view, but which I have not identified and analyzed beforehand, I usually lose by trading it. Occasionally, jumping on the bandwagon will reward you, but more often than not, you get caught out. It is part of a disciplined approach to not trade if your premarket analysis does not reveal a tradable opportunity that day.

Rule 2 is one that I have violated in the past, but never without being punished. To trade effectively requires total concentration and focus. There are no opportunities to work at 80 percent effectiveness and still do well. With your goal to avoid losses, you should turn off your trading system if you are not 100 percent focused.

Rules 3 and 4 are closely related. Both of them have to do with trying to get in on a move that is already well underway. The goal of day trading in a disciplined fashion should be to get in early on a move and exit before the move has expired and the price action has reversed on you. Day traders should not try to predict that a certain move will occur. They try to position themselves so that they can act should a move start and get a piece of that move. If you place a limit order (as you have to if you are trading on Island), it is certainly possible that you will only get a partial fill and the market will then move beyond your limit price, causing the rest of the order to be canceled. Trying then to enter an odd lot at a new price to catch more of the same move is a risky proposition. Likewise, watching a security move a dollar and not being able to get any stock, then continuing to chase the price of the stock is a bad idea. If you are continually missing entry points, you are likely to get filled only when the security reverses. Keeping to these two rules requires a lot of discipline, because there will be times when you see securities run for several dollars and chasing the stock will allow you to get a piece of the move. Console yourself with the knowledge that these represent a minority of cases. It is the majority of cases you need to account for.

Rule 5 should take care of itself as long as you follow the principle of getting out with profits early in the move rather than waiting for the move to expire and having to chase the stock to get an exit. Watching profits turn to losses has a devastating effect on many a trader's psyche. Having seen a profit on a trade, it is very difficult to realize a loss, even if the security is moving strongly against you. It is more likely that a trader will hold the position beyond any reasonable stop loss in the hope that things will turn in his or her favor. Invariably, things do not turn in his or her favor, and the trader is forced to exit when the pain of the loss becomes too great to bear. Even worse than this is that a trader can feel compelled to jump right back into the market to recover the loss. This can lead to an unwise trade that further compounds the losses. The rule, then, is to protect your profits at all costs, because you will never kill your capital by taking profits.

Rules 6 and 7 may raise eyebrows with many experienced traders, but I have found them to be my most valuable trading rules. The nature of the securities I search for to trade during Phase 1 means that those securities are trading off of some sort of extreme market reaction. For whatever reason, and I do not know what that reason is, the first move of the day in these securities generally does not last past the first 10 minutes of trading. I estimate that this phenomenon occurs in around 70 to 80 percent of securities that the premarket gap analysis identifies. The overall direction of the market also has an impact on the probability of the security reversing direction after 10 minutes of trading. A typical example of this phenomenon occurred when I traded VISX on Tuesday of the trading week covered in Chapter 6. The market as a whole was in a strong upward trend, so I preferred to look for securities that had pulled back to areas of support, and then to look for the first move up to enter a long position. VISX traded up strongly from near the open for more than a $2 gain, and it peaked at exactly 9:40 a.m. The next day the peak was at 9:50 a.m. for VISX. On Thursday MESG peaked at 9:40 a.m., and on Friday we saw TMCS bottom at around 9:36. The general concept is that for gapping securities, the force that drives their first move will run out early in the trading day, and the time this most frequently occurs is at, or close to, 9:40 a.m. If you do not feel comfortable initiating a position prior to 9:33 a.m., wait for a security to reverse its initial move. If you are waiting for a reversal of the initial move, it is better to look at a security whose initial move is in the direction of the premarket gap. The best Phase 1 opportunities come first from gap-down securities that move upward as soon as the market opens, or continue down for approximately 10 minutes, then reverse up. The second-best opportunities come from gap-up securities that drop at market open, or continue up at market open and reverse after around 10 minutes of trading.

Rule 8 was very difficult for me to adhere to when I first started trading. At the end of the day's trading, I would look at the intraday charts for a whole host of Internet securities, see strong moves that had carried the price actions through several dollars of appreciation or decline, and think that if only I could catch a couple of those moves I would be set. Of course, looking at those charts in hindsight is completely different from looking at the market as it is trading and trying to spot an opportunity to trade. What would happen is that I would see a security start to move, see positive confirmation on the Level II screen, and chase the stock to get some of the action. Occasionally, I would win, but more often I would lose, or get whipsawed swapping between long and short positions and not make any money. This is a stressful way to trade and should be avoided. To safely make money, you have to place yourself in a position to enter a position as a stock starts to move in the way you expect. To have a realistic expectation, you have to have studied the security's recent price history. You can then develop a premarket plan of how to trade it. Trying to jump on a train that has already left the station is risky.

Rule 9 should be known and accepted by all traders. Stop losses are essential for long-term survival. I try to keep my stop losses to $1/4 on shorts and less on longs. The reason for this is that there has to be some buying in the market to allow you to enter a short position, so there is always the chance that when you get filled on a short order, the price can continue up a little before falling again.

Rule 10 needs to be there as a reminder. As soon as you think you have a formula that will work in all instances, the market will prove you wrong. You have to constantly monitor the market's activity to understand whether it is likely to continue its trend or reverse. Always try to play an individual security that is heading in the direction of the overall market. You have to know whether longs or shorts are most likely to provide profits. You also need to know if gapping securities have been reversing at market open, 9:40 a.m., or some other time, or if they are tending to follow their premarket gap directions. This rule should always keep the thought foremost in your mind that the market will do what it wants, and that is your reactions to it that determine your results.

Rule 11 is a matter of discipline. The well-known patterns of securities gapping down to support or gapping up to resistance provide the best opportunities. Trendless securities that experience a spike, doubling or tripling their value overnight, can seem attractive, but generally these are securities with a small float available, which typically experience wild swings in price. These securities are too risky for a disciplined approach. They are not necessary to make good profits, so it is best to steer clear of them. What tends to happen with spiking securities is that there will be a wide spread between bid and ask (3/8 or more) and the same sort of spread between successive bid or ask levels, with few market makers at each level. This allows any excess demand or supply to move the security very rapidly, often more rapidly than it is possible to execute on very well. Occasionally, you will get it right and win big, but over time, the probability is that you will lose more by trading these securities than you will gain.

Rule 12 is an absolute requirement for safe trading. Often, I have seen what appears to be a perfect opportunity for a nice gain, only to find out that the security had a tier size of 200. It is tempting to trade on an ECN and go above the tier size to take a position. As we know, however, nothing is guaranteed in the market. If that position moves against you, getting out when you have more than the tier size can be next to impossible. Should the security suddenly change direction, it is amazing how quickly the opportunity to exit via an ECN can disappear, leaving you able to close out only a part of your position on SOES and hoping that an ECN provides an opportunity for exit, or that the move reverses in your favor. Neither is a situation you want to find yourself in.

Rule 13 is again a point of discipline. Particularly if you experience a losing trade in the morning and decide to close the trading system down for the day, there is often a temptation to look at the market again in the hope of gaining back your loss. Typically, this is a result of seeing either a buying or selling frenzy and trying to get in on the move. Jumping into a position is almost always a mistake. By the time you decide what to do, get your system started up again, and are able to act, the best entry point is long gone. The trading style to pursue is one that positions you to take advantage of moves in a security as they begin. This requires analysis and a plan for what you expect to happen to the security, and you only enter a position when the security behaves as you expect. For trading past Phase 1, this means that you will know the levels of support and resistance that have been established through the day and when one of those levels has been broken or respected.

Rule 14 should be followed without question at every occurrence. As you can see from the week's worth of trading illustrated in the last chapter, there are many occasions when you enter what appears to be an executable order only to wait two minutes or more to get a fill. If, during this time, the price action of the security makes you change your mind with regard to entering the position, the right thing to do is to cancel the order prior to taking the position. Order cancellations can be slow, however, and if the cancellation does not work its way through the system fast enough, you can get filled even after you enter the cancellation. You are then in the situation of holding a position that you just tried to get out of. The temptation is to say that the current move is a pullback and the initial direction of the price action will resume. This gives you hope that you will not take a loss and is most probably a mistake. If you try to cancel, get filled, and then hold, you are hoping that your most recent analysis is wrong and that it makes no sense. Don't yield to the hope that you can avoid a loss. A loss that results from a rule of discipline is a good thing, because it will minimize your total losses over time.

Rule 15 should be self-explanatory. The method of day trading I practice is to wait for a move in a security's price to start and then try to take a position for part of that move. If the move stops, I either have misread the situation or the stock is likely to reverse. In either case, I should not hold on hoping that the move will resume in favor of my position.

Rule 16 is intended to restrict your trading to stocks for which you are able to keep your stop losses. By making loss avoidance, or at least keeping them to a minimum, your prime goal when trading, you greatly improve your chances for success. To do this, you need to avoid securities that have the potential to blow past your stops, not giving you a chance to get out when you want. There are plenty of profitable opportunities in the market every day in securities that have good liquidity. There is no need to chase those that don't.

As stated previously, this is my set of rules, and I need to be constantly reminded of them. By keeping good records of your premarket analysis and trading actions, you too will be able to see where you have weaknesses. The next chapter offers some advice on what to track to make this sort of analysis easier. Before we move on to that, though, I want to share a recent trade in which I lost discipline and experienced a very rare day of losing.

When Things Go Wrong

The following is a trade report from the morning after a holiday party. The most obvious rule I broke here was that I was not 100 percent and should not have been trading. Normally, when I attend a midweek party, I try to schedule something for the next day that will keep me away from the trading system and the temptation to trade. That did not work out this time, however, and because the party had been a fairly quiet affair, I thought it was okay to trade. The fact that the party was fairly quiet was not the point. Attending the party disturbed my usual routine. I had less sleep than normal, leaving me tired in the morning. Anyhow, I made the mistake to trade when I was not 100 percent, which left me open to more mistakes.

Tick	#Typ	Symbol	B/S	Shares	Price	(P/L)	Comm	SystemTime	By
3192	3	RRRR	Shor	1000	$40^7/_{16}$		22.95	09:39:	ISLD
3606	3	RRRR	Buy	100	$41^1/_2$		22.95	09:41:	JPMS
3609	3	RRRR	Buy	900	$41^1/_2$			09:41:	JANY
						(1,062.50)			
11602	2	CORL	Buy	1000	$16^3/_4$		22.95	10:33:	ISLD
12157	2	CORL	Sell	650	$17^5/_{16}$		22.95	10:37:	ISLD
12158	2	CORL	Sell	200	$17^5/_{16}$			10:37:	ISLD
12159	2	CORL	Sell	150	$17^5/_{16}$			10:37:	ISLD
						566.40			

```
Total (Loss)      (496.09)
Commission        91.80
Net Loss          (587.89)
```

Chapter 7

This took place on December 23. I had done reasonable premarket preparation and had a good list of both long and short candidates to examine, depending on how the early trading developed. RRRR started to drop quite nicely, almost immediately from the open, and would have been a good candidate for a very early short, perhaps at 9:31 or 9:32. My problem, however, was that I was slow in assessing all my options. By the time I had determined that RRRR was a good early short, it was almost 9:40, and I hadn't really noticed. I entered the short position at 9:39. The price fell maybe 1/8 and then stopped. I then made a further mistake by holding the position after the price movement had stopped. When the price action started to move against me, I was slow in executing my exit and got stuck in the SOES queue. The price moved over $1 against me for a loss of $1062.50. Realizing what had happened, I was angry with myself. I got back half the losses later with a trade on CORL, when the market was in Phase 2 trading, but decided to stop there and take my loss. I deserved the loss for breaking the rules, and I take that as a $500 reminder not to do that. Before moving on, let's just see how many broken rules led to this loss.

First, I broke Rule 2 by trading when I should not have. Next, I broke Rule 6 by not respecting the 9:40 a.m. reversal time and not entering a position in the initial move of the security by 9:33 a.m. I broke Rule 9 by not having a stop in mind, which led me to get caught out without a quick way out of the position. Finally, I broke Rule 15 by not exiting as soon as the security stopped moving in my favor, at 9:40 a.m.

If I had been 100 percent, I would probably have been able to assess my options more quickly, could have been in a short with RRRR earlier, and could have gotten out before 9:40. Or I would have decided not to enter a position so close to 9:40 and would have looked at CORL as a potential gainer, given its previous history of gapping down to strong support and moving up nicely. As it was, I took the loss and the reminder to keep to my rules.

What I hope you take from this is that no matter how much success you have in the market, the potential to lose for no good reason is always there if you ignore the lessons of your trading past.

8
Keeping Track

In this chapter we will provide the final set of tools required to day trade using the methods discussed in this book. I have stressed at every opportunity the importance of discipline. Discipline for day trading means making a plan and sticking to it. To make that plan real, you need to write down what you expect to do and measure how you perform against your plan. This chapter has three sections, which mirror the activity of a trading day: the premarket analysis, the posttrade activity, and the tracking sheets for weekly monitoring. A fourth section discusses how I prefer to set up the windows on my trading system.

As I've said, one of the most important things you can do to ensure your long-term trading success is to measure your actions against your plan on a daily basis. This is often as much work as analyzing the market to make your trading decisions, but it's just as worthwhile.

Premarket Task Sheets

When trading the open, in particular, this is the most important task to complete every day. If you think you will get a long-term, reliable stream of income by logging onto your trading system at or around market open, getting some recommendations from an Internet chat room, and then trading like a champ, you are mistaken. To trade the open of the market requires that you identify which stocks are moving that day; which of those have real potential, as indicated by volume; what trends, support, and resistance are evident for those stocks on their daily charts; and how the market makers are positioning themselves on the Level II screen. In addition you need to know the tier size of the security you are thinking of trading, whether it is a candidate for shorting, and whether your broker can deliver the short to you. Remember, there is an opportunity cost to each trade. This means that while you are watching one security, another may be moving more in accordance with your plan, so it is important to not waste time looking for entry into a position you cannot take. In the next section I will discuss screen layouts that have helped me monitor four securities at a time, increasing my chances of seeing the best opportunity available that day. For now, however, let's look at the premarket security analysis sheets I use every day. They are illustrated in Figure 8-1.

Date:				Today's Preference: Long/Short
Symbol	Tier	Short	Daily Chart	Intended Play
Ups				
Downs				

Figure 8-1. Premarket security analysis sheet.

The security symbols are generated from the premarket report of securities gapping up and gapping down. Obtaining all this information allows you to identify a handful of securities each day that have moved with volume in the premarket. You will know how many shares you can trade and whether watching for a shorting opportunity is worthwhile. Most important, through technical analysis of the daily chart of that stock, you will know how the security has behaved recently. This will help you narrow down the number of securities you will monitor when looking to take a position in a security. The goal for short candidates is to find one that has gapped up to areas of resistance or price congestion on the daily chart. For long candidates, it is the reverse. You look for securities gapping down to areas of support. Once your technical analysis of the daily chart is complete, you can define what your intended play for each security will be.

In Chapter 6, I gave the longhand version of this information, which was derived from completing this worksheet for each of the gapping securities identified on each day. An example of a completed worksheet is given in Figure 8-2, which led me to taking a long position in COMS for a gain of $1 3/4 on December 22, 1999, as shown by the trade report below.

```
Tick   #Typ  Symbol  B/S   Shares  Price   (P/L)    Comm   SystemTime  By
2073   2     COMS    Buy   500     44               22.95  09:34:      SOES:PFSI
3569   2     COMS    Sell  500     45 3/4  875.00   22.95  09:42:      ISLD

Total Gain      875
Commission      45.90
Total Net Gain  829.10
```

In Figure 8-2, I have marked with an asterisk those securities that I would be paying particular attention to once the market opened. These are the securities with which I would populate my Level II windows and one-minute tick chart windows for monitoring. At the time of this report, the market was still moving upward strongly, so my preference was for longs if possible, and a number of prime candidates were unearthed by the premarket gap report. After the market had been trading for one minute, the Level II screens were showing particularly strong support on the bid side for both CORL and COMS, and I entered market orders on SOES

Date: December 22, 1999				Today's Preference: Long
Symbol	Tier	Short	Daily Chart	Intended Play
Ups				
TALK	A	✓	Possible exhaustion	Short if market also drops
GENE	A	X	Spike security	No Play
MLTX*	B	✓	Recent downtrend, gap up to resistance	Short
HHGP	A	X	Uptrend	No Play
ONTC	A	✓	Strong uptrend	No Play
GWRX	A	✓	Breakout for continuation	No Play
Downs				
CORL*	A		Moved down to support	Long
GEEK	A		Spike	No Play
COMS*	A		Uptrend, now down to support	Long
MQST*	B		Uptrend, now down to support	Long
RIMM*	A		Uptrend, now down to support	Long

Figure 8-2. A completed premarket worksheet for December 22, 1999.

for both (CORL for 1000 and COMS for 500 to keep within this account's margin requirements). SOES is not my first choice for taking positions under these circumstances, but there was no stock being offered on ECNs, so my choices were either a market SOES or jumping on the bid via an ECN and hoping someone would sell to me. Since I could see that the sizes for ECNs were not depleting on the bid, it seemed that no one was selling to the ECN bid prices, so SOES seemed my best option at the time. The SOES queue was so long, however, that even though I got a fill for COMS, I canceled the order for CORL because I saw evidence of bid support weakening prior to a fill on that order and did not want to get in under those conditions.

It is good discipline to file these analysis reports on a daily basis, and then to review how each of the securities you analyzed performed and check that your trading actions were in harmony with your plans. In the next sections I discuss the screen layouts that I have found make me most productive. Screen layouts are a very personal thing, and I recommend you use the following information only as a starting point for developing what feels most comfortable to you.

Screen Layouts

Most of today's trading software enables you to define several different page views, each with its own set of windows. I now focus on three different pages that I use at different times of the day and for different trading activities. The first one consists of four Level II windows, plus a small market minder, which monitors the last price and change on the day for the NASDAQ Composite and the net ticks figure. These Level II windows are used to monitor the four best market open plays that I have identified through my pre-market gap analysis. While I am looking for one of these four securities to show the anticipated behavior, I also keep an eye on the two indicators in the market minder to get a feel for how the NASDAQ market is performing overall. Both the NASDAQ Composite and the net ticks figure are broad measures of the NASDAQ market's health. They do not always head in the same direction during the market open, but when they do, it is a good indicator of whether there is excess demand or supply in the market at that time. If, on any given day, I have a preference for longs, see a security fall to levels of support on its daily chart, and see strong market maker support at the bid, then seeing both the Composite and the net ticks figure rise adds to my confidence in going long.

Once I have made a decision to take a position based on the Level II screen action and overall NASDAQ market performance, I switch to a different page. The second page has a Level II display: a one-minute tick chart set to track the bid price if I am long, or the ask price if I am short: a market minder of my selected securities for that day (plus the Composite and net ticks figure); and the order entry window. Most trading systems will automatically fill in a buy order if you double click on the ask price in your minder and a sell order if you double click on the bid price in the minder. This screen allows me to monitor everything I need to as I enter, hold, and then liquidate the position. The Level II screen has the attached dynamic time-of-sales window, which allows me to see whether the trades are on the bid or ask side (assuming the NASDAQ trade feed is reasonably up to date at that time).

The final page I use is set for six one-minute tick charts. In these windows I usually keep the charts of the composite, net ticks, and the four securities I am following, generally during Phase 2 trading. During Phase 2, I will only look at the Level II screen when I am either entering or exiting a position. When entering, I look to see if the expected support or resistance is holding at the price I anticipated. When exiting, I only use the Level II screen to assist me in selecting the order route and price level at which to trade. Phase 2 trades are driven by trends being in effect and defined trendlines of support or resistance being respected. The only place to see this is on a one-minute tick chart. The Level II screen tends to give you many false signals at this stage of the trading day.

This charting page can also be used if none of the securities being monitored move in the expected direction immediately after the market opens. Suppose a gap-down security looks good, but it continues to fall after the market opens. If the market indicators tell me the whole market is still headed down, I will not go long. If, however, my analysis tells me that a long is the right position to take and no other securities I am following are behaving as expected, I look for my long candidates to find their first bottom of the day and for a reversal up when demand comes into the market. This is the search for the point reversal discussed earlier in the book. If I see a long candidate continue to fall after market open, then see its bid-based one-minute tick chart start to rise (hopefully close to 9:40 a.m.), followed or accompanied by the Composite and net ticks figure reversing up, I will take a long position in the expectation that support is finally being found. Of course, once I decide to take a position, I switch to the page showing my order entry window. This is more risky than going long when a gap-down security starts to recover immediately after market open, so I tend to exit immediately if I see any signs of weakness either on the tick chart or the Level II screen.

What to Keep Track of on a Daily Basis

For each day that you are trading, I recommend you file the following documentation:

- The premarket plan
- Your market minder, showing opening prices for that day's securities
- A one-minute tick chart printed at least 20 minutes after each trade you make, making note of your entry and exit points and reasoning
- The daily chart for all the securities you are monitoring that day
- A short note stating how you felt that day, whether you traded to your plan, and ideas for improving your performance

At first blush, this may seem quite a lot of work and a lot of paper to track. I have found, however, that this type of record-keeping is the most valuable activity I undertake. With this type of documentation, it is possible to identify the type of trading you are most adept at, any mistakes you are repeating, and patterns in your behavior.

What to Keep Track of on a Weekly Basis

The most important weekly activity is setting aside time to perform whatever general market analysis you feel most comfortable with. If you like the point-and-figure charts of major market indexes, and you couple that with analysis of the NASDAQ bullish percentage (both available from the Chartcraft or Dorsey Wright Web sites), that is fine. I like these indicators and feel comfortable with the preference they give me for either long or short positions. Candlesticks coupled with conventional western-style charting are also an option.

Whatever method or methods you choose to determine your preference for either the long or the short side of the market must be viewed only as useful secondary factors in your trading decisions. The most important factor remains the supply and demand of the individual security. Nevertheless, having the appropriate preference for longs or shorts will help you stay away from some ill-advised positions.

Another measure of weekly performance, the only performance indicator that has any value, is the account balance. Throughout this book I have taken every opportunity to stress that disciplined trading should be your goal, not any specific monetary target. If, however, your account balance is not growing as a result of what you perceive to be disciplined trading actions, something is wrong. Weekly is the right frequency for me to keep track of my account balance. That way, I don't constantly fixate on having to find a trade that will give me X dollars to make whatever quota I have in mind. Weekly checking is frequent enough to bring my attention to any problems in my analysis or discipline that may occur and show up as poor returns in my account. I have discussed this in earlier chapters and will say it again here: *As soon as you try to take a specific amount of money out of the market or decide you need more money than you are getting at the moment, your mindset has changed to one that will drive you to take ill-advised trades, and the overwhelming probability is that you will end up losing.*

I also like to see which of the patterns I follow are yielding the best returns at the moment. As the market changes direction, you will find that gap-up or gap-down securities will alternatively provide the best opportunities for Phase 1 trading. Within each of these patterns, you will find also that the instant when the premarket gap starts to close changes. Typically, in times of a bull market you will tend to see gap-down securities start to appreciate immediately after market open, whereas gap-up securities will continue to appreciate into the open, only dropping after several minutes of trading. The opposite is true for bear markets: Gap-up securities tend to reverse down sooner than gap-down securities gap up. When the market is at a pivotal point or taking a breather in its trend, the behavior of gapping securities can be less predictable. By monitoring the prevailing behavior of these types of patterns, you will be better prepared when entering and exiting trades.

Monitoring your discipline is also an essential task. Monitoring your own behavior is always difficult. I find it helps to write down my plans for trading and then assess my discipline by reviewing whether or not I have kept to those plans. Typical plans include things like setting the number of trades you will allow yourself for the week, deciding which phase of market trading you are going to focus on that week, deciding which patterns you will look to trade, and so forth. Should you find yourself moving away from your planned activities, the best action to take is to cut back on the amount of trading you do until you are able to keep to your plans. Once you do keep to your plans, you can reward yourself by gradually increasing the number of trades you allow yourself for the week.

Conclusion

This, the shortest chapter in the book, contains possibly the most valuable advice. Keeping records of your premarket analysis and subsequent trading actions allows you to review what you are doing and identify what is going wrong if you start to lose more than you win. Every trader I know has gone through a bad patch, and to a greater or lesser degree has experienced losses, normally for one of the following common reasons:

- Loss of discipline, either not following the researched trading plan or breaking one's own trading rules.
- Getting caught in a rut: trading one pattern successfully, but continuing to trade that pattern after the nature of the market has changed, which typically leads to losses.
- Trying to trade all periods of the trading day. As noted, the different phases of the trading day have different characteristics, and different people will find their niche in different places. Stick with what you find you do well and avoid the rest.

By keeping the daily market preparation forms and posttrade chart printouts, you are able to monitor your effectiveness at identifying opportunities and executing on them. By performing weekly the tasks of identifying your preference for longs or shorts and monitoring your account balance, you can take a longer-term view of your performance and ability to keep the appropriate bias in the opportunities you seek out.

Chapter 8

Above all else, by reviewing your own actions, you will realize that there are no excuses for losses. The market moves in whatever way the majority decides. No one person can control that. The only things you can control are when you decide to enter and when you decide to exit a position, which can only be based on the reality of what the market is doing at that time, not what you hope it will do.

Afterword

One of the great things about the North American financial markets is that there is something for everyone. By this I mean that there are many different ways to approach them. Different people can hold opposing views and both be right with respect to risk tolerance and trading objectives.

My personal experience has led me to take advantage of two types of trading, first, the very short-term trading outlined in this book, and second, long-term buy-and-hold strategies. This works best for me. What works best for you may be something completely different.

Perhaps the most profitable strategies of all fall somewhere between the two approaches I follow, that is, positions in which one moves capital from security to security, holding a position for weeks or months, essentially for as long as it is perceived to be the best option available in the market. Timing trades in this fashion is immensely difficult, and nobody has found a way to get it right consistently. Or if anyone does know how to time trades this way, he or she is keeping it a secret. I, therefore, keep to the most predictable results I can find in the market, which appear at the very short-term and the very long-term ends of the spectrum.

In my short-term trading, I find that I loathe losses so much that I am more comfortable sometimes passing on potential gains in order to ensure that I do not experience losses. The brand of day trading I have illustrated here is not the only way to make money day trading, but it does take advantage of the most predictable moves each day. When the three things that need to occur for me to enter a position happen, I rarely lose money. Those three things are:

1. There must be a significant premarket move.
2. After the premarket move, the security must be trading at a level of support (to be a long candidate) or resistance (to be a candidate for shorting) as defined on the daily chart.
3. After market open, there must be strong market maker support for the security to reverse the direction of the premarket move.

I most commonly exit positions as soon as it appears the move in my favor is ending. I take my cue for this from the market makers. If I am long and support for the bid price weakens, I exit. If I am short, I exit if the market makers start to move away from the ask price. For a certainty, more profits are there for the taking by riding through small continuation patterns in moves like this. I see that situation almost every day; I get out when more profits were available. If you do try to hold through small pullbacks, however, you expose yourself to the risk of loss for those times that are not continuation patterns. When the direction of price movement really has changed and you have held on hoping that it was a temporary pullback, you often can't get out at a favorable price, and you end up losing money. Of course, trading in harmony with the overall market direction, as indicated by the daily charts and the one-minute tick charts of the NASDAQ Composite and net ticks value, will improve your odds of being able to correctly choose when to ride out small pullbacks. However, there are no guarantees when you do this. Whether you choose to ride out pullbacks in the hope of further gains needs to be defined by your risk tolerance, not by greed. If your actions are defined by greed, your account balance will surely become depleted over time.

Having experimented with all the forms of day trading I have heard about, I find the approach of trading reversals from premarket gaps at the open works best for me. I make small gains every day, miss out on many big moves of the day, and avoid the losses that chasing those big moves generates.

At the other end of the spectrum, holding a diversified portfolio of high-quality securities has proven historically to yield returns far better than fixed-income investments. I suspect that will be the case for the foreseeable future.

The one thing that I hope all readers take from this book is resolution to make a plan and stick to it, whatever type of trading you pursue. If, however, your plan is to buy good quality securities on dips and sell on peaks (as I hear all too often), do some more reading. Nobody who has been actively involved in the market for any length of time can do this consistently. This strategy most commonly results in some modest successes, followed by selling when the security has reached a perceived peak, after which the security appreciates still further. Seeing this, the urge to buy back in reappears, but by this time the security has consolidated at those levels, and the purchase is made just as the security falls to lower levels of support. Unfortunately, our trading decisions have to be made without future knowledge of price movements. There is no guarantee, if one sees regular peaks and troughs in the price history of a security, that those peaks and troughs will continue with the same regularity.

Remember what Dow said so long ago: A trend is in effect until a positive signal has been given that the trend has ended. Don't try to guess what is happening within a trend. It is, to all intents and purposes, unpredictable.

Index

%D line, 111
%K line, 111

Acceleration of trendlines, 60
Account balance, 259
Activities to avoid, 91–134
    assembling too many variables, 123–131
    derivatives, 92–96
    Elliott wave analysis, 117–121
    fair value, 128
    Gann analysis, 113–117
    Internet securities, 133
    IPOs, 133
    news reports, 134
    oscillators, 97–113 (*See also* Oscillators)
    over trading, 121, 122
    premarket trading, 134
    program trades, 128
    S&P futures, 123–126
    stock splits, 130, 131
    wrong tool at wrong time, 131, 132
Afterword, 267–269
Alcoholics Anonymous, 245
Appel, Gerald, 104
Archipelago (ARCA), 139, 174–176
Ascending triangle, 71, 72
Ascending triangle continuation, 84
At the money option, 93
Author's trading week (*see* Trading week)
Axe market maker, 145

Backwardation, 20
Bad patch, reasons for, 265
Bar chart, 37, 38
Bear alert, 196
Bear confirmed, 196
Bear correction, 196
Bear market moves, 49

Bearish breakout, 191
Bearish continuation rectangle, 81
Bearish engulfment, 187
Bearish Hirami, 188
Bearish resistance line, 189, 190
Bearish rising wedge, 85
Best ask, 26
Best bid, 26
Blumenthal, Earl, 195
Borrowable, 200
Bottoming formations, 54
Breakaway gap, 89, 90
Breakouts, 58, 61, 88–90, 190, 191
Broadening formation, 72, 73
Bucket shops, 41
Bull alert, 195
Bull confirmed, 195
Bull correction, 196
Bull move, 48, 49
Bullish breakout, 190, 191
Bullish continuation rectangle, 81
Bullish falling wedge, 85
Bullish Hirami, 188
Bullish percentage, 195, 196
Bullish support line, 189, 190

Call, 93
Candlesticks, 38, 39, 185–189
Cardinal square method, 115
Cautions (*see* Activities to avoid)
CBOE volatility index (VIX), 192–194
Chart patterns:
    candlesticks, 185–189
    point-and-figure, 189–191
Chart reading, 115
Chat rooms, 5
CNBC radio, 134
Cohen, A. W., 195

Commodity markets, 96
Complex chart forms:
  Elliott wave analysis, 117–121
  Gann analysis, 113–117
  oscillators, 97–113 (*See also* Oscillators)
Consolidation flag, 80
Continuation patterns, 77–88
  flags, 78–80
  head-and-shoulders, 82, 83
  interpreting, 85–88
  rectangle formations, 80, 81
  triangles, 83, 84
  wedges, 84, 85
Contrarian thinking, 192
Corrective waves, 118, 120

D line, 111
Daily charts, 5, 185
Dark cloud cover, 187
Datek, 42, 173
Day trading, 5–9
Dead cross, 102
Dell, 23
Derivatives, 92–96
Descending triangle, 71
Descending triangle continuation, 83
Direct-access trading, 161, 162 (*See also* Executions)
Discipline, 15–19, 77, 239, 243, 257
Divergence, 104
Documentation (*see* Keeping track)
Dog-dog owner analog, 7–9, 151
Doji, 186
Double top/bottom, 65, 66
Doubling down, 6
Dow theory, 46–52
Downward trendline, 12, 55–57

ECNs, 30, 139
Edge band analysis, 107
Einstein, Albert, 114
Elder, Alexander, 245, 246
Elliott wave analysis, 117–121
Elliott zig-zag correction, 119, 120
Entering positions, 267, 268
Evening star, 188
Executions, 161–183
  Archipelago (ARCA), 174–176
  getting shorts, 178–183
  Island, 168–173
  SelectNet, 176–178
  SOES, 162–168

Exhaustion gap, 89, 90
Existing positions, 268

Fading the trend, 145, 146
Failure swing top formation, 52, 53
Fair value, 128
Falloffs from bull, 59
False breakouts, 58, 61
Feedback, 245
Fibonacci numbers, 103
Five-minute chart, continuation pattern, 80
50 percent retrenchment line, 116, 117
Flags, 78–80
Flat correction, 119
Focus on process, 241–244
Full-service brokers, 42

Gamblers Anonymous, 247
Gann, W. D., 113
Gann analysis, 113–117
Gap-down security, 208, 209
Gap-up security, 208, 209
Gaps, 88–90
General principles (buy-sell strategies), 267, 268
Getting shorts, 178–183
Golden cross, 102, 103
Greed, 268

Halt condition, 25
Hammer, 187
Hanging man, 186, 187
Head-and-shoulders:
  continuation pattern, 82, 83
  reversal patterns, 73–76
Head fake, 146, 147
Hi-lo index, 197
Hirami patterns, 188

Impulse waves, 118, 120
In the money option, 94
Indicators of overall market direction, 38
Initial public offerings (IPOs), 133
Instinet, 30
Intel, 23
Internet securities, 133
IPOs, 133
Island, 168–173

K line, 111
Keeping track, 257–266

272 Index

Keeping track, *(cont.)*
  daily tracking, 263
  premarket task sheets, 257–261
  screen layouts, 261, 262
  weekly tracking, 263–265

Lane, George, 111
Lefevre, Edwin, 41
Level 1 data, 135
Level II screen, 28, 29, 135–137
  approaches to avoid, 140, 141
  break of downward trend, 152–157
  break of upward trend, 147–152
  components, 135, 136
  ECNs, 139
  fading the trend, 145, 146
  focus on group behavior, 147
  head fake, 146, 147
  market makers, 144, 145
  market participants, 137, 138
  what it shows you, 141–144
Liquidity, 31
Listed exchanges, 27–29
Long-term investing, 248
Losses, reasons for, 265

MACD, 104–106
Maintenance call, 194
Margin, 193, 194
Margin clerks, 193
Market makers, 144, 145
Market open, 9, 205–212
Market overreaction, 126, 127
Market secrets, 244, 246
MB Trading, 238
Measuring gap, 89, 90
Microsoft, 23
Midweek party, 255
Momentum oscillators, 97–100, 107
Monitoring your discipline, 264, 265
Morning star, 188
Moving Average Convergence Divergence (MACD), 104–106
Moving average oscillators, 100–107
Multiple tops, 65, 66

NASDAQ, 27–30, 138, 139
NASDAQ bullish percentage, 195, 196
NASDAQ Composite, 198
NASDAQ level II screen (*see* Level II screen)

Neckline, 74, 75
Net ticks value, 198
New Concepts in Technical Trading Systems (Wilder), 108
New York Knicks, 242
News reports, 9, 134
Nonchart indicators:
  hi-lo index, 197
  NASDAQ bullish percentage, 195, 196
  NASDAQ Composite, 198
  net ticks value, 198
  percentage of NASDAQ stocks trading above 10-week moving averages, 196
  relative strength, 197, 198
Nonfailure swing top formation, 53
NQDS feed, 131
NTDS feed, 131, 132
NYSE, 25–27

Obstacles to trading success, 244–247
One-minute chart:
  continuation pattern, 79
  defined, 4, 5
Online brokerages, 42
Opening patterns, 205–212
Options, 32, 92–96
Order-driven markets, 138, 139
Oscillators, 46, 97–113
  market open patterns, and, 208, 209
  momentum, 97–100, 107
  moving average, 100–107
  proper use of, 107
  range of change, 100, 107
  RSI, 108–110
  stochastic, 111, 112
Out of the money option, 94
Over-the-counter (OTC) markets, 27–30
Over trading, 121, 122
Overall trend, 38
Overreaction, 126, 127

Page views (trading software), 261, 262
Peer pressure, 60, 61
%D line, 111
%K line, 111
Phase 1, 10, 11, 15
Phase 2, 10, 11, 22–24
Phase 3, 10, 11, 23
Phases of trading day, 9–14
Pitfalls (*see* Activities to avoid)
Point-and-figure charting, 39, 40, 189–191

Index **273**

Point reversal, 13, 14, 66–68
Post-open periods, 212, 213
Premarket analysis, 199–204
Premarket gaps, 21
Premarket plan, 19–23
Premarket security analysis sheet, 258
Premarket task sheets, 257–261
Premarket trading, 134
Price action, 36
Price gaps, 88–90
Price movement, 129, 134
Primary trends, 48
Program trades, 128
Psychology (*see* Trading psychology)
Put, 93
Put-to-call ratio, 95

Quote-driven market, 138

Rainy day money, 16
Range-bound security, 57
Rate of change oscillators, 100, 107
Real Tick system, 138
Recordkeeping (*see* Keeping track)
Rectangle formations, 80, 81
Relative strength, 197, 198
Relative strength index (RSI), 108–110
Relying on others, 32
Reminiscences of a Stock Operator (Lefevre), 41
Resistance, 61–64
Retrenchment, 116, 117
Reversal patterns, 64–77
    head-and-shoulders, 73–76
    multiple tops, 65, 66
    point (spike) reversal, 66–68
    rounding formations, 68, 69
    tendency to enter too early, 77
    triangles, 69–73
Risk, 41
Risk tolerance, 268
Rounding formations, 68, 69
RSI oscillator, 108–110
Runaway gap, 89

S&P futures, 123–126
Sample trading week, 214–237
    (*See also* Trading week)
Screen layouts, 261, 262
Secondary trend, 48
SelectNet, 176–178
Selectnet preference order, 175, 177
Self-help organizations, 245, 246

Seven-candle pattern, 189
Short squeeze, 88
Short-term trading, 267
Shorts, 178–183
Single-candlestick patterns, 186, 187
Single moving average, 101
SOES, 162–168
SOES queue, 165
SOES tier size, 164, 165
Sorting software, 199, 205
Spike reversal, 66–68
Start-up money, 16
Stochastic creep, 97, 107
Stochastic oscillators, 111, 112
Stock splits, 130, 131
Stops, 240, 241
Sufficient volume, 200
Support, 61–64
Swing trading, 6, 8
Symmetrical triangle, 69, 70
Symmetrical triangle continuation, 83
Symmetrical triangle topping formation, 70

Technical analysis (TA), 33–36
    benefits, 34
    boredom (following a plan), 43–45
    criticism, 34, 36
    key concept, 34
    misconceptions, 41–43
    opposing tenets, 59
    tools, 36–40
Technical Analysis of Stocks and Commodities, 212
Tertiary trend correction within secondary trend, 87
Tertiary trends, 48
TESTA, 22
Three-candle patterns, 188
Tower bottom, 189
Tower top, 189
Tracking sheets (*see* Keeping track)
Trading against the gap, 208–212
Trading for a Living (Elder), 245
Trading psychology, 239–256
    focus on process, 241–244
    obstacles to trading success, 244–247
    stops, 240, 241
    trading rules, 247–255
    when things go wrong, 255, 256
Trading rules, 134, 201, 239, 240, 247–255
Trading software (page views), 261, 262
Trading week, 184–238

Trading week *(cont.)*
    Friday, 232–237
    market open patterns, 205–212
    Monday, 214–219
    post-open periods, 212, 213
    premarket analysis, 199–204
    Thursday, 227–231
    Tuesday, 219–223
    Wednesday, 223–227
Trend, 52–61
Trendlines, 55–58, 189
Triangle breakout, 191
Triangles:
    continuation patterns, 83, 84
    reversal patterns, 69–73
Triangular correction, 119
Two-candlestick patterns, 187, 188

Upward trendline, 12, 35, 55, 56

Vendor trap, 42
VIX index, 192–194
Volatility, 192
Volume, 129, 134, 200

Wave-three extension, 120, 121
Weak hands, 49
Wedges, 84, 85
Week of trading *(see* Trading week)
Weight-loss industry, 246
Weighting, 103, 104
Wilder, J. Welles, Jr., 108
Wit Capital, 129, 130

Zero sum game, 31
Zig-zag correction, 119, 120